The Richness of Augustine

THE RICHNESS OF AUGUSTINE

His Contextual and Pastoral Theology

Mark Ellingsen

WESTMINSTER
JOHN KNOX PRESS
LOUISVILLE • KENTUCKY

Book design by Sharon Adams
Cover design by Eric Handel, LMNOP
Cover illustration: Historiated initial "l" depicting St. Augustine (Vellum) *by Master of San Michele of Murano (early 15th century). Musee Marmottan, Paris, France/Giraudon/Bridgeman Art Library*

First edition
Published by Westminster John Knox Press
Louisville, Kentucky

This book is printed on acid-free paper that meets the American National Standards Institute Z39.48 standard. ∞

PRINTED IN THE UNITED STATES OF AMERICA

05 06 07 08 09 10 11 12 13 14 15 — 10 9 8 7 6 5 4 3 2 1

Library of Congress Cataloging-in-Publication Data

Ellingsen, Mark
    The richness of Augustine : his contextual and pastoral theology / Mark Ellingsen.— 1st ed.
        p. cm.
    Includes bibliographical references (p.) and index.
    ISBN 0-664-22618-3
    1. Augustine, Saint, Bishop of Hippo. 2. Theology, Doctrinal—Africa, North—History—Early church, ca. 30-600. 3. Pastoral theology—Africa, North—History of doctrines—Early church, ca. 30-600. I. Title.

    BR65.A9E44 2005
    230'.14'092—dc22

                                                                    2004057189

In memory of some special loved ones who led the way:
Anna Sangesland Nilssen (1879–1982)
Nikolai Nilssen (1881–1950)
Jergen Ellingsen (1895–1963)
Sigrid Siersted Ellingsen (1897–1991)
Gudrun Nilssen Johnsen (1909–1983)
Thoralf Johnsen (1907–1988)
Ruth Nilssen Aamot (1907–1998)
Ragnar Aamot (1903–1992)
Norah Nilssen Dalevold (1905–1967)
Einar Dalevold (1899–1989)
Marie Siersted (1902–1993)
Alfred Siersted (1899–1991)
Harry Siersted (1930–2000)

Contents

Acknowledgments

Writing Church History, writing about the giants of the past, is an act of remembrance. But writing about Augustine has been a real personal odyssey of remembrance for me. For St. Augustine has been an important part of my personal and professional life since I first was exposed to him in the Fall of 1967, as an eighteen-year-old college freshman. Along with some wise professors, he launched me into a career of pastoral work, Theology, and Church History. True enough, I have not devoted my whole career to his thought, but have wandered away into other topics, like Luther and the Reformation, the Middle Ages, Systematics, Homiletics, international ecumenics, the Religious Right, hermeneutics, African-American Church History, Christian social ethics, and sociopolitical commentary. Yet I never could escape Augustine, his insights, and his influence. He is everywhere in all of these fields (even Constitutional law, I found in preparing my most recent previous book). Even in my personal life, he was there, sometimes providing sound insights about my happy marriage and child rearing. Thus with this book I have come home—to a home I never really left.

When you return to your roots as I have with Augustine in writing this book, it sets you on many a walk down memory lane. Through happy college, seminary, and graduate school years, Augustine was there. Thinking of Augustine led me to remember his presence in my various ministries and faculty positions over the years. I have been reminded of the colleagues and teachers who have taught me about Augustine or who have joined me in fun, challenging conversation about his ideas. Three colleagues, David Wallace, Art Lewis, and Richard Wallace, especially come to mind as my special partners in "Augustinian crime" in the team-teaching we have done about him and his traditions over the years at the Interdenominational Theological Center. Working with these three friends has been one of the best things that has ever happened to me in academics. This part of the book gives me the chance to thank these brothers for the good years of conversation, support, and fun. I also want to thank another partner in admiring Augustine, Westminster John Knox's Don McKim, who made this book happen and has made it better with his work on the manuscript.

During most of my years with Augustine my best friend Betsey has been there alongside me, and we have spent some of our time together talking and thinking about his life and theology. Consequently, besides taking a moment here to thank her for the editing work she did on this project, I have also taken a few long and happy journeys with her down the memory lane of our more than thirty-year relationship as I worked on this book.

Such reminiscences have also led me often to think of a bunch of Norwegian immigrants, their children, and those they married, who helped raise me along with my beloved parents. Augustine was not a subject of discussion in the wild, raucous, and stimulating conversations of the Ellingsen-Siersted-Nilssen extended family. But the staunch Lutheranism of my Norwegian clan was more Augustinian than I realized until I started studying Augustine firsthand. I probably came to love him so much because without realizing it I was raised on him (at least on some of the best of his insights). In past books, I have mentioned this wonderful group. But now I have written enough volumes, prepared enough dedication pages, that all my closest relatives have had their book. With all the reminiscences associated with this one, it seems appropriate to dedicate this volume to beloved relatives who have gone ahead and now rest. So I dedicate the book to thirteen deceased loved ones (grandparents, aunts and uncles, and a wonderful older cousin), who have played big, important parts in my life. They were not writers or Augustinian experts. But this book gives me a chance lovingly to record for posterity a witness to their love of learning, love of life, love for each other, and love for God.

Abbreviations

Texts by Augustine

c. Acad.	*Against the Skeptics [Contra Academics]* (386–387)
c. Adim.	*Contra Adimantus, a Disciple of Mani* (394)
Adul conjug.	*On Adulterous Marriages [De adulterinis conjugiis]* (419–420)
Agon.	*The Christian Combat [De agone Christiani]* (396)
Anim.	*On the Soul and Its Origin [De anima et eius origine]* (419)
B. conjug.	*On the Good of Marriage [De bono conjugali]* (401)
B. vid.	*On the Good of Widowhood [De bono viduitatis]* (414)
B. vita.	*On the Happy Life [De beata vita]* (386–387)
Bapt.	*On Baptism, Against the Donatists* (c. 400)
Cat. rud.	*On the Catechizing of the Uninstructed [De catechizandis rudibus]* (399)
Civ.	*The City of God [De civitate Dei]* (413–426)
Conf.	*The Confessions* (399)
Cons. ev.	*Harmony of the Gospels [De consensu evangelistarum]* (c. 399/400)

Correct.	*On the Correction of the Donatists* (417)
Corrept.	*On Rebuke and Grace [De correptione et gratia]* (426/427)
Cura mort.	*On the Care of the Dead [De cura pro mortuis gerenda]* (422)
Div. qu.	*On Eighty-Three Varied Questions [De diversis quaestionibus octaginta tribus]* (388/396)
Doctr. Christ.	*On Christian Doctrine* (396, 426/427)
Enchir.	*The Enchiridion* (421)
Ep.	*Epistles*
Ep. *	*Epistles* [discovered by Divjak]
Ep. fund.	*Against the Epistle of Manichaeus Called Fundamental* (397)
Ep. Joh.	*Ten Homilies on the Epistle of John to the Parthians* (c. 406/407)
C. ep. Parm.	*Against the Epistle of Parmenianus* (400)
C. ep. Pel.	*Against Two Letters of the Pelagians [Contra duas epistulas Pelagianorum]* (c. 420)
Ep. Rom.	*Unfinished Commentary on the Letter to the Romans [Epistulae ad Romanos inchoata expositio]* (394/395)
Ev. Joh.	*Tractates on the Gospel of St. John* (c. 406/421)
Ex. Gal.	*Commentary on Paul's Letter to the Galatians* (394/395)
Faust.	*Against Faustus the Manichean [Contra Faustum Manichaean]* (397/399)
Fid. et op.	*Faith and Works [De fide et operibus]* (413)
Fid. et symb.	*On Faith and the Creed [De fide et symbolo]* (c. 393)
C. Fort.	*Acts or Disputation Against Fortunatus the Manichee* (392)
Gen. ad litt.	*Exposition of Genesis according to the Letter [De Genesi ad litteram]* (c. 399/415)
Gen. ad Man.	*On Genesis, against the Manichees [De Genesi adversus Manichaeos]* (388/389)
Gen. litt. imp.	*On the Literal Interpretation of Genesis, an Unfinished Book [De Genesi ad litteram imperfectus liber]* (393/394; 426/427)
Gest. Pelag.	*On the Proceedings of Pelagius [De gestis Pelagii]* (417)
Gr. et lib. arb.	*On Grace and Free Will [De gratia et libero arbitrio]* (426/427)
Gr. et pecc. or.	*On the Grace of Christ and Original Sin [De gratia Christi et de peccato originali]* (418)
Grat. Christ.	*On the Grace of Christ [De gratia Christi]* (418)
Haer.	*On Heresies [De haeresibus]* (428)
Imm. an.	*On the Immortality of the Soul [De immortalitate animae]* (387)
Adv. Jud.	*Against the Jews* (428/429)
C. Jul.	*Against Julian* (421/422)
Jul. op. imp.	*Against Julian: An Unfinished Work* (429–430)
De lib. arbit.	*On Free Will [De libero arbitrio]* (387/388–395)
C. litt. Pet.	*Against the Letters of Petilian, Donatist [Contra litteras Petiliani]* (c. 400)
Mag.	*On the Teacher [De magistro]* (389)

Mend.	*On Lying [De mendacio]* (394/395)
Mor.	*On the Morals of the Catholic Church [De moribus ecclesiae catholicae et de moribus Manichaeorum]* (388)
Mus.	*On Music* (387/391)
Nat. bon.	*Concerning the Nature of the Good, Against the Manichees [De nature boni contra Manichaeos]* (404)
Nat. et grat.	*On Nature and Grace* (415)
Nupt. et concup.	*On Marriage and Concupiscence [De nuptiis et concupiscentia]* (418/420)
Ord.	*On Order [De ordine]* (386–387)
Pat.	*On Patience* (417/418)
Pecc. merit.	*On the Merits and Forgiveness of Sins and On the Baptism of Infants [De peccatorum meritis et remissione et de baptismo parvulorum]* (411)
Perf. just.	*On Man's Perfection in Righteousness [De perfectione justitiae hominis]* (415)
Persev.	*On the Gift of Perseverance* (428/429)
Praed. sanct.	*On the Predestination of the Saints* (428/429)
Ps.	*Expositions on the Book of Psalms* (392/422)
Quant.	*On the Greatness of the Soul [De animae quantitate]* (387/388)
Qu. Hept.	*Questions on the Heptateuch [Quaestiones in Heptateuchum]* (419–420)
Retrac.	*Retractions* (426–427)
Serm.	*Sermons*
C. serm. Ar.	*Against an Arian Sermon [Contra sermonem Arianorum]* (418)
S. Dom. mon.	*Our Lord's Sermon on the Mount [De sermone Domini in monte]* (394–395)
Simpl.	*To Simplicianus* (396/398)
Solilq.	*Soliloquies* (387)
Spir. et litt.	*On the Spirit and the Letter [De spiritu et littera]* (412)
Symb. cat.	*On the Creed, Sermon to the Catechumens [De symbolo ad catechumenos]* (425)
Trin.	*On the Trinity* (c. 410)
Util. cred.	*On the Usefulness of Believing [De utilitate credendi]* (391/392)
Vera relig.	*On True Religion [De vera religione]* (390)
Virg.	*On Holy Virginity [De sancta virginitate]* (401)

COLLECTIONS IN WHICH ENGLISH TRANSLATIONS OF THESE WORKS APPEAR

CG	*Augustine's Commentary on Galatians,* trans. Eric Plumer. Oxford and New York: Oxford University Press, 2003

FC	*The Fathers of the Church.* Washington, DC: The Catholic University Press of America, 1947–1968
LCC	*The Library of Christian Classics,* Vol. 6, ed. J. H. S. Burleigh. Philadelphia: Westminster Press, 1963
NPNF	*Nicene and Post-Nicene Fathers.* First Series. Reprint. Peabody, MA: Hendrickson, 1995
WSA	*The Works of Saint Augustine: A Translation for the 21st Century,* ed. J. E. Rotelle. Hyde Park, NY: New City Press, 1990

Introduction

What Can We Make of All the Augustines? His Place in the History of the Church

It is difficult to imagine what can be said about Saint Augustine (354–430) that has not already been said. The last thing we seem to need is another commentary on Augustine. Indeed, the entire history of theology of the post-fifth-century Western church might be construed as a commentary on Augustine's thought. But other dimensions of this Augustinian saturation of Western Christianity, of the numerous diverse interpretations of his thought, occasion one more book on the subject (especially this one). We have not yet satisfactorily examined the ecumenical and pastoral implications of Augustine's thought.

What makes my approach unique is that I want to affirm most of the classical interpretations of Augustine, to claim that they are correct about the African Father. In so doing, however, I am offering an implicit critique of these earlier interpretive traditions as well as of much of the history of Western Christian thought. In essence, my argument is that earlier interpretive traditions are correct about Augustine; most of them have grasped some essential insights about his thought. But none of them has the *whole* Augustine. His thought is richer than its portrayal by his interpreters. Most of them merely stress a particular set of themes in his thought, and negate or ignore those themes that seem to

1

conflict with what the interpreters have stressed. Also missing in virtually all of the Western interpreters is Augustine's African roots, the degree to which he truly was an African Father.

This book, then, is about recovering this richness in Augustine's thought, to present an inclusive reading of the African Father that is itself inclusive of previous interpreters' insights. I can show that many of the classical interpreters are correct about Augustine. They accurately represent him. Each interpreter is especially accurate when considering texts written by the African Father that addressed pastoral concerns akin to those occupying the interpreter in question. This insight suggests that there may be a pattern to the history of Christian thought, that theological images logically lend themselves to addressing similar pastoral contexts in different settings and historical eras. Making this case is a long-term project for me, and making the case with regard to an inclusive reading of Augustine is a significant step along that road.[1]

SOME CLASSICAL INTERPRETATIONS OF AUGUSTINE

One can hardly conceive of the Protestant Reformation and its traditions without Augustine and the Reformers' distinct reading of him. For them, Augustine is *the* theologian of grace (*sola gratia*), the great enemy of everything Pelagian (of any behavioral prescription which implies that we must do something to save ourselves).[2] As such he is also praised for his role in the development of the doctrine of original sin. He is deemed as uncompromising in his insistence on the total sinfulness of human beings, on the forfeiture of free will. Modern heirs of the Reformers like Reinhold Niebuhr have likewise read the African Father in this way. In Niebuhr's case, he highlighted the social-ethical implications of Augustine's views in a way most compatible with Calvin's thinking (his belief that despite our egocentricity the structures of society can be transformed by the Gospel).[3]

On the other hand, the classical Roman Catholic tradition has interpreted Augustine's treatment of soteriology as affirming its own position on salvation, as the result of the cooperation of grace and our own efforts.[4] Likewise Augustine is cited by official Catholic documents to authorize the Catholic Church's affirmation of the Real Presence of Christ in the Sacraments and the status of the Mass as a Sacrifice.[5]

There is by no means unanimity within the Protestant house regarding Augustine and his theological heritage. The major traditions of Augustinian interpretation have been the Lutheran and Reformed heritages, but even John Wesley had a version of the African Father that served his view.

Thus Luther invoked Augustine to support his radical position on freedom from the Law, his belief that God commands the impossible, and that even redeemed Christians can never fulfill the Law of God.[6] This commitment is closely tied to the Reformer's belief that good works need not be exhorted, that they happen spontaneously.

In addition, Luther also portrayed Augustine as the source of his social ethic (the Two-Kingdom Ethic), which unlike the Reformed view maintains that government belongs to the realm of God's creation governed by the divine Law. Consequently, according to Luther and his version of Augustine, the Law of God, and not the Gospel, is to function as the norm for political judgments.[7] The Reformer also contended that Augustine supported his own view of the Lord's Supper, the belief that Christ is actually in the elements, though they remain bread and wine.[8]

By contrast, Calvin repeatedly invoked Augustine to authorize a number of his distinct views, and in so doing offers us a different version of the African Father. He saw Augustine affirming with him a view of the Lord's Supper as a ceremony of Christ's Presence, not in the elements but in the sense of summoning faithful recipients to a heavenly ascent to his Presence. Likewise the African Father is presented as a proponent of double predestination.[9] Another Reformed interpreter cited Augustine to authorize his advocacy of preaching the Law as a model for Christian life.[10]

Although John Wesley was not as self-consciously committed to endorsing the theological convictions of the African Father, his version of Augustine's thought closely resembles his own. Thus on the Methodist founder's account Augustine taught that good living and true faith belong together, since faith is full of good works.[11] Wesley's Augustine is a Pietist, preoccupied with sanctification and living the Christian life, not with justification by grace or the sovereignty of God as his Reformation interpreters viewed him.

There is a long history of debate over Augustine's theological method (the way in which he construes the nature of the Word of God in relation to contemporary experience of the worldviews or philosophies used to describe it). Some theologians insist on a *correlation* of the Word and contemporary experience (a *Method of Correlation*), in such a way that the prior analysis of that experience shapes the questions one brings to the Biblical text and the interpretation one has of it. Consequently, proponents of this approach read the Bible allegorically, seeking a text's deeper, rationally or experientially appropriate meaning. With this method, reason prepares the way for faith. The two are seen to be in harmony.

Other theologians (and interpreters of Augustine) operate with a more theologically conservative, *dogmatic* approach. They invert the commitments of the first method and initiate theological reflection with the Word of God understood as critiquing and shaping our experience. Proponents of this approach read the Bible literally, or at least when the text is read figurally as pointing beyond itself to more contemporary realities, the literal sense of the text is not abolished. This second approach also tends to contend that we never truly understand unless we believe and have been shaped by God's Word.

A third, mediating method has also been developed. It calls for a *critical correlation* of the Word of God and experience (the *Method of Critical Correlation*). Like the second, more dogmatic approach, proponents of this model see the Word of

God as critiquing and shaping the set of presuppositions we bring to the Word of God. Experience, after all, is said to correlate with and connect with the Word of God. Consequently, like the first approach (the Method of Correlation), theologians who hold to this third approach also insist that our prior analysis of experience shapes our understanding of God's Word. When we interpret the Bible this approach entails that we regard a text as functioning with different layers of meaning, each of which is related by the significations of the symbols employed in the text.

It is hardly surprising that each of these methodological approaches has proponents who claim Augustine as their inspiration. The first, the Method of Correlation, is exemplified by Paul Tillich. He sees Augustine as an ally for his Method insofar as the African Father is represented as positing the sort of ontological connection between the Word and experience that Tillich claims is presupposed in his method.[12] Almost eight hundred years earlier, another famous practitioner of this approach, Thomas Aquinas, invoked Augustine as a precedent for his positing a harmony of reason and revelation.[13]

The second, more dogmatic approach to theology is well exemplified by Karl Barth. He presents Augustine as his ally regarding the intimate relation between theology and proclamation and regarding the priority of the divine act in bringing us to understand the Word.[14]

Paul Ricoeur is an excellent representative of the third approach to theology. He too portrays Augustine as his ally. He invokes the African Father as positing a hermeneutic like his own that recognizes the richness of texts' meanings, their polysemous character.[15]

SO WHAT?

It is evident that this survey of theological options has presented some very different versions of Augustine. This is a book about determining whether the various theological approaches and denominational interpretations of Augustine are correct. As such, for students of Church History and Theology this volume can function as a helpful introduction to the differences among the teachings of the various denominations and as an overview of the major theological options in Western Christianity. In that connection, the diversity in Augustine's thought entails that every major doctrine and virtually every historic formulation of these doctrines come within his purview. Consequently, readers of this book are also going to receive a refresher/introduction to the core doctrines and issues dealt with in Theology, and the volume could well function in classes devoted to such doctrinal matters.

If the various interpretations of Augustine are all correct, if he really embraced all the distinct positions attributed to him, that has fertile ecumenical implications. It also may teach us lessons about how to do theology. For to the degree that I succeed in showing that the classical interpreters of Augustine tend to be correct about the African Father's thought when he was addressing pastoral and theological issues akin to their own, that may indicate that there is a pattern to the use of Christian concepts reflected in his theology. I will demonstrate that he tended to say the same thing about the classical doctrines when addressing similar pastoral concerns throughout his career.

Not only does this approach help us address the question of whether the diversity in Augustine's thought is a function of development in his career, of the difference between the later Augustine and the early Augustine. If such a pattern to the use of Christian concepts exists, it has significant ecumenical implications. To the degree his thought has legitimately generated distinct denominational traditions, it might be argued that they are reconcilable, insofar as their core convictions were successfully integrated by Augustine in his theology. And if these core convictions have not been successfully integrated by Augustine in his theology, that must entail that the Church needs seriously to reconsider the positive assessment the African Father has been given over the centuries. Judgments about the validity of Augustine's theology seem to be at stake in the conclusion one reaches about the ecumenical harmony of the core commitments of the various denominational traditions.

Identifying a pattern to the use of Christian concepts embodied in Augustine's thought also suggests a new model for theology, one that is more pastorally inclined. A theological proposal emerging from the lessons taught by this study of Augustine will do more than just articulate conceptuality. This new theological model will also be concerned with providing guidance regarding when the various classical theological conceptions are best employed. Insofar as it can provide such guidance regarding how to use theological formulations, the sort of pastoral, contextual model for theology suggested in this book can begin to bridge the all-too-wide gap between academy and parish. To appreciate the richness of Augustine's theology is to receive guidance not just about what to say, but about when to say it.

Chapter 1

The African Augustine and His Context

AUGUSTINE'S AFRICAN CONTEXT

In order to understand Augustine and the sort of concerns he addressed, it is necessary to examine his ancient North African context and his African roots. The place and time in which the African Father lived and worked (the region of the Roman Empire called the Maghrib, present-day Algeria) was genuinely multicultural. Three significant ethnic groups populated the region: Italian immigrants; Children of Phoenician immigrants (called Punics), who had lived in the region for nearly eight centuries; and Berbers of the Kabyle clan, indigenous Africans who in that era in this region (modern-day Algeria) prior to the Islamic invasions and subsequent intermarriage were (and continued to be) Black.[1]

Daily life in this part of Africa in the fourth century was thoroughly Romanized. That is hardly surprising given the great cultural impact Rome had had on the region and the higher standards of living many were enjoying since Roman occupation had begun in 146 BC. Indeed, this region was enjoying the greatest period of economic prosperity that to date it had ever known. That is not to say that the petty gentry families of Thagaste (Augustine's hometown) were particularly comfortable. Yet an ethos had been created in which upward social mobility was a real possibility, and the sons of these families seem to have been nurtured in a strong work ethic. Education in the ways of Rome was the key to success, and this explains why his father Patricius was determined to secure the best possible classical education for him.[2]

So thoroughly Romanized was this region of Africa that its Roman citizens, like Augustine, regarded native dialects of non-Romanized people as "Punic."[3] If one wanted to get anywhere in society, he had to speak Latin and adopt Roman ways. Thus it seems likely that Augustine's family spoke only Latin at home, and there is no evidence that he was fluent in any of the other languages spoken in the region in which he grew up. After all, Berber and Punic were the languages of the countryside and of the lower-class laborers.

Life in fourth-century North Africa was very public. Everything was on display, with nothing under the covers, not even sex. It was all discussed, debated, and complained about in public. Men lived "out of doors," publically disclosing in forums and conversations the most intimate details of their lives. Reputation was coveted above all else. Such concern about reputation entailed that the public sphere was very fragile. North Africans of the era developed impressive public-speaking skills, not just to praise but also to debunk their peers. In small towns, such jousting could lead to long rancorous feuds.

Although Roman entertainments, like chariot races and gladiator fights with wild animals, had been exported to Africa, rhetoric was the most typical form of entertainment (the e-mail or TV of the era). This rhetoric was emotional and moving.

Men of the region could be prickly, but also ferociously loyal to each other. Lifelong friendships and close extended-family relationships were a way of life.[4]

The society was patriarchal. Women were frequently beaten by their husbands.[5] The educational system was rigid, often enforced with beatings. One reason for such discipline was that the unruly behavior of some students mandated it. Augustine himself lamented the educational system of Carthage, noting that students often broke in on an instructor's lecture and seemed largely undisciplined.[6]

WAS AUGUSTINE BLACK?

Who was Augustine? None of the major historic interpretive traditions have really appreciated his African roots. Though most everyone heretofore has neglected it, a consensus is beginning to emerge that recognizes the likelihood of Augustine being of mixed racial background.[7] He himself reminded his contemporaries of his ethnic, cultural roots.

Perhaps nowhere is Augustine's identification with Africa clearer than in his postconversion interaction with Maximus, an older North African dialogue partner whom the African Father had first come to know during his earlier pagan

period. It seems that after Augustine's conversion to Christianity his former com-
patriot learned of his friend's new commitments and particularly targeted the
African Catholic veneration of certain African martyrs.[8] In response, Augustine
seems to have identified himself with Africa, as an African. He wrote in defense
of the practice of venerating such martyrs:

> For surely, considering you are an African, and that we are both settled in
> Africa, you could not have so forgotten yourself when writing to Africans as
> to think that Punic names were a fit theme for censure.[9]

Augustine's reference to the Punic language, which elsewhere he indicates he
understood, raises an intriguing question. Is Augustine referring to the Phoenician immigrants and the faithful Christians of this group who had been canon-
ized? If so, it would suggest his own Phoenician background. Subsequently in the
letter he followed up his rebuttal of Maximus:

> And if the Punic language is rejected by you, you virtually deny what has
> been admitted by most learned men, that many things have been wisely pre-
> served from oblivion in books written in the Punic tongue. Nay, you even
> ought to be ashamed of having been born in the country in which the cra-
> dle of this language is still warm, *i.e.* in which this language was originally,
> and until very recently, the language of the people.[10]

These comments could be taken as implying that the "Punic" to which Augustine referred and which he praised is ancient Phoenician, which could in turn suggest that he himself was of this ethnic background. In Roman North Africa,
however, the term "Punic" seems to have referred to anyone of a non-Roman cultural background. In fact, a number of scholars have concluded that the language
of the Phoenicians had largely been displaced in Augustine's lifetime by Latin and
Libyan (an ancestor language of modern Berber).[11] That Augustine himself used
the term "Punic" to refer to ancient Libyan seems evident in a point he made in
one of his sermons in *Ten Homilies on the Epistle of John to the Parthians*, as he criticized a group of heretics called Donatists. About these African Christians who
refused fellowship with the Church catholic, the majority of whom were residents
of small towns or farmers, and so were likely Berber in ethnicity,[12] he claimed:

> But these men, who much love Christ, and therefore refuse to communi-
> cate with the city which killed Christ, so honor Christ as to affirm that He
> is left to two tongues, the Latin and the Punic, *i.e.* African.[13]

Apparently when Augustine used the term "Punic" he intended to refer to indigenous African languages, especially ancient Berber (called Libyan). If so, his dialogue with Maximus was likely a defense of ancient Berber (not Phoenician)
traditions and could imply his identification with Berber culture.

Even more data suggestive of a Berber background in Augustine's family tree
can be identified. His mother's name, Monica, seems to have Berber origins, in
the name of the Libyan/Numidian god Mon. Another Berber custom that can

be identified in the African Father's family background is his choice of the name for the son born to him and his concubine, with whom he entered a seventeen-year relationship begun during student days. To name one's firstborn son Adeodatus [Godsend] as they did was a Berber custom.[14]

Of course none of these facts demonstrates that Augustine might have had Berber blood in his veins. In fact, Monica's Berber-derived name was typical of the Donatist Christians in this era, as they frequently employed Berber names. But, as already noted, the majority of Donatists were likely Berber in ethnicity. Consequently, can we assume that even if Monica's name and Augustine's embrace of the Berber custom of naming his firstborn son were the result of contact with the Donatist community (perhaps through his mother) it is possible that the reason the Donatist practices persisted in Augustine's family were because on his mother's side there was Berber family?[15]

One of the most provocative indications of the possibility that Augustine might have had a Berber background is suggested in his dispute with the young Pelagian bishop Julian. The Italian bishop had been quite critical of African Christianity for its bishops' condemnation of Pelagius and eventually successful demand that the pope do likewise. In response to Julian's rhetoric about "Punic donkeys," Augustine wrote:

> Don't out of pride in your earthly ancestry dismiss one who monitors and admonishes you, *just because I am Punic* [italics mine]. Your Apulian birth is no pledge over Punic forces.[16]

Augustine expressly identifies himself here as a Punic. Thus we can authoritatively rule out the possibility of his having an Italian ethnic background. But in view of his tendency to employ the term "Punic" for both Berbers and those of Phoenician origin, as well as other Berber-like cultural artifacts evident in his own family history, this quotation does nothing to discredit the possibility of his Berber ethnicity.

Is it not time for the academic community in general to take a hard look at the possibility of Augustine's ethnic Berber background and how that might affect the way that we interpret him? It is not an option that most college or seminary instructors typically put before students, and until they do that he will continue to be presented as a European doing a proto-European theology. Only when we give Augustine's own context the attention it deserves can we begin to appreciate the contextuality of his thought. Failure to do so by his great interpreters accounts for why they have appropriated only pieces of his thought and failed to understand it in all its richness.

AFRICAN CONTEXT AND AUGUSTINIAN THEOLOGY

In one sense we might say that Augustine's theology is so rich because of the wide variety of pastoral issues he addressed, and that this wide range of issues was occasioned by doing ministry in a multicultural context like his. In making this suggestion, we need to keep in mind that "race" is a modern concept and that the Roman Empire did not exhibit a racial consciousness as is characteristic of modern Western society. However, the quotations just cited emerging from Augustine's dialogue with Julian and Maximus do indicate an ethnic awareness, even a kind of ethnic rivalry.

Readers acquainted with the modern European and African ethos know that encounters with ethnic diversity and the ethnic rivalries that often ensue from such encounters create a multicultural environment. The ethos of Augustine's multicultural ancient North African context was not all that different.

Although this sort of multiculturalism may have contributed to the wide range of Augustine's theological commitments, I believe that there is another reason contributing to the rich diversity of his thought. Such diversity is more a function of the African Father's fidelity to the whole of the Biblical witness. As subsequent chapters will reveal, most of the diverse images embraced by Augustine have roots in Scripture. This observation has implications for understanding the character of the pastoral-contextual model of theology implied in his thought. Augustine's theology leads us to consider whether the rich diversity of the Biblical witness might entail that the most Biblical theology is one like his, which breaks with the prevailing systematic models in favor of the patterned theological diversity embodied in his thought.

AUGUSTINE'S CAREER AND THE DIVERSITY OF HIS THOUGHT

Some have claimed that the rich diversity of Augustine's thought is a function of its development in distinct stages. There is no question that the African Father experienced a significant spiritual pilgrimage. This pilgrimage is well known, but it is helpful to summarize it inasmuch as I will refer to its various stages throughout the book.

I have already alluded to Augustine's earliest educational endeavors. His father sought to ensure for him the finest classical education available, and he set out on a course of study to become an orator and teacher of rhetoric. But his studies, particularly of the famous Roman lawyer-orator Cicero (160–143 BC), led him to conclude that oratory could not be divorced from the quest for truth. He never renounced that lesson.

The young student's quest for truth led him to study and eventually endorse a dualistic Persian religion, *Manicheism,* which taught that humans are trapped in the cosmic struggle between good and evil, light and darkness. After nine years of practicing this religion, however, Augustine came to renounce it, as a result of his study of Neo-Platonic philosophy. He took up this study after leaving Carthage to come to Milan, where he hoped to find a better climate and better students, for the rhetorical instructions he offered. In Milan he encountered

another milestone. The great bishop and rhetorician Ambrose (born c. 339) came
into his life.

Augustine had no real interest in Christianity at this time, for he had rejected
the religion of his formidable mother in part because of his perception of the
unsophisticated, philosophically naive character of the Bible's literal sense. However, the young rhetorician did attend a number of worship services led by
Ambrose in order to learn from his rhetorical technique. By Augustine's account,
hearing the great preacher's sermons, his "spiritual" reading of Scripture, made
the Bible truly credible and meaningful to him for the first time. It was the beginning of his intellectual conversion to Christianity. (It may be that he was more
influenced at this stage by continuing pleas of his mother, who had accompanied
him to Milan and who greatly admired Ambrose. But some scholars believe that
the greater influence at this stage may have been Ambrose's theological mentor,
Simplicianus [d. 400], who was heavily immersed in Neo-Platonic allegorical
interpretation of Christian Scripture.)[17]

This intellectual conversion was not itself the beginning of Augustine's identification with the Church. That transpired only as a result of his exposure to early
African monasticism, and specifically to accounts of the life of the great early
monk Anthony. Overcome with joy, Augustine was baptized and returned to
Africa, determined to live as a monk. It was not to be. He was reluctantly
ordained a priest in 391 and four years later consecrated Bishop of Hippo, a position he held until his death in 430.

During his career as a Christian writer, Augustine addressed the whole range
of human issues, but we may categorize it in four distinct phases. Each was generally occasioned by the problems, challenges, and heresies he encountered. One
set of writings, his earliest, is directed against Manicheism. A later set of writings
sought to dialogue with and refute *Donatism* (a heresy that rejected the validity
of the ministries of those priests who had in some way lapsed during a period of
persecution, as well as the ministries of those priests whom they had ordained).
His next target was the heresy of *Pelagianism* (a heresy that denied original sin
and taught that humans had freedom to choose between sin and perfection).
Finally, late in his career, Augustine sought to refute the charge that Christianity
had undermined the Roman Empire, during which time he composed his great
work, the *City of God*.

Of course, one who has traversed such diverse spiritual ground changes. In
that sense the diversity of Augustine's thought may be related to its development.
However, another way of assessing his career is to regard it as a series of periods
during which he addressed different concerns. Viewed in this light it is hardly
surprising that we would discern a rich diversity in Augustine's thought, and that
this diversity would be related to the distinct periods in his thoughts.

As I have already suggested, however, this book demonstrates that the diversity of Augustine's theology is not merely a function of the development of his
thought. We will observe a consistency throughout his career that reflects the pat-

tern to the use of Christian concepts to which I have previously alluded. When addressing similar concerns throughout his career, he tended to rely on the same theological conceptions. Thus it is only because certain pastoral concerns predominate in some periods of his thought and not in others that we can identify differences in Augustine's theology from one era to another. The diversity in his thought is ultimately a reflection of his pastoral approach to theology, of his development of a Pastoral-Contextual Theology that addressed the full range of spiritual questions.

Chapter 2

Bible and Theological Method

Scholars have spoken of an Augustinian synthesis of reason and faith. When this insight is coupled with the African Father's famed spiritual pilgrimage through classical learning, Neo-Platonism, and Manicheism, many of his interpreters have been led to attribute to him an allegorical approach to the Bible (bypassing the Bible's literal meaning in favor of "deeper" spiritual meanings purportedly hidden in the text).[1] To an extent, Augustine's Medieval interpreters were correct to identify with such a hermeneutic, with the so-called Augustinian Synthesis of reason and faith (Proverbs; John 1; Rom. 1:20).[2] Especially early in his career, the African Father worked with this set of assumptions, with a hermeneutic not unlike the Method of Correlation model that has dominated much Post-Enlightenment Theology. He interpreted the Bible in light of a set of philosophical assumptions, correlating the Biblical text with these assumptions by reading it allegorically.[3] As Augustine continued to develop his theology and appreciate the Biblical witness, however, he relied less and less on these original hermeneutical assumptions. One finds him undertaking a literal reading of the Biblical text, seeking to absorb experience and reason into its narrative world, much like the dogmatic method of theology. This approach is largely endorsed in the modern era by Karl Barth and Hans Frei.[4]

Both of these hermeneutical approaches appear from time to time through-out Augustine's career, with a sort of consistency not noted by interpreters. He never abandoned allegory and the endeavor to relate reason to faith when he sought to offer apologies for Christian faith or dealt with sanctification. But when dealing with heresies or expositing the logic of the Christian faith, he concentrated more on the literal sense of the Biblical text as the norm, if not the source of hermeneutical conclusions. And when concerned with apologetics in more implicit ways while explicating the faith, the African Father employed something like the modern Method of Critical Correlation. Augustine's contextually conditioned use of these distinct hermeneutics, allegory and a kind of narrative approach to Scripture, provides significant insights into his own theological method. Identifying the ways in which he utilized these distinct hermeneutical approaches also furnishes insights about the most effective use of these hermeneutical alternatives throughout Post-Augustinian Church History, as in the twenty-first century and beyond.

TOWARD AN ALLEGORICAL-APOLOGETIC HERMENEUTIC

As with most matters pertaining to understanding Augustine, it is well to begin biographically with his spiritual pilgrimage. Augustine observed that reading Cicero taught him to love Wisdom. In his youth Scripture seemed unworthy in comparison to Cicero.[5]

Looking back on his journey, the African Father remarked that it was better for him to have read the Platonists before reading Scripture. This had helped him, he concluded, more clearly to see the difference between the Biblical witness and Plato.[6]

As a result of his spiritual journeys, Augustine began appreciating what once offended him about Scripture. In fact, he came to regard these characteristics as indicating its profound mystery.[7] Indeed, Augustine subsequently claimed, while explaining and defending the Trinity, that the Bible suits itself to babes, using words taken from the corporal realm to raise readers to things transcendent.[8]

A turning point in the young Augustine's new appreciation of Scripture was when he first came to endorse Ambrose's letter-spirit distinction, and as a result did not merely read Scripture literally.[9] A kind of Pauline Law-Gospel distinction was implied in his appropriation of this hermeneutical perspective. For instance, in his *Confessions* where he describes his appropriation of this hermeneutic, Augustine speaks of God withdrawing so that we might return, that He has descended so we might ascend to Him. We must become lowly enough to hold the lowly Jesus as God.[10] But contrary to the conclusions of many interpreters, it is by no means clear that this letter-spirit distinction always entails allegory for the African Father, or even for Ambrose for that matter.[11]

A number of Augustinian commitments entail or are at least compatible with an allegorical reading of the Bible. They emerge when he seeks to relate faith to philosophy or concerns himself with issues of living the good life (sanctification). Thus in *On True Religion,* philosophy functions in Augustine's view as the framework for understanding faith.[12] The Christian religion, he claims at one point, always existed. Only after Christ did it come to be called "Christian."[13]

In two other works with an apologetic agenda, the same concern to relate faith to reason and philosophy emerges. For when theologians operate with such an agenda, because the Bible was not written with the avant-garde philosophy of the day with which the theologian is in dialogue, the Bible can no longer be read literally. Thus in *On the Usefulness of Believing,* a work of apologetics and anti-Manichee polemics, the African Father contended that no one doubted that the soul is immortal, that all religion is concerned to make it blessed (preoccupied with salvation).[14] And in the *Soliloquies* he claims that reason can demonstrate God to the mind.

On True Religion also addressed apologetics combined with concern about lifestyle (sanctification) issues, and so it is not surprising to find he urged readers to use reason in order to turn to God. He also asserted that Plato saw the way of salvation, for like the catholic faith he called the human race away from desire for temporal goods to the spiritual. Christianity is construed as making Platonic truths generally available to common people. Indeed, Plato himself was nearly Christian, Augustine contends. Examples of similar assertions abound throughout Augustine's career. Not just in apologetic contexts, but also when refuting the claims of the Manichees, the African Father claimed that what faith affirms reason also understands.[15]

This sort of correlation of reason and faith, understanding reason and philosophy as gateways to faith, is evident in Augustine's adoption of a kind of natural theology in similar contexts of pastoral concern with apologetics. For example, as late as his *City of God,* the African Father claimed that there is nothing in pagan theology for which Christian faith cannot account. Philosophers from all parts of the world, including the Egyptians, are said to believe in the true God and in the creation of all. Earlier he had claimed that what Plato and his devoted interpreter Plotinus say of God is true. In a similar vein, in his *On the Trinity,* Augustine even asserted that anyone who sincerely seeks what is above is really seeking God.[16]

In this context, specifically while dialoguing with the relationship between faith and philosophy, seeking to persuade his reader (apologetics), Augustine affirmed a construal of Scripture most suggestive of an allegorical approach to Scripture. He claimed that Scripture makes the deep mysteries of philosophy accessible to all.[17]

Later in his career, as he sought to relate the Trinity doctrine to our rational judgments of what is of value, Augustine even went so far as to endorse something like a Cosmological Argument, or at least to contend that the world testifies to God's existence. The Universe, he asserted, proclaims its dependence on a supremely good establisher. Its nature leads to the conclusion that there must be a Creator.[18]

Earlier when critiquing Manichee denials of the goodness of creation, he asserted that every rational creature (by its relation to the whole) proclaims the Creator.[19] In the famous discourse on memory in the *Confessions,* while seeking to know God from an anthropological starting point, he claimed that God is in the mind.[20] In *On True Religion,* similarly concerned with an apologetic agenda, Augustine claimed that Truth is higher than our minds, that the unchangeable substance of our minds is God.[21]

AUGUSTINE'S USE OF ALLEGORY

Express affirmations of an allegorical approach to hermeneutics appear first in the Augustinian corpus in works refuting the Manichees. Writing against this heresy, in response to charges of immorality in the Old Testament framed by Faustus, a Manichee leader, Augustine expressed an openness to reading the Old Testament Prophetic narratives either allegorically or literally. No matter, he insisted, one must read them as having moral and religious character.[22]

In *On True Religion,* a work as already noted that was at least in part devoted to the apologetic agenda of sorting out the relation between authority and reason, he specifically expressed an openness to allegorical interpretations, albeit at some points in a guarded way.[23] In another work directed against the Manichee critique, the African Father urged first retrospectively that we not read Old Testament Law literally,[24] and even expressly affirmed a fourfold sense of Scripture:

> The whole Old Testament Scripture, to those who diligently desire to know it, is handed down with a four-fold sense—historical, aetiological, analogical, and allegorical. . . . In Scripture, according to the historical sense, we are told what has been written or done. Sometimes the historical fact is simply that such and such a thing was written. According to the aetiological sense we are told for what cause something has been done or said. According to the analogical sense we are shown that the Old and New Testaments do not conflict. According to the allegorical sense we are taught that everything in Scripture is not to be taken literally but must be understood figuratively.[25]

In the same treatise Augustine noted that the need for allegorical interpretation was no accident. Endeavoring to persuade his old Manichee friend Honoratus of faith's rationality, the African Father suggested that some things in Scripture that seem to offend were put there on purpose, so that we might look for their hidden meaning.[26]

Allegory was still used later in Augustine's career in contests similar to those which characterized his earlier use of this hermeneutic. In the final book of his *Confessions,* while dealing with issues of Christian living in the context of his exegesis of the Creation accounts, Augustine engaged in an allegorical interpretation of Genesis 1:28 (though it is not clear if he actually read it figuratively, i.e., retaining the text's literal sense while indicating it points to a meaning beyond itself).[27]

In 396 or later, when noting what we consider in our sober senses (dialoguing with reason), along with a certain concern about holiness, he claimed that phrases ascribing severity or evil to God and the faithful that seem wicked should be interpreted allegorically.[28] But he did not do this in a sermon delivered early in the fifth century, as he read the text of Jesus' interaction with the prostitute (Luke 7:37) narratively while attending to the Donatist rejection of fellowship with sinners.[29]

If we return to the earlier 396 treatise, *On Christian Doctrine,* it will be noted that Augustine also recommended that we interpret figuratively if a Biblical commandment seems to enjoin a crime.[30] He himself apparently recognized the validity of a more literal approach along with his commitment to the appropriateness of allegory. Thus in one of his later sermons he seemed to advise that the interpreter should let the nature of the exegeted text determine whether to interpret literally or figuratively.[31]

The African Father's ongoing use of an allegorical hermeneutic is evident even as late as 413 or sometime in the next decade and a half when dialoguing in the *City of God* with philosophical critiques of Christian views of eternal life, and so engaging in apologetics.[32] He claimed in reference to Biblical accounts of Paradise that nothing forbids understanding the text allegorically. Even if there is no historical reference, he had no objections, though he still claimed to believe in the historical truth manifest in the narrative.[33]

In another part of this treatise, Augustine more strongly insisted on noting the historical facts of certain Old Testament texts even when engaging in allegorical interpretation. In this case he was engaging not so much in apologetics as in tracing the logic of Christian faith, the history of the City of God. (His approach may have been more figural than allegorical in this case.)[34] When the context changed in one of his earlier epistles, as he sought to refute the Donatist heresy, he insisted that allegory must be subordinate to Scripture's plain sense.[35]

At any rate, it is evident that Augustine relied on an allegorical interpretation of Scripture throughout his career, though this hermeneutic did predominate in the early years of his involvement in Christianity. The transition to greater appreciation of the literal sense of Scripture may be a function of his devoting more attention to apologetics and issues pertaining to Christian responsibility (sanctification) than he did in his later years, when his agenda was more preoccupied with refuting the heresies of Donatism and Pelagianism or with depicting the logic of Christian faith, either by laying out its relation to world history or by writing documents with a catechetical flavor.

Modern Versions of Polysemy: A Method of Critical Correlation

Augustine did not totally reject the commitment to a passage of Scripture having multiple, polysemous meaning, even on some occasions when he emphasized the Biblical text as his starting point for theology and focused on its literal meaning. Indeed, at several points, something in between his literal, Narrative approach to Scripture and its commitment to the priority of God's Word in shaping the experience of the faithful is combined with his allegorical sympathies and their corresponding commitment to a philosophical starting point for reflecting on the Word. Commitments like these are of course most reminiscent of the modern Method of Critical Correlation.[36]

This sort of theological method is apparent in Augustine's *On the Trinity* in a context in which he sought to explain and exhort faith in the Trinity while subsequently showing how the Triune God is reflected in the human mind and self-knowledge. Essentially the African Father insisted in that context that we must believe first, that the Word of God is prior to our experience and understanding, and yet Greek philosophical assumptions function for him as a basis for interpreting what the Word reveals. The movement here is from revelation to philosophy to faith/understanding.

Augustine operates with these assumptions as he first claims that you cannot see or know God if you do not love Him.[37] But, he adds, it is impossible to love what is entirely unknown. The mind at least has to have a picture of what it loves.[38] Likewise in self-knowledge there is a sense in which something of one's own mind and of the value of knowledge is already known and loved.[39]

Augustine expressly invokes Greek philosophical assumptions at this point in explaining how we come to recognize and believe in the Biblical witness concerning Christ. The Bible stimulates our faith not by focusing on mental images, but on the Idea of human nature already in our minds.[40] By this philosophical knowledge our thought about Christ is shaped. Augustine adds that the dynamic is not precisely the same in the case of the Trinity, and yet here too his reliance on Greek philosophical assumptions about the need to know the universal form in order to believe and recognize a concrete reality is no less diminished. To believe and understand the Trinity, he argues, we must love God. But how can we love what we do not to some extent know? We know love, he contends, which is comprised of loved, lover, and love itself. Since God is love itself, we already know God to some extent through this love which He initiates in order to make it possible for us to love. Saturated in this divine love, we can know the triune God in loving the love that makes us love.[41]

This movement from the Word (Christian images) to shaping our experience and from the experience we bring back to our understanding of the Word is precisely the circularity posited by modern proponents of the Method of Critical Correlation. It is not surprising that this combination of prioritizing the Word of God over experience, yet rendering the interpretation of the Word dependent on human experience and philosophy, should emerge in the dual context Augustine addressed—explaining the content of faith, though with an apologetic agenda. It is different in those contexts when Augustine's concern focuses on expositing the logic and content of faith apart from the apologetic agenda. Then his reliance on philosophy's role as a support in interpreting Scripture is virtually diminished, as he noted in a 396 letter to Eusebius. Liberal studies are not germane in these contexts, as the African Father claimed, but only Holy Scripture and ecclesiastical documents.[42] The authority of the Word of God, and faith that is derived from it, is deemed sufficient and even necessary for understanding.

AUGUSTINE'S NARRATIVE HERMENEUTIC

In contexts in which Augustine endeavored only to clarify, explain, or exhort the content of Christian faith, he sought not so much to demonstrate the intelligibility of Scripture as to assert its authority. He does so by claiming the apostolicity of the Biblical writings or that they have been transmitted to the Church through Apostolic lines by the bishops. In numerous instances he even uses the stronger language of divine inspiration.[43] Indeed, in such contexts he goes so far as to contend that Scriptures are justly called divine.[44] He even refers to "sacred and infallible Scripture."[45] In fact, the Christian faith itself is said to be infallible.[46]

In several other contexts the African Father affirmed Biblical authority in this strong sense. In a dialogue with Jerome, explaining his reasons for disputing some of the eminent translator's work, he contended that the Bible is without error.[47] In disputes with heretics, he argued that Scripture tells no lies, does not deceive, and that the Biblical authors were not mistaken.[48] This claim for the Bible's reliability, indeed its infallibility, is even extended at one point in the *City of God* when Augustine, while laying out the logic of faith, encounters human conjectures about the origin of humanity. In a context similar to that faced by modern Fundamentalism he insisted on the Bible's reliability even concerning chronological information.[49]

Reason and philosophy have no role in verifying the authority of Scripture in these instances. In fact, at one point in his *Confessions* as he sought merely to exposit the logic of Christian faith, Augustine insisted that, as in the case of many truths that must be believed on the word of others, one can believe in the authority of Scripture on the word of those who believe in the Bible. On these grounds, he observed, what he once deemed absurdities in Scripture now served for him as a reminder that it is a book for all that could be read easily and yet preserved the deepest part of its mystery.[50]

Given these commitments, something like modern versions of Narrative Theology or Neo-Orthodox *Heilsgeschichte* views of Scripture (which hold that core Biblical accounts pertaining to salvation really happened, though their historical veracity cannot be verified with ordinary critical tools) emerge in the *Confessions* and elsewhere when Augustine concerns himself with expositing the logic of faith. As these modern approaches contend that the Bible lures us into the world it depicts and then we in turn have our experience shaped by that world, so the African Father contends in such contexts of exposition that the Word of God impacts our experience, revealing what we cannot know of ourselves.[51]

This commitment to understanding the Word as shaping or interpreting the experience of the faithful is typical of the theological perspective of the *City of God*. We are lured into this world history. Interpreters claim that for Augustine the Bible is the basis of a Christian culture.[52] Elsewhere, in a sermon that tells the story of Jesus' encounter with the woman who was a sinner (Luke 7:36–50), Augustine contends that Bible stories are said to be represented "before the eyes of the heart."[53]

Another way of embodying these commitments is to affirm the methodological priority of the Word in Scripture to our philosophical speculations about it. Augustine does this when expositing the faith (sometimes as embodied in The Creed) or when combating heretics who rely on reason as the ground for faith. In these contexts the African Father expressly asserts that faith precedes reason, that "you must begin with faith and not rather with reason."[54] He made the same point in other ways by claiming that only the pure in heart truly know God and that to discern God, the mind must be trained by the Rule of Faith. When responding to the despair caused by philosophical speculation, he once observed that nothing would remain stable in society if we believed nothing that could not first be scientifically established.[55]

Such methodological commitments in these contexts, specifically to begin theologizing with the assumption of Biblical authority against the Manichees, led Augustine to endorse a kind of Ontological Proof for God's existence, as he contended that Reason knows a reality (Truth) beyond itself to exist, and the very nature of God demands that this reality be identified as God. His comments here effectively subordinate reason to faith in a way that did not characterize his arguments for God's existence when dealing with apologetic concerns.[56] There is a systematic character to the African Father's thought in the sense that what he says in a given context is consistent throughout his career. Yet he nevertheless displays a conceptual richness if we consider his thought when he addresses radically different contexts and issues.

There are times when at first glance Augustine seems to correlate reason and faith in ways that might lead casual readers to conclude that he is opting for a kind of allegorical approach to hermeneutics or at least to the sort of the Critical Correlation Method previously considered. If interpreted in this way it is easier to see why many scholars have overlooked the African Father's occasional, contextually conditioned employment of a Narrative hermeneutic.

For example, we can identify the Narrative hermeneutic's subordination of reason to faith in remarks in *Nature of the Good, On the Predestination of the Saints, Enchiridion,* and *Usefulness of Believing.* In the case of the first of these, while refuting Manichee teachings Augustine claims that Christian truths are known through both reason and faith. However, he immediately follows this comment with references to the Biblical witness, so that "the less intelligent who cannot follow the argument may believe on divine authority, and so may deserve to reach understanding."[57] Faith, it seems, precedes reason after all.

In his work on predestination, critiquing Semi-Pelagianism, the African Father noted that thinking is prior to faith. He immediately added, however, that in what pertains to religion and piety we are not capable of thinking anything of ourselves. Consequently, he concluded, faith must be a gift of God making the rest possible.[58] When the African Father connected faith and reason, he frequently portrayed the right use of reason as dependent on faith or on the Word of God.

In the *Enchiridion,* a work devoted to a summary of Augustine's thought with an eye toward the Gospel's influence on Christian life, he echoed many of the same themes regarding the priority of faith over reason. True wisdom is piety, he contended.[59] In response to questions of how reason does or does not support faith, Augustine noted that we must begin with faith, not reason. Faith that works by love endeavors by purity of life to attain sight, so the pure in heart know the vision of supreme happiness.[60]

While describing his spiritual pilgrimage and the nature of religion (its logic) in *Usefulness of Believing,* he claims that even though we owe knowledge to reason and our beliefs to authority, it is still the case that authority, the source of our faith, is prior to reason. Indeed, he argues, God alone must provide wisdom, for without faith we would not even seek God.[61] Augustine posits a similar prioritizing of faith over reason in *On True Religion,* a treatise that begins with apologetics but moves to exposition of the logic of faith and conversion. He adds here, perhaps because there is also an apologetic interest in view, that reason is not entirely absent from authority.[62]

Augustine offers an observation along the same line when expositing doctrine in a work whose overall purpose was devoted to laying out his metaphysics while taking cognizance of apologetics. He contends that things we hold according to faith and that reason also demonstrates are fortified by Scripture, so that the less intelligent can follow.[63]

The *City of God,* a work devoted to expounding the emergence of the two cities as they have impinged on human history, and so of the unfolding of the logic of Christian faith, is another treatise in which this prioritizing of faith and God's Word over reason and experience is evident. We previously noted how in segments of this treatise devoted to apologetics, the African Father notes that there is nothing in pagan theology for which Christian faith cannot account. Philosophers from all parts of the world (including Egyptians) believe in the true God creating all.[64] But in the same work, perhaps because of the treatise's overall agenda and lack of preoccupation with apologetics, he also referred to Christianity's superiority to all philosophy and claimed that it is rarely and only with great effort that a mind soars to the unchangeable substance of God.[65] He makes a similar point in *On Christian Doctrine* when dealing with internal, nonapologetic questions about the meaning of Biblical signs. He contends in this context that Christians can claim what is true in Plato.[66]

Although these comments could be taken as the African Father's endorsement of a natural theology, he clarifies elsewhere what he intends in these remarks. In *On the Spirit and the Letter,* though willing to say that God can be known through invisible things of creation, he insisted that though we may come to God in this, we shall not glorify Him as He deserves.[67] Likewise, in the *City of God,* as he explains how it is that Plato holds so many truths about God, Augustine notes that some have speculated that the great philosopher was exposed to Jeremiah during travels to Egypt. While affirming this unequivocally at points in his career, the African Father amends the claim, but not without holding onto his belief that Plato was exposed to Hebrew Scriptures while journeying in Egypt.[68] There is no compromise here in these contexts in his insistence that Greek and even Egyptian thought, which interestingly he deemed older than that of the Greeks, is not older the Prophets (as long as Abraham is considered a prophet).[69] In contexts where the logic of faith is being articulated, the story of Christianity told without specific polemical or apologetic concerns, Augustine's commitment to prioritizing faith over reason is quite evidently unequivocal. In fact, at least at one point in this great treatise, when responding to the critiques of reason, he dramatically emphasizes this point, actually breaking the reason-faith synthesis that characterizes his thought, and instead contending that faith believes the incredible (1 Cor. 1:21, 25; Rom. 1:22).[70]

The Literal Sense and the Bible's Historicity

The priority of faith over reason has implications for advice Augustine offers about reading Scripture, advice that is necessary in order to maintain the reader's faithfulness to the literal sense. To get to the literal sense, to what Scripture reveals, Augustine contends that we must put aside ourselves and our (critical and philosophical) presuppositions. Thus he advises in contexts in which his aim is not apologetics that the key to interpreting Scripture is a godly temper, not criticism.[71]

In a similar context, devoting attention to how we are to understand ambiguous signs, he urges readers to study Scripture with an awareness that knowledge puffs up (makes one unduly proud). Echoing the Lutheran Reformation's Theology of the Cross, Augustine exhorts us to come to the text with charity (especially Christ's Cross).[72] Other times, while preaching on the genealogies of Luke and Matthew or when exhorting faith, he counsels that we not be disturbed by what we do not yet understand or be puffed up by what we do understand.[73]

Augustine never or rarely abandoned the synthesis of reason and faith, even when he addressed issues related to the logic of faith. Thus in *On Christian Doctrine*, in a section devoted to interpreting unknown signs in Scripture, the African Father nevertheless reiterates the importance of human knowledge. For the sake of the necessities of life, he asserts, we must not neglect human arrangements. However, he adds, these branches of learning are only useful in matters related to bodily senses—objects past or present, and in reasoning.[74] In a manner most reminiscent of Neo-Orthodoxy, contemporary Narrative Theology, and even of the Protestant Reformers, he states that what is learned from other sources that is hurtful must be condemned. If useful, such knowledge is already in the Bible.[75]

Given Augustine's commitments to Biblical authority and the previously noted comments regarding Biblical infallibility in contexts in which he merely exposits the logic of faith, it is interesting to observe how in some situations he takes positions suggesting the infallibility of the Bible on all matters and in other contexts limits the authority of Scripture. He takes a strong view of Biblical authority at one point in *Usefulness of Believing*, as he asserts that *all truth* is in Scripture in a context in which he is describing his faith pilgrimage and responding to the Manichees, but concerned with difficulties in interpreting Scripture.[76]

This set of hermeneutical suppositions entails a move the African Father makes in the *City of God*, as he attempts to correlate certain events from pagan history with contemporary Biblical incidents.[77] Elsewhere in the text, a related though somewhat distinct way of understanding the relation between the Biblical accounts and secular (critical) history emerges. He claims that the most trustworthy chronicle of the past is offered by one who is also a prophet of future things. Whatever in secular histories runs counter to divine authority should be deemed false.[78] Although in one sense this comment could be taken as a rejection of the authority of secular histories when they conflict with the Biblical testimony, in another sense a kind of accommodation acknowledging the validity of these histories might be in play, not unlike the concept of *Heilsgeschichte* in modern theology.[79] Augustine contends here that prophetic/eschatological themes are more important than historical accuracy.

At other points the convergence between his thinking and *Heilsgeschichte* theology is even more apparent. Historical events of the Bible, he claims in those contexts (as he addresses those who only believe on rational grounds), cannot be known, but only believed on grounds of credible testimony. "I should not believe the Gospel unless the authority of the Catholic Church moved me so to do."[80] Elsewhere, in a work concerning epistemology, he claims that with regard to historical events, we must believe in order to understand.[81] In any case, when merely expositing the nature of Christian faith or when encountering critiques of Biblical authority head-on in outright polemics, then Augustine asserts the absolute authority of the Bible in all spheres of knowledge. This has been a pattern for most subsequent theology.

It is different when Biblical authority is described with a view toward the Bible's impact on Christian living or when encountering critiques of its authority in the contexts of preaching or teaching in an ad hoc apologetic, rather than polemical modes. (The context I describe here is not the same as when one's sole purpose is academic or systematic apologetics. Such apologetics are more ad hoc. Systematic, academic apologetics tend to rely on allegorical understandings of the Bible.) We can identify some compromise of an unequivocal insistence on the Bible's historical veracity in *Usefulness of Believing*, as he addresses those who challenge the veracity of Christian faith even while explaining the nature of faith in Christ. Miracles, Augustine claims, make fools more ready to purify their lives and morals under the constraint of authority. This is why Christ did miracles. He did them for the sake of morals.[82]

In the *City of God*, the subject of the Bible's miracles is discussed when, while continuing to narrate the End of the City of God, Augustine addresses critics of Christianity who object that miracles no longer happen. The African Father notes that the closed canon puts the miracles of the Bible in everyone's minds, as they are fixed. Miracles still happen, but not everyone hears of them.[83] If it is hard to believe the Miracle of the Resurrection, he notes, it is even more miraculous that the world has believed, and that itself is a miracle that suffices.[84] The miracles of today bear witness to Christ's Resurrection.[85] In another way of making the point he contends that miracles no longer happen because they are no longer needed as they once were to help the unbelieving world, and their continuation might lead the faithful to focus on visible things. If criticism intends to imply that they never happened, he appeals to widespread acceptance of Christ's Resurrection and Ascension to heaven.[86]

One can identify similar lines of endorsing the Bible's authority, its literal sense, without necessarily insisting that everything the Bible says pertains to every sphere of human knowledge. Thus in his *Treatise on the Merits and Forgiveness of Sins and on the Baptism of Infants*, written against Pelagianism, Augustine maintains that Scripture does not speak on all issues. When it is silent, he contends, we should use restraint (when dealing with issues about which the Bible is not clear, like whether the soul is propagated).[87]

Of course, the different versions in the Gospels have been sources of concern for the Church since their canonization, if not before. Thus it is not surprising that Augustine addresses this matter, contending for how much sense it makes to have different versions of the same story of Jesus, as he writes against Manichees in an effort to defend the reliability of the Biblical witness.[88] In other works, addressing similar challenges, the African Father notes the slight discrepancies among parallel accounts, but deals with them by claiming that the Bible deals simply with round numbers, that the Bible often expresses the whole under a part.[89]

In an exposition of the literal sense of the Book of Genesis, primarily in dialogue with the Manichees and their critical approach to Scripture, Augustine takes a position most suggestive of Post-Liberal Narrative Theology and other approaches indebted to the philosophy of Ludwig Wittgenstein. (All of these modern theologians refer to the Bible's meaning and truth only in the religious realm, so that these claims cannot be discredited by other academic disciplines.) Consistent with the suppositions of these theologians, the African Father claims in this context that Scripture's inspiration pertains only to salvation. The Bible is true, even if at odds with rational perceptions about the physical world.[90]

In much the same spirit, Augustine counsels when dealing with ambiguities in the Bible that we must make allowance for the condition of Biblical times when undertaking Biblical interpretation. (At this point he is referring to Old Testament polygamy.)[91] Since the Bible is not about science and history, he claims that history is helpful in interpreting Scripture with regard to the course of an historical narrative. Science is also helpful, he asserts, in those Biblical narratives concerning the existing state of things—the nature of animals, trees, and so on.[92]

No matter how the Bible is read, by whatever means, loyalty to its literal sense seems nonnegotiable for the African Father. Thus in several instances when dealing with criticisms of the literal sense of Scripture, he insists that the miracles of the Bible, even if treated figuratively or symbolically, give us no reason not to believe them.[93]

SCRIPTURE AND TRADITION

Catholic that he was, it is hardly surprising to find Augustine to be a theologian who affirmed the authority of both Scripture and Tradition. The African Father advocated appeal to Tradition (reception by the churches) to determine the canonical Books, in at least one case in order to authorize inclusion of certain apocryphal books in the canon.[94] When decisions were to be made about ecclesiastical matters, he appealed to both the Bible and Tradition, allowing the latter to function especially in cases where Scripture laid down no definite rule. When engaged in apologetics he advocated appeal to the Rule of Faith (early versions of The Creed) in order to clarify the ambiguities in Scripture.[95]

Indeed, against the Manichee heretics, Augustine contended that the reason for believing is not found in the Scriptures alone, but is grounded in the Catholic tradition. As he famously uttered, "For my part, I should not believe the gospel except as moved by the authority of the Catholic Church." By his account, it is the ancient and universal character of Tradition (established through consensus among the bishops and the people over time) that renders its claims authoritative.[96]

Augustine's Credal orientation is evident at other points. The Creed, he contends, makes the Catholic faith known ("faith," that is, as that which is believed as distinct from the faith by which one believes). In The Creed and The Lord's Prayer the three graces faith, hope, and love are exemplified. The Creed is said to be milk for babes, but food for the strong when spiritually apprehended. For Augustine, The Lord's Prayer has to do with affirmations of hope.[97] It is evident that for the African Father most of the time there is no Biblical hermeneutic apart from Tradition. On a number of occasions, however, when heretics were appealing to tradition to make their points, the African Father opts for the authority of Scripture alone.[98] This is a significant insight for appreciating the rationale for the Protestant endorsement of *sola scriptura*. It is to be affirmed when the Tradition seems to sanction heterodox views.

FIGURAL INTERPRETATION

We previously observed some ambiguity about Augustine's use of the letter-spirit distinction, whether it entails his reliance on figural interpretation or allegory. The letter-spirit distinction has characteristically been taken to mean that we are not to take the figurative sayings of Scripture literally.[99] But at least in sections of *On the Spirit and the Letter* devoted to expositing the faith, this is not what it means for Augustine. In this work against the Pelagians he notes that the distinction really means that the letter of the Law admonishing us to avoid sin kills if the life-giving Spirit is not present.[100]

In connection with the letter-spirit distinction understood in this way, we find something like the Law-Gospel distinction posited by Augustine elsewhere in *On Christian Doctrine*. Scriptures are said to teach humans that being entangled or in love with the world, drawn away from the love of God, they are compelled to bewail their condition and then will be led to fix attention on God.[101] In a similar manner Augustine noted that Biblical texts ascribing severity to God are to be understood as addressed to those not subduing their lust.[102]

The letter-spirit distinction is also construed by Augustine as a reminder that grace lies hidden under a veil in the Old Testament, but is revealed in the Gospel.[103] He advises us to read the Old Testament as a shadow and figure of things to come.[104] These remarks seem more amenable to understanding the letter-spirit distinction as a reference to respecting the literal sense of the Old Testament and so to advocate reading the Bible figurally, not allegorically.

But there is a clear ambiguity, if not outright diversity, in how Augustine relates the Old and New Testaments. In a work against the Manichees and in his *Confessions* as he describes his faith pilgrimage, he refers to the need to read the Old Testament "spiritually," not "literally," in a manner that sounds like the espousal of allegory.[105] In both of these instances Augustine is not as concerned with giving reasons for his views as in the *Usefulness of Believing*, when he expressly affirms allegory in demonstrating the value of the Old Testament.[106] The texts cited above focus only on the nature of Biblical authority. As such, they are less apologetic in intent than *Usefulness of Believing*.

Augustine could be critical of allegory, noting both its strengths and weaknesses. We observe this in *On the Trinity* as he explains the Trinity from its (obscure) reflections in the nature of human beings. In that context, he expressly addresses allegorical readings of the Old Testament and its relation to the New Testament, noting how enigmatic allegory is. His point seems to be that just as the Trinity is obscure in human nature, so the use of allegory can, but does not always, obscure.[107]

Similar patterns regarding Augustine's attitude toward the use of allegory and figural readings, not literal readings (though in this case his attitude toward allegory is ambiguous), are evident in his insistence in *On Christian Doctrine* that the Bible is not to be read literally in all cases. In this case, in a context where he addresses the exegesis of ambiguous signs, he appeals to the Pauline letter-spirit distinction in such a way as to authorize some departure from the Bible's literal sense.[108]

I reiterate that in all cases, though, even when the Old Testament is read allegorically and not literally, Augustine still insists that no one doubts that the narrated Old Testament events really took place.[109] In the midst of all his hermeneutical diversity, there are some continuities. The African Father refuses to neglect the Bible's literal sense. Such commitment to the Bible's literal sense is evident in his unambiguous effort to correlate the two Testaments figurally, in accord with the literal sense, in other treatises when he is not engaged in apologetics or philosophical discourse.[110]

In any case, there is general scholarly agreement that in Augustine's career we see an increasing preference for figural over allegorical interpretation.[111] As we can observe, however, this is not a function merely of development in his thought. The increased preference for the literal sense in later years seems to be more a function of Augustine's decreased engagement in apologetics, as he gave more attention to internal church matters of the unfolding of the logic of Christian faith for society.

Figural interpretation may also mean that the readers of Scripture, hearers of the Word of God, experience themselves as figures of the Biblical accounts, such that the Bible's world overcomes and orients the experience of its readers and hearers. I have already noted how often Augustine's hermeneutic embraces this viewpoint. It is especially typical of the *City of God* and other works, as we are lured into the story of world history presented by Augustine's account.

We do not find as much figural interpretation of this type in Augustine's sermons. For example, in his *Ten Homilies on the Epistle of John to the Parthians* we can identify more exposition of Bible stories in Augustine's preaching than the employment of a narrative, storytelling approach.[112] Yet in these cases he does launch his exposition from the Biblical text. He does not commence with philosophical speculation. And in most cases he is engaged in dialogue with Donatism.

Why we do not find as much storytelling preaching in Augustine, given his reliance on a Narrative hermeneutic at points, especially in the context of laying out the logic of faith, is an intriguing question. One might speculate that it is indicative of the impact of Roman rhetoric and its preoccupation with eloquence on the African Father. Of course, in the case of these particular sermons we need to keep in mind that 1 John, the subject of these sermons, is itself not a narrative genre, and so Augustine's use of an expository approach in these cases may be more stylistically appropriate to this genre. And when Augustine preaches on narrative-like texts but employs more expository styles of preaching, he is also preoccupied in those cases with other agendas, like exhorting Christian living or merely recounting the Biblical story without reflection on what it has to do with his hearers. In any case, in a number of sermons, even some directed against Donatist separatism, he actually employs a Narrative approach.[113] It seems that like Augustine's theological hermeneutic, his homiletical style was contextual. He was a proponent of both allegory and figural interpretation, and the distinction between these approaches is forfeit at the peril of compromising an inclusive portrait of Augustine.

MAKING SENSE OF THE LITERAL SENSE

Some interpreters (Bertrand de Margerie, G. H. Allard, Curtis Freeman, and S. M. Zarb), influenced by DeConstruction and other post-Enlightenment models of interpretation, contend that Augustine himself does not believe in a single literal meaning, that he is a proponent of polysemous meaning.[114] There are certainly instances where Augustine says things that either outrightly affirm or at least give support to this conclusion. Typical of his pattern in using allegorical exegesis, these instances occur when the African Father is engaged in apologetics, or is at least dialoguing with philosophical questions.

In a treatise in which he addresses epistemological questions in dialogue with his son (though with theological issues in mind regarding God's use of sign), Augustine notes that words do not indicate the mind of the speaker. For one may speak of one thing while thinking of something else. Sometimes what the speaker says, Augustine claims, does not convey the same meaning to those who hear him.[115]

When addressing the diversity of opinions about the meaning of Genesis 1 and seeking to bring harmony, Augustine concedes that he does not know the mind of Moses. He suggests that Moses may have meant several things, and that perhaps Moses foresaw all the various valid meanings of his words. Later, though, in the same work, with a focus on glorifying God, Augustine suggests that Moses did not see what his words came to mean.[116] These comments remind one of those texts cited above that seem to reflect something like the Method of Critical Correlation in his thought. Not surprisingly the present texts share the twofold agenda that characterized the other texts—an apologetic agenda related to a concern to exposit Christian beliefs.

The subjectivism that seems to underlie these comments is not the only epistemology employed by the African Father. By contrast, when explicating the logic of faith while responding to false teachings and skepticism he posited the normative accuracy of our clear perceptions and the objectivity of truth.[117] It was such an epistemology that allowed Augustine clear to appeal to the idea of just one meaning to the literal sense, in *On Genesis Literally Interpreted*, as he urges that we choose the author's intended meaning:

> When we read the inspired books in the light of this wide variety of true meanings which are drawn from a few words and founded on the firm basis of Catholic belief, let us choose that one which appears as certainly the meaning intended by the author.[118]

It is apparent how there is even diversity in what Augustine means by the "literal sense" of Scripture, and as in the case of his hermeneutic this diversity is related to differences in context. When addressing philosophical, apologetic issues or seeking harmony, Augustine seems to endorse a polysemous understanding of the literal sense. But when the issue is simply an exposition of the faith or a refutation of heresies that challenge the ordinary, plain meaning of the

Biblical text, then Augustine insists that the literal meaning means just that, the single plain meaning of what the author intended.

Signs

In closing, we can gain further clarity about Augustine's hermeneutics by examining his discussion of signs. The same sort of pattern of favoring allegory and polysemous meaning, of subordinating the literal meaning of language to some deeper truth when addressing apologetics and other philosophical issues, is again apparent in Augustine's treatment of this topic of signs. The most detailed, though not the only, discussion of this topic emerged in *On the Teacher,* the dialogue with his son about how truth is attained (epistemology), though not without concern about the logic of faith (about how God uses signs). His reflections on signs at this point closely parallel his hermeneutical and ontological orientation that I previously noted in *On the Trinity,* a book devoted to apologetic aims of showing how the triune God is reflected in the human mind and self-knowledge.

Given Augustine's general preoccupation with memory (especially to be highlighted in the next chapter), it is not surprising that because he contends we learn by remembering, it follows that words are mere "signs" of what we remember, as when we use words in prayer, though we need not tell God anything.[119] All words are names (can function as names), in his view. We cannot point something out without a sign; even gestures are signs.[120]

Augustine's apologetic concern in this work emerges, as he subordinates language to philosophical realities, after the fashion of Greek philosophy. He contends that words carry the mind to the things of which they are signs. This is the basis for conversation.[121]

Given these commitments, it follows that knowledge conveyed by the sign is more important than the sign (the word) itself. Thus knowledge is better than the words.[122] Ultimately, nothing is learned from words. If I know the meaning of a word it teaches me nothing; if I do not know its meaning, again it teaches nothing. We must know the object signified by the word if it is to be intelligible. Words bid us to look for things, but do not show them to us.[123]

In this apologetic mode, Augustine presents Christ as a way of indicating how Revelation is possible through biblical signs. For given the Greek philosophical presuppositions with which Augustine works in this dialogue (and most of the time), Christ is identified with the Eternal Wisdom that is the source of the universal forms and so of all knowledge to which the signs refer. As such, Augustine can portray Christ as the inner teacher who acquaints the soul with realities signified by signs.[124]

Augustine's subordination of signs to our experience is evident in these contexts even to the point of his claiming that when concerned with things present to our senses, but not presently existing before us, we do not speak of the things themselves, but of images derived from them imprinted on the memory. Indeed, in a manner reminiscent of the perspectivalism indebted to the distinction posited by the great German Enlightenment philosopher Immanuel Kant between noumenon and phenomenon (a belief that absolute truth cannot be found since all experience is relative to the observer who puts her/his imprint on it), the African Father claims that we cannot speak of the images as true or false, for they are private.[125] If anyone hears others speak of their memories, provided the hearer has similar experiences, Augustine contends, the words do not teach such persons. He/she merely recognizes the truth of what has been said by the images that are already in the memory. Words merely put the student on the alert.[126]

In the same context, Augustine also opens the way further to polysemous meaning of signs (and so the Biblical text) as he notes that words do not indicate the mind of the speaker. It is possible to speak of one thing while thinking of something else. Sometimes what a speaker says does not convey the same meaning to those who hear him or her.[127]

An additional example of Augustine's subordination of signs (and so of Scripture to experience) can be identified in his earliest commentary on The Book of Genesis, written to refute the Manichees. He claims that before the Fall communication was immediate. Signs only became necessary, he argues, after the Fall. Likewise in a sermon on John 8:13–14, stressing sanctification and living the Christian life, Augustine claims that Scripture will not be needed when Christ returns.[128]

In another treatise, *On Christian Doctrine*, while addressing the question of the true sense of Scripture and so without the apologetic agenda of the passages already cited in this section, Augustine offers an analogy between Christ being made flesh and the relation between our thoughts and their articulation in speech.[129] These reflections entail that just as our own thoughts are really present in the words we utter, so God is really present in the Word of God. Such theological implications are nearly articulated expressly at another point in the treatise as Augustine claims, while considering questions of how Scripture is to be interpreted, that by Biblical signs (the material things of the world) we are lifted into the presence of the invisible.[130] (It is interesting to note here that the African Father insists on stressing the sovereignty of grace in these contexts as he contends that interpreting a text correctly depends on God's aid.)[131] At least when not engaged in apologetic endeavors, Augustine contends that the language of Scripture renders the divine reality present.

When exhorting faith, the African Father offers other reflections about the Bible's language that are not suggestive of allegory, but are more characteristic of the literalist approach of contemporary Neo-Orthodoxy and Narrative Theology. He notes that terms in Scripture are not to be judged by their use in the world.[132] Again it is evident how in contexts in which apologetics are not part of his agenda, the Augustinian synthesis of reason and faith, of nature and grace, clearly makes the divine side of these dialectics the senior partner.

CONCLUSION: WHAT TO MAKE OF AUGUSTINE'S
CONTEXTUALLY CONDITIONED DIVERSITY

Augustine himself offers some valuable guidance regarding how to order and make sense of the diversity in his hermeneutic. He addressed the question of how to interpret Scripture, whether allegorically as affections of the soul or literally, in *On True Religion*, a work with an overall apologetic aim. However, he answers the question in a segment devoted to extrapolating the nature of faith, with special concern to critique idle curiosity. In that context, he urges appreciation of the one truth that divine providence has spoken by human corporeal creatures. The answer to the question of how to interpret the Bible is in his view to be found in diligent study of Scripture.[133] In other words, he seems to advocate that we are to let the Bible itself, the genre of its literature, determine how it is to be interpreted.

In another treatise as he deals with the nature of Scripture's ambiguities and specifically with how those in error try to dodge Scripture's literal meaning, the African Father insists that what is literal should not be read figuratively. For people are likely to avoid the literal meaning whenever it teaches something contrary to their opinion or enjoins or praises something that is not sanctioned by the custom of their companions.[134]

Of course, Augustine was aware of the numerous texts in Scripture that do not seem to lend themselves to literal interpretation, that are apparently obscure and have no plain meaning. In contexts devoted merely to expositing the content or character of the Biblical faith, he responds with the comforting thought that the obscurities in Scripture are divinely arranged, given by God in order to subdue our pride.[135] One seeking in faith and love has the mysteries of the Bible opened, he contends.[136]

In other works, Augustine provides an additional reason for appreciating the obscurity of Scripture. He says in the *City of God*, while laying out the logic of Christian faith, that such obscurity is good in causing many opinions about truth to be discussed. But in this context he insists again that whatever is said when interpreting the Bible should be confirmed by an obvious text.[137] He makes the same point elsewhere when focusing on internal theological issues about the nature of faith as he advises his hearers to feed on the plain parts of Scripture and to be exercised by the obscure.[138] Once again we note how an authority is conferred on the literal sense in a way that the other senses of Scripture do not have.

In view of his willingness to concede obscurities in Scripture and his own embrace of diverse hermeneutical approaches, it is not surprising to find Augustine also conceding an openness to a variety of interpretations of Scripture in his *Confessions*. His only stipulation is that the meaning of each interpretation must be true. The meaning one derives from a text need not be identical with the author's intention, Augustine insists. For the author may not have seen all the meanings of what he wrote. Indeed, in the context of stipulating openness to a variety of Biblical meanings despite objections to such variety, Augustine

even suggests that some references in the Creation Accounts are to be read allegorically.[139] Allegorical interpretation is embraced in contexts where appreciation of theological diversity is at stake. Allegory seems to be a tool for catholicity
in that sense.

The same point regarding openness to a variety of interpretation is also
affirmed in *On Christian Doctrine*, as Augustine continues to address matters
related to the internal logic of faith. He adds that an interpretation is not opposed
to sound doctrine if it is supported by other Scripture.[140] In other words, Augustine has no problem with different interpretations if the unity of faith is not
undermined.[141] Sometimes texts are read literally, sometimes figuratively, sometimes both ways (figurally). It all depends on the nature of the Biblical text, he
observes. Some texts lend themselves especially to literal interpretation, while
others are more suited to allegorical readings.[142]

Because the literal meaning of a Biblical text has priority, Augustine contends
that this meaning is to be chosen first over the other senses of Scripture unless it
cannot be related to good morals or true faith. Only then is the text is to be interpreted figurally/allegorically. (It should be noted here that he makes this claim in
a context in which he is dealing with the reality of ambiguous signs in the Bible.
It is when dealing with such texts that for him allegory is appropriate. As previously noted, for Augustine the Bible itself determines when certain hermeneutical approaches are appropriate and when they are not.)[143]

How are we to reconcile different interpretations of obscure texts? Augustine's
formula is deceptively simple, yet most profound. We are to practice the rule of
love, he claims. For the meaning is not our own. Tolerance for diversity and pluralism is espoused in these remarks. We are to love the truth uttered by interpretations other than our own. He elaborates on this point in a context in which he
addresses his enemies and critics of his interpretation of The Book of Genesis. At
the same time the African Father even speaks of a flood of meaning that may
come from Moses.[144]

What is laid out clearly in Scripture are matters of faith and life. This insight
is to be used in dealing with obscure texts, he urges.[145] We are to interpret
ambiguous texts, it seems, with these agendas in view.

We are left with the task of trying to order the contextually conditioned
diversity in Augustine's hermeneutic. Perhaps Augustine's remarks in *On Christian Doctrine* make the point most clearly and concisely. Because love is the end
of Scripture, we are not all wrong about the Bible, he contends, if love is built
up by one's interpretation. (In his *Expositions on the Psalms* he makes a related
claim, that all Scripture is about Christ [esp. *His Cross*] or is about Christ and
His Church.)[146] This is certainly consistent with his claim that the Bible's concern with matters of faith and life should guide our interpretation. It is also
consistent with his contention while exhorting faith in sermons that if nothing else were said of love in Scripture nothing more need be said than that God
is love.[147]

In this spirit he offers a rule for interpreting figurative statements: Because Scripture teaches nothing but love, the interpretation must serve the rule of love.[148] In addition he urges that a Biblical text must be read literally if the text refers to doctrine or purity of life.[149] Another somewhat related canon within the canon is proposed by Augustine: In contexts in which he is reflecting on the character of the Christian living (sanctification concerns), he claims that the Bible is a record of our faith to encourage our hope and manifest our love.[150]

The last observation's insight could be deemed compatible with contemporary Narrative Hermeneutics. In essence the African Father's point seems to be that the Bible is not about history and science, that its primary meaning and the nature of its truth claims is about faith, hope, and love. Then he proposes another criterion (this one in a context where he merely deals with internal theological questions about how to interpret Scripture): Whenever there is ambiguity, consult the Rule of Faith.[151]

In closing, it is relevant to consider what Augustine himself says regarding the diversity in his thought. Later in his career, while acknowledging at times in contexts of dialogue with Pelagianism that he had rethought his positions on the relationship between grace and faith, Augustine still claims a continuity with his past writings. He contends in these documents that when he had spoken of free will prior to the later Pelagian controversy, even then he had still deemed some actions to be done from necessity, yet he had nevertheless not forfeited the contention that the individual is responsible for such deeds.[152] Each heresy, he notes, introduces its own new questions.[153]

From his later anti-Pelagian perspective, Augustine cites earlier treatises that he claims made clear that the beginning and end of faith is God's gift.[154] He further notes that even in his earlier works when he was not aware of Pelagians he did write about grace apart from merits. Even in his *Confessions*, Augustine claims, he had taught what Pelagius later criticized as he called for God to give what He commands, and in Augustine's own claim to have been converted by God.[155]

Nevertheless, the African Father remains aware of how contextual even his stress on unconditional grace must be. This awareness on his part is evident in his warnings regarding how predestination must be preached with sensitivity to when hearers are prepared to hear it, that the doctrine must be preached with sensitivity to people of slower understanding.[156] In fact, he advised that when dealing with those who do not persevere, it is better to speak of others, not of those in the congregation.[157]

Augustine also acknowledges the theological diversity in his thought, how he affirms commitments that seem contradictory (just as I have identified in this discussion his use of different hermeneutics). The nature of Scripture demands such diversity in his view. Thus he claims that grace and free will must be taught because both have their proper voices in Scripture.[158]

An appreciation of pluralism in Augustine's thought is not to accuse him of relativism. For example, The Golden Rule in his view is not altered by the diversity of national customs. Other examples could be cited.[159] He even claims in his *Retractions* to adapt his words to the situation he addressed:

> Because this [the origin of evil in the human will] was the subject we proposed to debate, there is not discussion in these books [against the Manichees] of the grace of God whereby He has predestined His elect and Himself prepares the will of those among who make use of their freedom of choice. But wherever an occasion occurs to make mention of this grace it is mentioned in passing not as if it were in question. It is one thing to inquire into the origin of evil, and another to seek the means of returning to man's original good estate and even to a better one.[160]

It is evident that Augustine realizes that when it comes to theology (even his hermeneutic), it really is a matter of context. But this insight has largely been neglected by most of his interpreters. This explains why we have systematized him, rather than learn all that we might from his use of distinct theological methods.

Implications for Theology Today

Augustine's contextual use of Scripture embodies sound insights that prefigure the way the Bible has been used by many of his heirs. His use of allegory and the Method of Correlation for apologetics or comforting despair makes logical sense. It explains the dominance of such a theological model since the Enlightenment, preoccupied as the Western church has been with the task of trying to demonstrate the relevance and intellectual credibility of the Christian faith.[161] A more dogmatic approach was evidenced in Augustine when preaching or articulating the logic of faith. Modern proponents of such approaches have not been so preoccupied with the apologetic task.[162] Likewise, just as when in contexts where he needed to assert the authority of Scripture, Augustine uses the language of divine inspiration and even infallibility, so his modern heirs (in the Fundamentalist and Evangelical Movements) seem to assert these points in response to the perceived erosion of Biblical authority and challenges to the historic faith.

We have also observed in Augustine something in between these two methods, a commitment to the literal sense of Scripture, but understood in a polysemous fashion to enable the introduction of philosophical and other interpretive categories into theological conclusions. As this approach surfaced in contexts in which Augustine was dealing with apologetics to some extent while articulating the logic of Christian faith, so modern advocates of this approach are not as systematically committed to apologetics, while not forgetting this agenda.[163]

Similarly the contextual pattern of Augustine's manner of relating reason and faith, as well as of the relationship between the Law and the Gospel (old and new covenant), is suggestive of patterns in the thought of his theological heirs (Heb. 8:8–13; 2 Cor. 3:6; 5:17). I have already noted how Augustine posits the continuity of reason and faith when addressing issues other than polemics with Pelagianism (especially for apologetic purposes). It is interesting to note that at least two prominent interpreters of Augustine who likewise posited the continuity of reason and faith had pastoral purposes in view similar to the African Father when they posited these commitments. The apologetic concern to reach out to all is evident in the theologies of both Thomas Aquinas and John Calvin. And as Augustine was concerned to affirm the goodness of the physical creation against the Manichees, so Calvin was concerned to affirm a strong doctrine of creation.[164] The affirmation of the continuity of reason and faith seems closely linked to these two pastoral purposes throughout the history of Christian thought (especially the history of Augustinian interpretation).

The continuity of reason and faith is not the only position that Augustine took on this issue. As we have noted, at several points in his career he insisted on the importance of reason in matters of faith, on our inability to comprehend God, most notably when he encountered the Manichee overemphasis on reason or against Pelagianism in all its forms.[165]

Although other interpreters have not typically highlighted this appreciation that sometimes the African Father posited a dialectical relation between reason and faith, some like Martin Luther have seen him as an ally in the sense of inspiring their own dialectical thinking. Thus Luther not only follows him in rejecting a correlation of reason and faith (in polemical contexts the first Reformer spoke of reason as the "devil's whore"). The first Reformer expressly deemed Augustine as an ally in teaching that God commands the impossible and in maintaining a letter-spirit (Law-Gospel) dialectic, even hinting that the African Father was a proponent of freedom from the Law. In making these affirmations the Reformer was responding to Pelagian-like views, just as these same concerns inspired Augustine's insistence on the contrast between reason and faith.[166] In fact, it is in response to Pelagius that Augustine himself asserts in *On Grace and Free Will* that God commands the impossible and in the same work as well as in *On the Spirit and the Letter* posits the Law-Gospel distinction. In his *Commentary on Paul's Letter to the Galatians* he goes so far as to claim that you can "act as you desire, so long as you are acting with love."[167]

A pattern in the history of the interpretation of Augustine is evident in this data. Interpreters of Augustine tend correctly to portray the African Father's thought when they are addressing pastoral concerns similar to the ones Augustine was addressing when he articulated the points stressed by the particular interpreter in question. This is because his interpreters naturally gravitate to those Augustinian treatises in which the African Father was addressing concerns like the ones that motivate them. Such dynamics seem to confirm my thesis that there may be a pattern to the use of Christian concepts throughout the history of the Church, that some concepts more logically address certain perennial pastoral issues better than others. We will observe this pattern again and again in subsequent chapters.

Note again that this conceptual diversity did not imply a relativism for Augustine. Sometimes the genre of Biblical texts determines which hermeneutical approach best serves. The Book of Psalms is not intended to be read literally like the Gospels and Epistles are. The diversity and conceptual richness of theological methods, hermeneutics, and various doctrinal construals are still brought together in a coherent whole. Ultimately for Augustine, the diversity exists to give testimony to and is bound together by Christianity's testimony to the love of God in Christ.[168]

Chapter 3

God/Trinity/Christology

Given Augustine's acknowledgment of the similarities between Christian teaching and Plato (Neo-Platonic philosophy), which we have observed especially in contexts when he engages in apologetics or polemics with the Manichees, it is not surprising that the African Father's view of God is clearly indebted to the insights and concepts of this philosophy. He even expressly acknowledges this indebtedness in an apologetic context in the *City of God* and elsewhere.[1]

There are obvious examples of Augustine's reliance on themes compatible with Platonic thought, especially in the first half of his career when addressing apologetic contexts or when engaging in polemics with the Manichee heresy and its belief in a vulnerable, material god of light who had to contend with evil. Among these is his affirmation of the immutability of God (which also appears when he seeks to minister to despair).[2] Such an unchanging God does not have a body or extension, but is purely spiritual and invisible.[3] He also insists that this God is omnipotent.[4]

Other characteristics of God that Augustine notes in these contexts largely in the first part of his career include his identification of God with the Light of Truth, his insistence that God is everywhere and nowhere, neither finite nor infinite, able to be everywhere present, not confined in any place, able to come without leaving where He was.[5] Augustine proceeds to identify God with Being and with the Ultimate Good or with Truth.[6] He also at least implies that this Being is absolutely simple, at one point referring to this simplicity in the sense that all the divine qualities are one.[7]

In these same polemical or apologetic contexts, the African Father does not limit himself only to Neo-Platonic themes for depicting God. In *On Christian Doctrine,* he draws the logical implications of his reliance on Greek thought for construing God, contending that God is ineffable and cannot be described.[8] While recounting his own spiritual pilgrimage (a kind of apologetic quest) in his *Confessions* he speaks of God as Loveliness/Sweetness (in comparison with sin), as Beautiful and fairest.[9] God is portrayed as the Power of our souls, as free from care for Himself and full of care for us.[10]

The impassability of God is implied in these contexts describing Augustine's spiritual pilgrimage or coping with despair, as he asserts that God abides in Himself while we are tossed from trial to trial. However, Augustine adds, if the Lord did not hear our sorrow we should have no hope.[11]

Augustine also further develops his points regarding the impossibility of locating God in compelling ways, noting that while nothing can contain God, yet He is in all things. Even if one goes to hell God is there. As the world is from God, so it is in Him.[12] God, he contends, is more inward than the most inward place in the heart and loftier than the highest. He is highest and nearest, most present and most hidden, wholly everywhere yet nowhere limited in space. At one point Augustine compares this to how our rational capacities allow us to be in many places while still in one place (in our bodies).[13]

In addition, Augustine notes that God is not limited to some space for He penetrates the whole world, as light penetrates the entire atmosphere. In a profound image he compares God to an infinite sea penetrating a sponge, and that sponge is creation.[14] Presumably God permeates all that is in the universe! In another early work, *Two Books of Soliloquies,* he compares God to the light of the sun, noting that as the earth is only visible with the light of the sun, so the intelligible world (reason and the realm of the universal forms) is only visible with the light of God.[15]

Augustine's reflections in the *Confessions* and his earlier polemical works further elaborate on the implications of his Neo-Platonic-influenced affirmation of the impassability of God. Thus in the *Confessions* he claims that in God nothing (including events of the past) dies, for God is infinite and unchanging. Consequently, he concludes, all our tomorrows and yesterdays are present in God.[16] Time is *in* God.

These commitments occur near the end of his *Confessions,* as he addresses philosophical (and so apologetic) concerns about time and eternity. The African Father claims that for God the years are as a single day, and today is eternity. A similar point is made in *Tractates on the Gospel of John* and in his *City of God.*[17]

Along the same lines Augustine also contends in his early apologetic work *On True Religion* that in eternity there is neither past nor future. He elaborates this point in noting that in eternity there is no changeableness and so no time that is characterized by movement.[18] (The idea that time is a function of movement is most suggestive of Einstein's Theory of Relativity.)

WHERE GOD IS

In contexts where Augustine relies heavily on Greek philosophical suppositions, it is not surprising that he enhances his apologetic agenda by positing ontological connections between God and human nature. In some cases this enables him to posit arguments for the existence of God. The affirmation of this set of commitments is hardly surprising given the tasks at hand when doing apologetics or justifying his own faith pilgrimage. In these contexts the theologian's aim is to indicate the rationality of faith in God.

In his *Confessions,* as he seeks to know God from an anthropological starting point, Augustine contends that we must turn inward to know God.[19] He proceeds to explore the riches of memory in order to gain this knowledge. The power of memory is great, he contends. It is limitless in possibilities. The mind is not large enough to contain itself. His question then becomes where can that part of the mind be which the mind itself does not contain.[20]

In pursuing this point, the African Father notes that to seek God is to seek happiness. All seek happiness, and it lies in the memory. We know happiness like one knows truth; it too lies in the memory.[21]

Of course, Augustine notes, some things are in the mind before we ever learn them. We can remember things, but they are not present.[22] Likewise God is in the mind, but not limited to memory, he argues. We can be certain He dwells in the memory, because we remember Him since the first time we learn of Him. How then did we learn of Him? We learn of Him only in Himself. God Who is truth resides everywhere, replying in one act to all who seek counsel.[23] In other words, Augustine contends that God is where the pleasant memory of my wedding day is, where the slaves' vision of freedom is though never having experienced freedom themselves. These realities are in our memory and yet transcend it, existing in a kind of fourth dimension.

While still preoccupied with similar philosophical, apologetic questions, Augustine notes that in all the things the mind traverses in search of God we do not find any sure place in the mind save in God. For in God all that is scattered in someone is brought into one.[24]

A similar line of thought appears elsewhere with regard to Augustine's consideration of God's relationship to the universal forms. We do not learn from others by their words, but listen to the Eternal Wisdom of God (Christ), the giver of the forms, Who dwells in us.[25]

To make the point in another way, the general truths of reason are not taught, but are already in the mind. Thus when they are known it is not because of the teacher's words, but through contemplation, by God making them manifest inwardly. The teacher's questions merely help the mind to bring truths to light, to hear the Inner Teacher. Because there is often no interval between the moment of speaking and the moment of knowing, students sometimes suppose they have been taught externally by the teacher. In fact, it must be taught by Christ, Who dwells in us.[26]

The reliance on Platonic conceptions, specifically Neo-Platonic Mysticism, appears in another context, later in Augustine's career, in his *Expositions on the Book of Psalms* (which may still be in the same era as the anti-Manichee documents). Augustine contends there, in the best traditions of the great Neo-Platonist Plotinus, that the soul thirsts for God, that God could be known only through withdrawal from sensuality. However, the Deity is not to be found in the soul or in pure thought, for God transcends the soul. Of course, such mysticism seems also reflected in one of his sermons as he identifies God as the soul's spouse and also in some of his accounts of his spiritual experiences in the *Confessions.*[27]

Augustine makes a similar point regarding the reality of God and how to find him at points when he elaborates on the relationship between God and happiness. The two go together, Augustine claims; knowing God leads to happiness.[28] Happiness must go beyond the mind to Wisdom, because the things of the world are not permanent, as Wisdom is, for the things of the world were made from nothing.[29]

In knowing God we also love ourselves, Augustine contended. For in God are all the benefits in which the happy life (eternal truths) are found.[30]

Arguments for God's Existence

In *On Free Will,* an earlier polemic against the Manichees that included a dialogue with reason, Augustine offers something like an argument for God's existence. In the best traditions of ancient Greek philosophy he notes that Reason is humanity's superior faculty.[31] He then proceeds to assert that only what is eternal and unchanging is above Reason, and that that reality is God.[32] Such a reality exists, he contends, for it is obvious that Truth is superior to our minds. And if nothing is more excellent than such wisdom, then it is God, he concludes. Since God must be Truth, this truth superior to our minds that unequivocally exists entails that God must exist.[33] Again it is evident how the definition of God makes possible the conclusion that God exists.

In the previous chapter I noted references in Augustine's writings to this argument, and especially in apologetic contexts, to appeals to other dimensions of the created order to prove God's existence.[34] It is evident how useful Platonic thought was to his view of the doctrine of God, particularly in apologetic contexts and in polemics that challenged the sovereignty of God.

CONSTRUING GOD IN THE LATER WORKS AND WHEN PREACHING AND TEACHING

Augustine's reliance on Neo-Platonic concepts for construing God is not the whole story concerning his treatment of this doctrine. In his *Retractions* later in his career he noted with displeasure his earlier praise of Plato and the Platonists.[35] Yet this critique never led him to repudiate the basic Greek philosophical conceptuality he used to depict God. Of course, when he does use the concepts of changelessness, simplicity (a belief that all God's qualities are one), or Wisdom to describe God, and likewise when he seems to continue to rely on the sort of Neo-Platonic modes of knowing God in a sort of mystical fashion, he is typically dealing with apologetic concerns, refuting heresies like Manicheism or Pelagianism that challenged God's sovereignty, seeking to offer comfort, or exhorting Christian behavior, just as he used these concepts for the same purposes in his earlier writings. (The two new developments are that he employs such Platonic themes to depict purely spiritual, angelic existence and also in polemical circumstances expressly to deny the validity of female attributions to God.) Among the works in which he refers to God's immutability are *On the Trinity, On Patience, On the Spirit and the Letter, Tractates of the Gospel of John,* and the *City of God.*[36]

Regarding the unchanging character of God, when responding to critics in *On the Trinity* Augustine addresses what to make of Biblical texts that imply that God has reacted to worldly events, such as references to divine jealousy and wrath. The African Father noted that Scripture rarely employs things spoken properly of God. And when dealing in his *City of God* with eternity, which is unchanging, Augustine claims that when the Bible teaches that God became angry after being gentle, it is the ones who find Him changed who changed, not God, Who in eternity has already done all things that have already happened or will happen.[37]

Other images suggesting Augustine's attribution of Neo-Platonic conceptions to God during the second half of his career, especially when dialoguing with reason, offering comfort, or recounting his faith pilgrimage, include the identification of God with Wisdom, with the Good, or with the Light.[38] In the *City of God* and elsewhere, especially in contexts concerned with apologetics (discussing the rationality of the faith) or when recounting his own faith pilgrimage, he notes how God is found through the mind—suggesting again his endorsement of a kind of Neo-Platonic Mysticism. As was previously noted he also affirms the simplicity of the divine being (simple in the sense that its qualities and substance are one).[39]

While explaining the origin of the earthly city, the African Father affirms God's impassability with regard to the fact that He never changes His mind. God is said to permit evil where it exists.[40]

Just as in the earlier part of his career, Augustine portrays God in such a way that He cannot be located in any particular place. While describing the eschatological vision Augustine claims that God is wholly in heaven and wholly on earth, that He will be all in all. He makes a related point in *On the Trinity*, as he claims in response to unbelievers that were we to multiply the brightness of the sun's light a thousand times, or did so times without number, God would not be there.[41]

Time and Eternity

Another consequence of the reliance on Neo-Platonic conceptions for describing God emerges in the later works when the African Father articulates the logic of the Christian faith. He provides some profound insights about the nature of God's existence in eternity, in relation to time. As the universal forms of Greek philosophy are not changed by the passage of time, so all time is encompassed in the Godhead.

In the *City of God,* Augustine summarizes this insight. First he notes that God's Mind does not pass from one thought to another. This entails, he adds, that all that takes place does so in an immutable moment.[42] In short, everything is in the present for God. Or as he puts it in one of his sermons, eternity is an everlasting day. The Father is said to be Light. These points are most suggestive of the insights of Albert Einstein concerning the relativity of time, that at the speed of light there is no time.[43]

In *On the Trinity* Augustine makes a related point. He claims that God knows all things in a way that what is past does not pass, and the future is present.[44] This insight could offer a helpful way of resolving the perennial predestination versus free will debate. On Augustine's grounds at this point, divine foreknowledge of the exercise of human free will and divine election are simultaneous. This is a potentially rich ecumenical insight, which might make possible the building of bridges between proponents of predestination and of free will.

Another point about the divine nature that seems to be a consequence of the African Father's continuing dialogue with Greek philosophy emerges in the *Confessions* while he is articulating the logic of Christian faith. He claims for God to live and to live happily are one thing, because He is His own beatitude.[45]

What leads Augustine to rely less on Platonic conceptions in his later writings is related to development in his thought. But that is not the whole story. Because the later part of his career is less concerned with apologetics and polemics with the Manichees, more geared toward polemics with the Pelagians and exposition of the logic of faith, his shift seems related to new contexts being addressed in his later years. As I have noted, however, in apologetic or polemical contexts even in these later works he continues to rely on the Platonic conceptuality more characteristic of his work in these contexts in his earlier period. Thus we observe a consistency throughout Augustine's career in his use of these themes.

Perhaps the closest Augustine comes to a repudiation of the use of Neo-

Platonic conceptuality for describing God is when he merely exhorts faith or tries to explain its logic. At these times he relies less on these concepts or makes very clear that he rejects the implications of how Platonic assumptions might entail that the Good was merely produced by emanation from God. In fact, in these contexts we find the African Father more expressly articulating the Will of God as the source of all that transpires in the cosmos, and even in God's inter-Trinitarian life. Such a stress on God's Will as the cause of all corporeal change is especially evident in *On the Trinity*.[46] This too represents a break with Neo-Platonism, which identified the (ultimate) Good with a reality beyond movement, will, and rest.[47]

A similar example is evident in the *City of God*. The African Father contends that God may create radically novel things by changing His will, because God's knowledge is one of diversity. Likewise, in *On the Trinity* he concedes in a manner foreign to classical Greek philosophy that things happen to God in time. Yet, he continues, God is not accidentally changed by these events any more than friendship or money are changed by different interactions or exchanges.[48]

The Love of God and Divine Wrath

The way in which the African Father refers to the love of God and its relation to His wrath also illustrates, at least in some cases, a stress on the Will of God in a way not easily reconciled with the Platonic assumptions. In many contexts, especially when engaged in polemics or when exhorting Christian life, he posits a dialectical relationship between divine wrath and love. In an early-fifth-century text, *On Patience,* he contended that God is both wrath and love, loving humans to drive away the sickness but hating them as sick (Ps. 5:1–7). The emphasis on God's Will is evident in this case. Likewise in earlier works, when exhorting Christian life, he placed more emphasis on divine wrath in the sense of demanding works.[49]

The same vision of God is evident in Augustine's *Enchiridion,* a work devoted to addressing a similar concern about living the Christian life. At one point, when dealing with the consequences of sin, he contended that God's anger at sin is wholly just. However, the African Father added, He is not only just, but also merciful and deigns that His unmerited mercy should shine more brightly in contrast with unworthiness of its objects. A similar vision of God's wrath serving His love is in a sermon devoted to living the Christian life.[50] Augustine did not totally reject Greek philosophical assumptions in this work. As the Greek universal forms are purely rational and not affected by physical matters, he contended in a context concerned to refute those who claim that we save ourselves by working faith that God's anger is not a disturbed feeling.[51]

God is also portrayed as characterized by a dialectical tension of wrath in love in various texts where Augustine teaches double predestination, which as we shall see in chapter 6 is most evident when writing against Pelagius. Such texts can be identified even in the *Enchiridion.*

In different contexts, when expositing faith's logic or proclaiming faith, even when exhorting Christian living, along with comforting despair or when merely describing the character of Christian life, a different picture of God emerges. In these cases, in many different works, Augustine emphasized more unambiguously that God is love.[52] In at least two of his sermons he makes this point powerfully in other ways, contending in one that love is God and in the other that God is a friend.[53]

An emphasis on the priority of the love of God over divine wrath is affirmed in other ways in contexts where faith was being exhorted or its logic simply being explicated. In *On the Trinity* he asserts that God is the very love that links all His creatures together (1 John 4:16).[54] This construal of God is also implied in references to election that only talk about the elect (apparent affirmations of the doctrine of single predestination [1 Tim. 2:3–4]).[55] For if God only elects to salvation, it is evident that divine love must have the final say in the divine essence.

In anti-Pelagian contexts or in contexts concerned to refute the false claims of reason, another way of asserting the love of God was by defining the righteousness of God in such a way that the stress is on God's Work of making the faithful righteous. He makes an observation in several works addressing this concern that were central to the Protestant Reformation. He contended that God is righteous in making us righteous when He justifies the ungodly.[56]

Other examples of Augustine's emphasizing God's love over His wrath when he either exhorted faith or comforted despair are evident in the *Confessions.* He likewise portrays God in this way in such contexts in a sermon given prior to 410 when he describes God as the Maker of Good Who disposes evil. Such a loving God is also evident in these contexts as he refers to God hearing our sorrow or in his *Expositions on the Book of Psalms,* contending that goodness is peculiarly the quality of God. At one point in this treatise Augustine establishes the priority of divine love by claiming that God's derision of sin is really the power He gives us to understand sin's vanity. Elsewhere while catechizing he also claims that even the reason for the Incarnation is love.[57]

THE WILL OF GOD AND GREEK PHILOSOPHICAL CONSTRUALS OF GOD

These trends, placing more stress on God's Will and actions when expositing the logic of Christian faith, are also evident in the earlier works. For example, while expositing the faith with some apologetic concerns in the background in his *Confessions,* the African Father claims that although God does not will by a succession of acts, He never ceases to do good, yet is ever in repose because He is His own repose. God is ever in action, yet ever at rest. He makes time, but does not move in time.[58]

In a similar context of exhortation to the logic of faith that also includes a polemic against Pelagianism, Augustine claimed that without any temporal change in Himself, God is said to do by a sudden act of the will what was already ordained. God has already done the future. While addressing a similar context in his *City of God*, still unwilling to say that God changes, Augustine does concede that the Bible's references to God "repenting" (Gen. 6:6–7; 1 Sam. 15:35) refer to the natural causes divinely willed.[59] Portraying God as a God Who acts in these contexts distances the Christian God from the universal forms of Greek philosophy that were regarded as impassable.

Another way in which Augustine breaks with the Greek conceptions is in contexts of dispute with the Manichees, as he tries to argue for the goodness of God against them. He does so by insisting that in the case of sin God in His foreknowledge does not exercise compulsion.[60] In this sense God does not always get what God wants; He is vulnerable to our exercise of personal responsibility. The forms of Plato and Plotinus do not exhibit such vulnerability.

This construal of God differs somewhat from remarks in a later work, *On Patience* (which may not have been written by Augustine). In that text the author notes that God does not suffer, but is patient. Wrath is more evident in this text than in the earlier work, probably because it is not just preoccupied with comforting despair (accounting for the concern to assert divine patience), but also with urging Christian living (which introduces the need to assert divine wrath as a threat and motive to live Christianly).[61]

TRINITY

Augustine offers a rich, profound variety of images to depict the Trinity doctrine. In his early treatise *On Faith and the Creed,* he more or less accounts for this variety and points out why we should not commit ourselves to just one Trinitarian image, as he claims that we cannot say anything rash about the doctrine.[62] This diversity is even evident in the work he devotes wholly to the subject, *On the Trinity.*

The Trinity is affirmed throughout the Augustinian corpus. It is fundamental to the African Father's doctrine of God. As he puts it, the Trinity is not something in God, but is identical with Him.[63] Thus in his *Confessions* he claims to identify the Trinity in Genesis 1, contending that in the word "God" we recognize Father, in the "beginning" in which God created we see the Son, and that we see the Spirit moving over the waters.[64]

Elsewhere in the *Confessions* he claims that God is a Trinity like existence, knowledge, and will are found in human beings.[65] Drawing such analogies between the Trinity and human life is typical, since, as he notes in the *City of God,* all God's creatures intimate the Trinity.[66] In other works, the African Father notes the trinitarian character of human nature in being comprised of memory, intelligence, and will, or insofar as we are people who are, know that we are, and delight in our being.[67]

Similarly in *On the Trinity* the African Father notes the tripartite character of the mind—the remembrance, the understanding, and the love of itself. Another way he puts it is that the Mind, the knowledge of it, and the love of itself is a trinity.[68] Likewise, there are three functions of knowledge—memory, understanding, and will (or love)—as well as a mental trinity of memory, imprinted image, and the agency by which the two are conjoined.[69] Even love is said to have a tripartite character. When human beings love, they really love love. Consequently in love there are three—the lover, the object of love, and love itself.[70] In the *City of God* he even contends that there is a trinity in philosophy—physics, logic, and ethics.[71]

Just as in his general treatment of the doctrine of God, Augustine does not neglect reliance on Platonic categories in developing his Trinitarian reflections. Thus in *On the Trinity* he affirms that God is Being, so that we can only talk about the Persons of the Trinity in terms of relation, not as distinct substances. God's essence must equally be true of all the Persons, since God is simple (all His qualities are One).[72] Yet, he insists, because of this it follows that any of the divine Persons exercising these qualities must be One with the others, but that their One substance must also be Three. For all qualities in the Godhead are One, identical with the divine substance. Thus the Trinity is simple because it is nothing more than the One God, Who is inseparable from the Three.[73]

Having stressed the unity of the Persons, their distinction only by virtue of their relationships, Augustine proceeds to offer images for depicting these relationships. In one of his earlier writings he describes how the Three can be One in the sense that the fountain, river, and water in a vessel are all distinct, yet all are water. Similarly, he contends the tree is comprised of root, trunk, branches—all distinct yet one.[74]

With regard to the relationship between Father and Son, the Credal formulation's reference to the Son being begotten of the Father, Augustine contends in *On the Trinity* that we cannot speak of when the Son was begotten of the Father, for nothing took place in time, that the proceeding of the Spirit as well as the begetting of the Son continues to happen.[75] He then compares the Son's begetting to how our words are born of our knowledge (albeit with the important differences that the words in us are not only always born of knowledge and that our words are never everlasting).[76] Thus the Son is begotten of the Father in the sense of the Father uttering Himself.[77]

When the Word's content is the same as the content of knowledge, we say it is a true word. Thus the Son is like the Father in all things.[78]

The African Father then turns to the question of how the Holy Spirit fits in this relationship. In an earlier writing he depicts the Holy Spirit as the communion of the Father and the Son. The Spirit is identified as the Deity embracing both, as the mutual love and Father and Son. In a later work, *On Christian Doctrine,* he speaks of the Father as unity, the Son as equality, and the Holy Spirit as the harmony of unity and equality.[79]

Elsewhere, especially in *On the Trinity,* Augustine also affirms the *Filioque* (the Spirit's procession from the Son).[80] One argument he makes for this conclusion is that such an affirmation is mandated by the fact that God is Spirit, just as both Father and Son are Spirit.[81] Augustine's position on this matter has been crucial in the Western church's adoption of the *Filioque.* We see in *On the Trinity* that this affirmation is essential to the African Father's treatment of the doctrine.

In this treatise and elsewhere, Augustine at one point describes the Trinity as lover, beloved, and love. The Holy Spirit is the love between Father and Son:

> Therefore the Holy Spirit, whatever it is, is something common both to the Father and the Son. But that communion itself is consubstantial and co-eternal; and if it may fitly be called friendship, let it be so called; but it is more aptly called love.[82]

The Father loves the Son and the Holy Spirit is the love Who makes them One (like two become one in the love of a Christian marriage).

Augustine's insistence on the unity of Godhead leads him to claim that love belongs to the whole Trinity, not just to Spirit alone. Likewise the Trinity can be called Spirit in its entirety, for the Spirit is the unutterable communion of the Father and the Son.[83]

This theme of the unity of the Persons also manifests itself in Augustine's insistence that all Three share the same attributes and teach the same, for the working of the Trinity is inseparable.[84] When one of the Three Persons is mentioned as the author of any work, the whole Trinity is to be understood as working.[85]

These commitments lead Augustine to posit a Christocentric Trinitarianism, especially in contexts when explaining faith. Whatever is done by the Trinity is said to have been done by all the Persons, he contends, just as the qualities of existing things never operate apart from each other. Consequently, the whole Trinity assumed human nature![86]

CHRISTOLOGY

Given his renown as the great theologian of grace and the emphasis he places on love in his hermeneutic, there is a sense in which Augustine is correctly identified as a Christocentric theologian. He makes this point expressly near the beginning of the *Enchiridion* as he seeks to explain the starting point of faith: "But the sure and proper foundation of the catholic faith is Christ."[87]

Most of the great Christological controversies and the Decision of the Council of Chalcedon endorsing the doctrine of Christ's Two Natures transpired after Augustine's lifetime. Nevertheless, his views on this range of issues are still most relevant for the tradition that followed him and for theology today.

There has been a debate among modern interpreters of Augustine regarding a thesis advanced by the great nineteenth-century German scholar Adolf von Harnack. He maintained that Augustine's conversion to Christianity was merely intellectual and that only gradually did he embrace a Catholic Christology. This led Harnack to portray Augustine's Christology as primarily focused on His humanity.[88] In short, Harnack made Augustine a proponent of modern Liberal Theology. Not surprisingly he has had his critics. I will show that both sides are correct, in certain contexts.

Not surprisingly, Harnack's thesis works best regarding some of the African Father's earlier writings (a point that Harnack himself conceded). Thus in *Of True Religion,* an early work of apologetics, Augustine writes that Christ's appearance in the flesh liberates our nature, for it teaches human beings not to despise the body or sex. Christ's whole life provides an education in morals, he claims.[89] Another example of a text that seems to authenticate Harnack's reduction of Augustine's Christology to the status of a mere example for Christian life is evident in another early treatise, *On Faith and the Creed.* Augustine claims that the Incarnation God gives us is an example of humility. We see this humility, the African Father claims, in His taking on the whole of human nature in womb of a Virgin.[90]

It seems evident that Harnack's interpretation applies well in specialized contexts—where Augustine is doing apologetics or concerned with exhorting living the Christian life. It is clear, however, that very catholic conceptions of Christology are evident even in his earlier treatises, when he merely seeks to exposit the logic of the Christian faith. For instance, in *On Faith and the Creed,* he criticizes both Modalists (who taught that that Word could not be God unless He is with the Father) and Arians (who relegated Christ to a creature).[91] In this same early work, he even discusses why Christ must be fully human. If He were not, Augustine asserts, our nature would not be assumed and would not be saved. In a later work, the *Enchiridion,* he further elaborates on this point and contends that Christ must be God in order to redeem us and is human in order to show our sin and give us an example.[92] In a later Epistle he provides a concrete analogy for understanding the Two Natures of Christ in One Person, comparing their union to the union of body and soul.[93]

It is quite evident how thoroughly committed Augustine was to affirming the divinity and humanity of Christ after the fashion of this doctrine's eventual codification at the Council of Chalcedon later in the fifth century. The other ways in which Augustine depicts Christ include his claim that the Humanity of Christ is the supreme Sacrament/Mystery, revealing the supreme Mystery, His divinity, as well as His identification of Christ as Physician and as the hidden God.[94] Among his other Christological claims are: (1) Christ is to be seen in all of Scripture. (2) By Christ, God sought us when we did not seek Him. (3) The grace of God is displayed in the Incarnation, for it testifies to how much God love us.[95] In the next chapter, we will examine in more detail how the African Father portrays the works of Christ (the doctrine of the Atonement).

Antiochene or Alexandrian?

One of the major Christological debates that would begin in Augustine's lifetime and extend throughout the Church's history is the dispute between proponents of Antiochene Christology (which stresses the distinction of Christ's Two Natures) and those of the Alexandrian School (which emphasizes their unity). One finds affirmations of both strands in Augustine's thought, though once again in a very clear pattern.

In many of his earlier writings, the Antiochene vision prevails. However, one also finds it in later writings. In all cases this vision of how Christ's Two Natures relate emerges when the African Father addresses apologetic concerns, exhorts readers/hearers to live the Christian life, or reflects on the Last Judgment. Thus, responding to criticisms of the Biblical testimony regarding Christ and the Trinity, Augustine claims that there are two kinds of Biblical passages that refer to the Son: Those referring to Him in His divine essence, and those relating to his incarnate life.[96] Such a distinction without contending for the appropriateness of attributing what is proper to one Nature to the other (the so-called *communicatio idiomatum*) is characteristic of the ancient Antiochene Christology.

The Antiochene view is also evident in a 417 Epistle dealing with apologetic questions. Christ's Body is said to be in heaven; different characteristics are to be attributed to each nature, Augustine contends. Something like this point is also made clear in one of his anti-Manichee works concerned with Christian responsibility and in a sermon on the Last Judgment.[97] In his earlier works, especially in response to heretics or when dealing with Christian responsibility, the Antiochene Christology appears, for example, in *On Faith and the Creed,* as the African Father claims here and elsewhere that Mary was not the Mother of God (of Christ's divinity).[98]

However, at some points in *On the Trinity,* a work in which he posits an Antiochene view when dealing with rational critiques of Christology and the Trinity doctrine while expositing faith and how Christ cures our pride, Augustine claims that Mary is the Mother of God.[99] This affirmation is characteristic of the Alexandrian position, for Mary is properly Mother of God only if, like this early African position, we attribute to the divine nature of Christ what is properly true of His humanity (Mary's role as Jesus' mother).

The Alexandrian Christology is also evident elsewhere in this treatise and in other documents where Augustine seeks to exposit faith or dialogues with the Arians or Manichees. In these contexts he claims that Christ's humanity was exalted, that the Son of God Himself was crucified on the Cross, and refers to Jesus as the "human God."[100] Again like the Alexandrians, these affirmations are possible only if what is attributed to one of Jesus' Natures may also be attributed to the other.

The pattern in Augustine's thought is perhaps a lesson for deploying the various historic Christologies. Antiochene construals work well for doing apologetics

or when exhorting Christian living. The Alexandrian model more likely functions when the logic of faith is propounded.

Mariology

Augustine's endorsement of a high view of Mary as per his reliance on the Alexandrian Christology is evidenced at other points in the Augustinian corpus. In the
best traditions of Mariology, the doctrine functions as a testimony to Christ.

When expositing the faith along with a concern for exhorting the Christian
life, Augustine insists that Christ was begotten and conceived without carnal lust,
such that he brought with Him no original sin. He was born from one who had
no lust.[101]

In connection with Mary's lack of lust, Augustine also teaches her Perpetual
Virginity in one of his sermons and elsewhere.[102] Also out of his express desire
to honor Christ, he does not wish to speculate about whether Mary sinned, a
point some have argued substantiates her Immaculate Conception (the belief that
she was not conceived in sin).[103] I recommend we take him at his word on this
point and not speculate about his position on this doctrine. In any case, for
Augustine the heart of these reflections, as typifies much of his theology in contexts of exhortation to faith, is Christ.

THE HOLY SPIRIT

Augustine's reflections on the Holy Spirit also emerge not just with regard to the
Spirit's role in inter-Trinitarian relations, which we have observed, but also with
regard to the Spirit's actions among the faithful. Not surprisingly, there is a
stronger presence of the doctrine of the Spirit in his writings against the Pelagians
than in his treatises against targets who deny free will and Christian responsibility, like the Manichees.

Given Augustine's general preoccupation with apologetics (maintaining a dialogue with Greek philosophy) and polemics with the Manichees, both of which
lead him to assert free will, it is not surprising that we find relatively few references
to the Holy Spirit in this era. If we want to assert free will or the virtues of Reason, there is little place or need for the Spirit (James 2:14–36; Mark 16:16). Consequently, about all Augustine says about the spirit in the anti-Manichee writings
is that the Spirit has in fact been given, but not just to certain special teachers who
were leaders of the movement.[104] When in one of these earlier writings he undertakes a discussion of what the Spirit does, it is not as the giver of gifts or the agent
of good, but only as enabler to spark the free will to do good (Rom. 8:13–14). He
makes this point when trying to assert in the midst of his critique of the compromise of grace that we can do good works (exhorting the Christian life).[105]

In his later works, especially when exhorting faith or responding to the Pelagian heresy, there is a stronger emphasis on the gift character of the Spirit (1 John

4:13; 1 Cor. 2:10–11).[106] Among the Works of the Spirit are: (1) Writing the Law on the heart; (2) Renewing in us the image of God; (3) Anointing us with charity (especially the love of God); and (4) Functioning as the Church's soul.[107]

When Augustine's concerns are more related to living the Christian life in this period he does continue to use more like cooperation language (the Spirit "co-operating with our strength").[108] This cooperation language is diminished the more the primary concern is with exhortation to faith or refuting Pelagius, and the less his preoccupation is with living the Christian life.

Thus in such contexts the Spirit is identified as the finger of God leading us to do good works.[109] In receiving the Holy Spirit, Augustine contends, there arises in the soul delight in and love of God, though not by free choice. In fact, he adds elsewhere, the dead person cannot be aroused to confess sins except by the Lord crying within him.[110]

The theme of being drawn by the Spirit to "delight" in the good, helping the faithful resist contrary impulses, suggests that when addressing the Pelagian heresy or exhorting faith the African Father believes that the Spirit makes good works happen spontaneously among the faithful.[111] In fact, in response to undue use of rational speculation, he insists that the Holy Spirit intercedes or prays for us.[112]

Because the Holy Spirit is love (the love between Father and Son), when given to human beings the Spirit is said to pour the love of God in their hearts (both to unite the souls of all the faithful just as the Spirit unites Father and Son, and also to kindle and enflame them with love of God). Humans, Augustine contends while explicating the faith, have no means of loving God unless it comes from God.[113] Elsewhere the Spirit is identified as the fire of love, proclaiming that God is love.[114]

In another text, when exhorting faith Augustine contends that this love poured out by the Spirit draws us to faith.[115] Even when explicating the logic of faith along with exhorting Christian living, Augustine says that the Spirit binds us to God.[116] In fact, in his *Confessions* while dialoguing with reason's feeble attempts to understand mysteries of the faith (a sort of apologetic agenda), he claims that the Spirit lifts us up above our concupiscence passions, and unclean-ness of spirit.[117] The love that the Spirit provides changes recipients.

Insofar as the love we receive from the Spirit directs us back to the Spirit's role in binding Father and Son through love, in dealing with the Work of the Holy Spirit we are inevitably brought back to the Trinity doctrine, to be reminded of the Spirit's divinity. It is fitting in a chapter devoted to the variety in Augustine's thought for depicting God that we are reminded of the role he sees for the Spirit in uniting the diversity within the Godhead. In his view, the Spirit is the Holi-ness of Father and Son.[118] In fact, Augustine contends, the Spirit shares all the faculties of the other Persons of the Trinity. Thus he can refer to the Spirit as God's Will and also His love.[119] Many in one, but all subordinate to the divine love well summarizes Augustine's thought on this range of issues.

Chapter 4

Creation and Providence

Asserting the goodness of creation (Gen. 1:31) and creation out of nothing (*creatio ex nihilo*) was absolutely essential for Augustine in his early dialogue with Reason (prevailing Greek philosophical conceptions of his day) and with the Manichees. While not overlooking the realities of affirming sin and evil, he nevertheless frequently extols the physical beauty of the universe. He also finds a way to affirm the transience of the world while still referring to God's goodness, construing the creation like a work of art formed from one body by another.[1] This image allows him to construe creation as giving external evidence to what the (divine) mind first perceived within itself.

As in the case of the doctrine of God, Augustine's earlier thought about creation, preoccupied as it is with the apologetic task and with polemics against the Manichees, is much indebted to Neo-Platonic conceptions. Of course, subsequently in his *Retractions* in a context not concerned with apologetics he claims to regret this.[2] Early in his career he distinguishes the sensible and intelligible universes, regarding the universe as an immense ensouled animal.[3] But he later expresses regret about the first view and the latter commitment he subsequently claims was a rash view, though he never denies it.[4]

Augustine's commitments to asserting the goodness of creation lead him in his later works to affirm, contrary to the Manichees, that even the fleshly elements of creation are valuable to us. In fact, he asserts, entities are good simply because they exist. Thus even the devil is good.[5]

This manner of construing the goodness of creation entails that insofar as it is still in existence since the Fall, creation (even the means of procreation) remains good even in sin.[6] Likewise the beauty of the universe remains in place. In fact, when describing the Christian life in his *Expositions on the Book of Psalms,* he asserts that the creation in all its beauty is engaged in praising God.[7]

Augustine's elaboration on the goodness and beauty of the creation offers a sophisticated insight. Explicating in the *Enchiridion* the faith with a view toward its implications for living the Christian life, he notes that what has been created is not supremely and equally and unchangeably good, when taken separately. Making a point most suggestive of possible indebtedness to the ancient Roman philosophy of Stoicism and its affirmation of the rationality of the cosmos, Augustine notes that as a whole created realities that are not equally good when taken separately are very good because their ensemble constitutes the universe in all its wonderful beauty.[8] The goodness and beauty of the created order pertains to its totality. Or as he puts it elsewhere, the whole is better than each of its parts.[9]

The African Father makes a similar point early in his career against the Manichees in *On Free Will* when he contends that just as differences in brightness among parts of the universe contribute to the perfection of the whole, so the universe requires greater things and lesser things in relation to one another.[10] In a work devoted to apologetics, *On True Religion,* Augustine also contends that all that is in the universe is created to ensure its beauty. What we abhor gives pleasure when we consider the universe as a whole.[11] All is good.

Augustine expresses a clear appreciation of the beauty of the creation throughout his career, especially in apologetic contexts or when offering comfort to those considering the sufferings we encounter in our fallen world. No words, he claims, can describe the myriad beauties we are given to contemplate in the universe, like the grandiose beauty of the ocean, the activity of the bees, as well as arts, poetry, and music. And all can recognize its beauty, he contends.[12]

Of course, Augustine insists on a balance in the way in which we love the things of the world. There are things in the world that we ought not love, he asserts. The desires of the flesh and the pretensions of this life are not to be loved. Of course, we are to love what God made, Augustine contends. However, he adds, we must choose either to love the things that pass away with time or not to love the world and live forever with God. For if the things of the world are fair, the One Who made them is fairer.

God does not forbid our love of the things of the world, Augustine adds. But, he insists, God will not have one seek bliss in these things. The end of esteem for them should be the love of their Maker. To do otherwise would be like the betrothed loving the ring more than the lover.[13]

In view of the Augustinian appreciation of the beauty of the universe as a whole, it is logical that the African Father reflects on how the various components of the universe relate. Thus in the *City of God* Augustine posits a hierarchy of being according to the order of nature. God as Supreme Being must have given being to all beings. But insofar as He gave more being to some, an order to nature has been arranged hierarchically. There is a glorious harmony of various ranks. For example, in this order, intelligent life is the highest. Not only are echoes of Stoicism evident in these and earlier affirmations of the rational order of the cosmos. (Even when operating with his more literal, Narrative hermeneutic Augustine may employ philosophy in an ad hoc manner.) In the best traditions of Stoic endurance without passion, Augustine asserts in different contexts, when not considering the human situation in relation to sin, that human beings are less free if governed by passion instead of reason.[14] In part, he adds elsewhere, God's decision to govern by means of ranks and differences among the creatures is a function of the realities of the fallen world.[15]

Also in the *City of God* Augustine offers a profound comment with rich constructive implications for our post-Darwinian world. He claims that part of the harmonious beauty that God has established in the universe is by means of the principle of "survival of the fittest."[16]

Several other significant features of Augustine's view of the created order should be noted. In the previous chapter I mentioned how he posited the trinitarian character of all living creatures. Their very existence raises the triune question of who made the universe, how, and why. All living creatures are triune in the sense that they are, know, and love.[17]

Another feature of the created order that Augustine posits is that it is governed by the Law of God, which is written on the hearts of all by the presence of Holy Spirit. A natural law (understanding the Law of God as built into the structures of creation) is expressly affirmed (Rom. 2:12–16).[18]

DIALOGUE WITH NEO-PLATONISM

I have already alluded to Augustine's tendency, especially when engaging in apologetics and when dialoguing with the Manichees in his early work, to rely on Neo-Platonic conceptions to construe the created order. Thus in *On Free Will* against the Manichees he contends that all created things owe their existence to the form in which they were created. And every corporeal form derives its existence from the supreme form, which is truth, Who is God.[19] Even later in his career, in the *City of God,* again in contexts where he seeks to refute certain false teachings, Augustine echoes these Platonic commitments, contending that every corporeal object has a form. Participation in the form entails that the object participates in something belonging to the ideal world. And the One Who both created matter and is supreme in the ideal world is God.[20] Again it is apparent how throughout his career the African Father tends to make similar points when addressing similar pastoral concerns.

I have noted the African Father's tendency to utilize Greek philosophical insights when concerned to offer apologetics. Thus at the end of his *Confessions* as he explicates the Biblical creation accounts, though in a dialogue with the Manichees and with his apologetic agenda, Platonic construals emerge again in his reflections on the need for matter to have forms. In the discussion, though, he clearly asserts that these forms were themselves created.[21]

TIME, ETERNITY, AND THE SIX DAYS OF CREATION

Augustine's reflections on how creation transpired are also thoughtful and timely. In the *City of God* the African Father contends that it is silly for critics to reflect on time before creation when God was active, for there was no such thing as time before the universe was made. Elsewhere he claims that the universe was not created in time, but with time.[22]

Angels play a major role in Augustine's narrative of creation as well as in his depiction of the history of salvation. They are used by God as messengers to human beings. They are also identified as part of the City of God. They have been created by God, though we do not know precisely when.[23] Angels are said to gain knowledge of God by the presence of an immutable truth in their souls. They know this better than we know ourselves. Augustine believes that angels know every creature in the wisdom of God and carry out His orders in creation.[24]

Augustine also teaches that some of the angels fell. However, he rejects the Manichee idea that the devil has an evil nature. The difference between the angels, he insists, is a matter of different choices and desires, not a matter of different natures.[25] Such views regarding the fall of certain angels and the context for his remarks on the topic prefigure his treatment of the doctrine of sin.

Augustine finds a way to affirm the transience of the world while still referring to God's unchanging role as Creator. Or as he puts it in his *Confessions* and elsewhere, the created realities with movement have the vicissitudes of time in them.[26] Yet God is ever at rest, though always working.[27]

Elsewhere in the treatise he notes that things must constantly change, cease their existence, in order that new things come into existence, to serve the whole. (The words we speak follow this principle.) All that goes to make a whole does not exist at one moment. Yet, he insists, God does not pass away. For God did not simply make the world and leave it; as it is from Him, so it is in Him.[28]

The *Confessions* also includes the African Father's reflections on creation's relation to time from God's eternal perspective. He begins that discussion by noting that the heavens and earth must have been made, for they change. And, he argues, they must have been made by God because God is good and they are good. Because God is beautiful, the heavens and earth are beautiful (Ps. 27:4; Zech. 9:17). Compared to God, though, they are not good and beautiful.[29] Augustine proceeds to note that the heavens, though not coeternal with God, partake in His eternity. That is why their creation is not in the enumeration of days, he contends.[30]

To the question of what God was doing before making heaven and earth, Augustine notes the problem of how God could be a true eternity in which a new will (to create) should arise in Him. With some frivolity the African Father suggests that God was preparing hell for those who raise such questions. He notes, more seriously, that in eternity nothing passes, but all is present.[31] Time and the universe began together, so there was no time when God was not creating, for there was no time before creation.[32] Augustine seems to contend in these reflections, which have some apologetic intent, that God is still creating.

The African Father's further elaboration on time lends more clarity to his views on the duration of creation. We cannot say that past time or present time is long, he comments, for the past no longer is. A period of time like a month is also not present, since much of it is still to come. Yet the past and future do exist, or else the past could not be described and the future could not be prophesied. Future and past *are,* only as present. They exist in the mind.[33]

To these points Augustine adds that time is measured by its passing, passing from that which does not yet exist, by way of that which lacks extension (present), to that which is no longer. In the mind time is measured. What is measured is not the thing itself, but its impress on the mind.[34] Of course this psychological sense of time corresponds with physical time for Augustine. Thus he claims that time springs from changes in the universe and that it is the result of motion.[35] Consequently, it follows, given these suppositions, that the future is not long, for it does not exist. The past is long, merely as a long memory of the past. History, then, is like reciting a psalm we know. Our expectation is that the whole is to be read, but when beginning, some is used up and some is still to be said.[36]

These points allow Augustine to deal with the question of how God creates. They entail that before all times God is Creator, for nothing is hidden to eternal knowledge. Like when a canticle is sung, nothing is unknown to the singer, both what has been sung and what remains to be sung.[37] In eternity God is Creator, for He knows all time, like a singer who knows a song knows the song in its entirety.

Augustine deals with the problem of the length of creation with apologetics in view in his *On Genesis Literally Interpreted.* He claims that since God's creative act is single and simultaneous (in establishing eternal patterns of created realities, rather like Platonic forms), the six days of the Genesis accounts might (but do not necessarily have to) be construed or articulating articulate categories for our mind. Augustine also interprets the light God created as the divine likeness of intellection. Thus since God illumines us by working our intelligence, creation was presented in that sense as continuous (Ps. 104). However all that can be known (the Greek universal forms) is already in existence. Thus creation is in that sense complete, created all at once simultaneously like a tree is created all at once in its seed. God's creative illuminating light is sequential and simultaneous like new days happen on earth (the sun rises), but day and night occur simultaneously all over the earth once and for all. In his *City of God* Augustine makes a related affirmation of God's continuing work in creation through natural means by referring to God as a fountain from which all blessings flow and of His creative energies without which no earthly goods can be generated.[38]

Augustine's Views of Creation and Post-Einsteinian Ontology

Many of Augustine's reflections on the topics of time and eternity, as they relate to his vision of the created order, have striking similarities to ways of dealing with these realities emerging since Einstein. Though such a topic is worth another volume, several of these points of convergence can be noted in passing.

Of course, atomic theory is not modern; it has roots in ancient classical thought. In one of his letters the African Father engages in this conceptuality, noting that the various atoms, if they comprise reality, cannot have come together by chance. With a comment most suggestive of today's Intelligent Design Theorists, he notes that the coming together of the atoms must be accomplished by God's Providence.[39]

In a manner most suggestive of Einstein's view of time, the African Father contends in his *Confessions* that because the created realities can change from one form to another they may be put in motion and so have in them the vicissitudes of time. Anticipating Einstein's insight, he claims that time is not yet absolute, but only came into existence with creation. Augustine adds to this that all temporal realities must die if the beauty of their temporal sequence is to be preserved.[40] This death is not a contradiction of the goodness of creation. These observations are certainly convergent with the Theory of Relativity insofar as both presuppose that time is related to motion.

Augustine's vision of eternity, that in it nothing passes, but all is present, is also in line with Relativity's idea that at the speed of light there is no time.[41] The African Father's concept of God being ever at rest yet always working is most consistent with the concept of eternity (regarded as the speed of light), a reality at which all events are simultaneous.[42]

Augustine's reflections on how God continues to relate to the universe are also compatible with modern reflections on how God relates to the world. The African Father's concept of God being like an infinite sea and creation a sponge penetrated by the sea makes it readily apparent how he can contend that God did not simply make the world and leave it, for it is in Him.[43] An ocean cannot abandon a sponge thrown into it. In the same framework, his comments in a sermon that God is in the world, though not like the sky is in the world, for He is everywhere present, make perfect sense.[44] The sponge in the ocean has the ocean's water all over and in it. God permeates every nook and cranny of the cosmos (Jer. 23:23–24).

PROVIDENCE

In a sense, Augustine's reflections on God's continuing role in creation entail that his view of Creation intersects with the doctrine of Providence. The doctrine also includes consideration of the emergence of evil and how God continues to rule the creation.

At many points, especially when dealing with sloth, interpreting his own spiritual pilgrimage, or in his famed account of world history (the two cities), Augustine could affirm a strong doctrine of Providence, asserting that all that happens, even evil, is the Work of God (Gen. 19:24–25; Job 1:12). Yet in other contexts, when concerned to address or affirm human responsibility or when in dialogue with the Manichees, he balances this with an acknowledgment of our responsibility for evil and an assertion that God simply foreknows, but does not compel what will happen and has happened (Gen. 6:6; Mark 6:5). He seems to concede this paradox in the *City of God* as he asserts that the providence of God transcends human reckoning.[45]

A fundamental commitment of Augustine's view of Providence, one that undergirds much of what he said earlier in his career, appears also in his later works. He contends in his *Enchiridion* that human beings in Paradise were able to destroy themselves by an act of the will. To have maintained a life of righteousness would have required sustaining by a Creator.[46] Thus at least in contexts where the logic of faith is depicted along with concern for living the Christian life, Augustine teaches that grace was required by humanity, even before the Fall.

A theme that is especially consistent in his work is the claim that Evil is the absence of good, that it has no substance. This allows him to contend that God did not create evil, since evil has no substance (is not a part of His creation).[47] As he puts it in the *City of God,* evil is a function of our doing, not of substance, just as water is not evil but one can drown in it.[48]

The African Father's reflections on miracles when dealing with apologetics offer intriguing and potentially useful insights for modern apologetics. Miracles like in Biblical times have not been allowed to continue, he contends, lest the mind always seek visible signs and the human race grow cold by becoming accustomed to what kindled faith.[49] However, he hastens to add in his *Retractions* that he does not intend to imply that miracles have ceased. His point is only that the experience of tongues when hands were laid on the baptized in Baptism no longer happens.[50] (It is significant that Augustine did not interpret the Pentecost experience as the gift of glossolalia, but as the Holy Spirit conferring on believers the ability to speak the language of all people.)

Another intriguing insight about the nature of divine providence pertains to how Augustine accounts for God's rationale for creating and human beings and for ruling the universe. He does not enjoy people, the African Father contends. He only uses them. For God is not in need of anyone. Thus His use of creatures is not for His own advantage, but is simply for our benefit. In the same spirit

Augustine nicely relates creation and redemption, contending that in both God takes seed and develops its potentialities.[51]

Free Will

In his earlier writings, especially when seeking to assert free will against the Manichees, Augustine affirms free will, though not in such a way as to deny God's foreknowledge of the future, a foreknowledge of what happens by necessity. This foreknowledge, he insists, does not rob us of our will to happiness or unhappiness. By His foreknowledge God does not exercise compulsion in future events. God is not the agent of what He knows will happen. In his *City of God,* Augustine makes a similar point against the Stoic determinism as he contends that divine foreknowledge does not cancel human free will.[52]

Elsewhere in the same context Augustine insists that although not everything that happens is what God ordained, He may still use suffering to work good. Every creature in that sense by its diverse movements proclaims the creator by attaining a beauty appropriate to itself in the stability of nature. In short, everything is for the best.[53]

A concern to affirm God's goodness in Providence while still respecting free will is evident in other early treatises devoted to refuting the Manichees. Thus Augustine claims that even what is lacking in creation is fittingly ordered by God. Evil may come to us, but only with God's permission (Deut. 33:39; Isa. 45:5–7). Similarly, in a work of this period devoted to apologetics, he contends that God harmonizes good and evil so that the universe, even with its sinister aspects, is perfect.[54] In one of his Sermons while exhorting to good works he claims that God gives pain, but only to bring us to health. In another he compares God to a father or a doctor, not always giving child or patient what is requested in order to strengthen him or her.[55]

In other writings devoted to apologetics, God is said to permit good people to endure persecution and that He judged that people would serve Him better if they served Him freely. Augustine assumes a distinct, though related position in a sermon exhorting Christian life as he claims that God blinds and hardens merely by withdrawing aid.[56] God is not construed as totally in charge of all that happens in these contexts.

When dealing with despair or exhortation to Christian living and cathechesis throughout his career, Augustine contends that God permits temptation or that there is no sin without divine permission. In one of these cases the devil is identified as the agent of temptation, though only with God's permission.[57] Invoking the concept of divine permission does not relegate God to vulnerability in these contexts.

The Mystery of the Divine Rule

As already noted, there is a paradox in Augustine's treatment of divine providence, insofar as his affirmation of free will and a God Whose power is somewhat limited stands juxtaposed in other contexts to the affirmation of a sovereign, all-powerful God. In his apologetic treatise *On True Religion,* we find a hint of his way of resolving this apparent tension:

> The art of medicine remains the same and quite unchanged, but it changes its prescriptions for the sick, since the state of their health changes. So divine providence remains entirely without change, but comes to the aid of mutable creatures in various ways, and commands or forbids different things at different times according to the different stages of their disease.[58]

The impact of Greek philosophy on Augustine's view of God in contexts in which he does apologetics is again evident. But he here seems also to concede that perhaps his different construals of God's actions in governing the world is a matter of which one is most effective in particular contexts.

Also paradoxical in Augustine's own mind was how God governs. In *On True Religion* he noted that we cannot say how God's Providence deals with humanity, for God has willed it to be handed down through history and prophecy.[59] Providence is known only a posteriori.

A Sovereign God

As noted, a different conception of divine sovereignty appears in contexts in which Augustine is dialoguing with the Pelagian heresy or our sinful pride. In these contexts, God is frequently portrayed as the agent of both good and evil. Critiquing human vanity in his *Confessions,* he enthusiastically extols the beauty of the transitory natural order by which God causes both birth and death. With a similar agenda at one point in his *Expositions on the Book of Psalms* Augustine asserts that the events of the world are not moved by chance, that every motion, from the snow to the rain to the sting of the gnat and the shipwreck, transpires at the command of God (Ps. 148:7–8). And in *On the Merits of Forgiveness of Sins and on the Baptism of Infants* he claims that sometimes God even withholds blessings from saints in order that they might discover that it is only from God that they receive delight (Rom. 9:19–23).[60]

Further examples of such a strong doctrine of divine sovereignty in anti-Pelagian contexts are evident. In his *On Grace and Free Will,* Augustine contends that sometimes children of unbelievers get grace, and children of believers do not, that such things happen through God's secret providence. In another treatise he adds that the faithful must merely condescend, not murmur against God.[61]

In other anti-Pelagian contexts the African Father refers to God letting some live longer because He foreknew that they would fall, or taking other baptized persons from this life lest wickedness overtake these Christians. Augustine also observes that the reason why some are taken away before falling and others remain and fall is a matter of God's inscrutability (implying that all of these events are God's providential work).[62]

When addressing in the *City of God* the false human pride or the veneration of false gods he sees in his adversaries, Augustine concedes that it is true that the hardships Romans suffer from barbarians came from divine providence. However, though evil is the work of God according to remarks in this context, God also is said to work good. His mercy is bestowed even on the impious people of Rome. For God makes the sun rise on the good and the bad. When he turns to laying out faith's logic, but also when exhorting the Christian life, Augustine contends that God's patience and His scourging have a good and loving purpose. They are an invitation to the wicked to do penance.[63] Or as he puts it elsewhere in the treatise, punishment serves the purpose of inspiring sanctity, of testing the saints.[64]

In a treatise devoted to refuting Pelagianism Augustine continues to emphasize a strong doctrine of divine sovereignty. God, he claims, has the wills of all in His power. He hardens hearts.[65] He does whatever He wills in the hearts of the wicked. Then Augustine adds a very significant point: All the wickedness is done by humans, but the turning was accomplished by the Lord.[66] This set of conceptions offers a bridge between the strand of Augustine's thought that stresses divine sovereignty and the other strand that affirms free will. When Augustine stresses the action of God, he does not reduce human beings to mere robots.

When the Pelagian polemic is combined with some sort of exhortation, a portrait of God Who is somehow less in control of things is introduced. We encounter the concept of divine permission, which entails that not everything that happens in the cosmos is the Work of God.

In such a mixed context in *On Nature and Grace,* Augustine says of God that in some sense He forsakes us to sin, so we do not become proud. Evil, he adds, can be used by God's mercy to bring about good, a point he also makes when comforting despair or when exhorting Christian living with a polemic against heretics.[67] The idea that God can bring good out of evil is most suggestive of the views of one of Augustine's most important interpreters—Martin Luther and his Theology of the Cross.[68]

The same commitments are evident in the *City of God.* Augustine claims that God permits angels and sinners to do evil, but makes good use of it, and so God's providence is not impeded by this. He makes this claim while laying out the logic of faith along with a concern to assert grace against Pelagianism.[69] The idea that God permits sin and evil appears in another mixed pastoral agenda (the endeavor to exhort Christian living while dialoguing with the apologetic agenda) in the *Enchiridion.*[70]

While doing apologetics or addressing related agendas along with responses to critics of God's providential goodness in other works, Augustine tries to account for the existence of evil. Divine providence is said to show that through evils it brings about by the agency of inferior beings who find pleasure in doing evil, the good are admonished to seek the unchangeable. In one of his expositions of Genesis he claims that all that transpires is set in motion by God, and though each lives according to its own bent, none would proceed along were it not God still regulating them. In this connection Augustine speaks of a distinction between "first causes," originally inserted by God in the world, and "secondary causes," which God foreknew would develop in the future. In another early apologetic work devoted to the Book of Genesis the African Father offers a distinction between realities that God makes and realities like evil that he regulates but does not control.[71] Note that in these contexts there is a bit weaker affirmation of divine sovereignty, insofar as evil is not worked by God.

A very strong affirmation of divine sovereignty, of God's action in all the events of the universe, appears in the *Confessions* when Augustine reflects on the despair and also the false beliefs he had held, including a failure to take his sin seriously enough. He claims that God sent him the torture of his toothache and that God takes His creatures in death.[72] Yet even in this same work he seems to compromise these affirmations of divine agency, as he contends that free will is the cause of evil. Of course, the context was a dialogue with the Manichees.[73]

Elsewhere in the *Confessions* when simply recounting his own faith pilgrimage (a context with similarities to exhorting to Christian living), Augustine takes a position rather like when he exhorts living the Christian life. He contends that evil is a perversion of the will.[74]

Correlating Divine Action and the Human Will

In the *City of God* Augustine asserts a position on divine providence that again takes it seriously while also affirming human free will. In the context of criticizing the philosophy of Stoicism and its belief that fate necessarily determines what is, the African Father contends that it does not follow that although God causes something to happen there is no power in the will. But our will does what God wanted it to do.[75]

Elsewhere in the treatise, he claims that because God foresaw what was in our will does not mean that we have no power. Thus we are still responsible for our sin, he insists. He proceeds to contend that God permitted humankind to sin, linking the idea to divine foreknowledge.[76]

At another point Augustine makes a further effort to relate divine sovereignty to human free will. While explicating the logic of faith, the priority of grace in dialogue with the Stoic rejection of freedom, he claims that just as God is not under necessity because we say He must live in eternity and know all things, so when we say we must choose freely our liberty is not compromised.[77] Along the same lines, when tracing out the logic of faith while dealing with eternity, the African Father claims that God causes us to will what we will.[78]

These contexts of exhortation and describing the logic of the faith continue to demonstrate Augustine's commitment to asserting both the divine initiative and a role for the human will in depicting the maintenance of the world. However, the action of God is prioritized.

Again the *City of God* provides some good examples. At one point, while articulating the logic of faith, he claims that things not meant for eternal life follow the directions of divine providence. Thus even the dissolution that is death is not annihilation but progress.[79] The human will is not forgotten in this context. Thus Augustine claims that a person would not become evil if the person's will had not chosen to do so.[80] This appreciation of human responsibility for evil may be presupposed in what seems like a more unambiguous claim to divine sovereignty by Augustine when, while describing faith, he contends that divine providence explains the establishment of kingdoms.[81]

When trying to explain the faith in this same treatise along with critiques of paganism, Augustine contends again for a potential mediating position: "What we choose to do freely is done of necessity." God is said to be the source of the causes of all things.[82] Along the same lines, while describing the logic of faith elsewhere in the treatise, the African Father claims that we are to appreciate that all temporal things and earthly necessities are given by God.[83] While expositing the faith, particularly divine providence, the African Father claims that God can do whatever He wills, creating many things that seem impossible. Whatever is pleasing, the faithful person attributes it to God.[84]

Also in the City of God while presenting the logic of faith, without any additional preoccupation with refuting Pelagianism, Augustine posits a vision of divine providence in which God is even less sovereign, is in fact limited. (Typically it is in the most virulent anti-Pelagian polemics that Augustine emphasizes a strong doctrine of divine sovereignty.) Thus in this context he claims that the wicked do many things contrary to God's Will. Of course, he hastens to add, all still tends toward good ends.[85]

It is evident that not just when dialoguing with the Manichees, but also when concentrating solely on the logic of faith, Augustine portrays God by as not being totally in control (albeit still eschatologically in control). As another example, when simply expositing Scripture in a preaching context, Augustine contends that God is the Maker of good and the disposer of evil. God knows where to place us, and may use the evil one's choice to order the evil. God does not cease to work in continuing to govern what He made.[86] At least insofar as the evil one's work seems to operate independently of God, we can see again that, when exhorting or expositing faith, Augustine's God, though ultimately in control, is not in control of all that transpires. A role for the creatures' wills is affirmed. We can also identify this pattern in passages in his City of God, where, while laying out the logic of faith, Augustine portrays God as foreseeing all things.[87] Divine foreknowledge implies that what God's creatures do on their own is not irrelevant to the agency of God.

God is portrayed a bit more as being in control of the creation, at least by giving permission for evil, when exhortation is combined with apologetics or refuting heretical notions (like anti-Pelagianism) or when exhorting Christian life (rather than merely proclaiming or describing the Good News of the Gospel). One example emerges in the City of God when Augustine claims that God makes contrasts and antitheses, as a beautiful poem is characterized by contrasts.[88] This passage clearly attributes even evil to God. It emerges in a context when Augustine is articulating the logic of faith, but is in dialogue with cosmological concerns about angels in such a way as to suggest an apologetic preoccupation. Recall that when exposition of the logic of faith is mixed with another agenda, then a more sovereign God is typically portrayed by the African Father.

When laying out the logic of faith while trying to distinguish Christian belief from Stoic necessitarianism, Augustine insists that we still have power of will. Nevertheless, he argues, some things happen against our will. What happens against our will, he adds, is God's will.[89]

We have already observed that we find the language of divine "permission" of providential activities even in the *City of God*. They emerge whenever the African Father combines the agenda of depicting or exhorting the faith with a critique of heretical trends. Other examples in the treatise include Augustine's claim, while dealing with despair over our evil along with a concern to affirm grace against polemical targets, that God permits newly baptized infants to be attacked by demons. In a similar context he contends that the devil is under God's Power; God permits us to fall under the devil. Since God is ultimately in control of things, even to the point of permitting evil, it follows that His Providence rules all that He has created.[90]

Likewise, when dealing with exhortation to Christian living (addressing the Last Judgment) in this work, a similar vision of divine providence is apparent. Augustine contends that no good can be done without God's help and that there is no sin without divine permission.[91]

A somewhat different theological vision emerges elsewhere in Augustine's *City of God* as he deals with despair over our evil, but is still concerned to affirm grace against polemical targets. In that passage he holds that fallen humans have not been left without God's mercies. They are in reach if we will pay the price of law and education.[92] The language in this case clearly connotes cooperation in such a way as to undermine divine sovereignty. However, the point here pertains to a kind of civil righteousness, to matters of education, not to achieving the righteousness of God that saves.

In the *Enchiridion*, in a mixed pastoral agenda in which the African Father both exhorts Christian life and responds to Pelagian challenges, both strands of his treatment of Providence seem to appear. On one hand he claims that the Will of God is never defeated, and that God permitted evil. Yet on the other hand he contends that much is done contrary to God's Will.[93] A mixed pastoral context results in a mixed portrayal of divine providence.

I have already noted how the African Father attempts to reconcile the two strands pertaining to Providence, especially when providing a general overview of the logic of faith and sometimes when exhorting Christian life. He tries to affirm God's role in determining what happens while still affirming a role for the will. Another very interesting example of his effort to synthesize these strands of thought emerges in *On Nature and Grace*. While seeking to promote Christian responsibility in a context with a critique of Pelagianism in the background, he claims that necessity and free will are not opposed, for we hear and smell many things against our will.[94]

The contextually patterned richness of Augustine's thought is not in logical contradiction. The same diversity is evident in his Anthropology.

ANTHROPOLOGY

There are clear evidences of Augustine's reliance on the dualistic conceptions of Greek philosophy. These occur in earlier writings as the African Father dialogues with the Manichees (as like them he contends that the soul holds a higher position than the body), or while engaging in apologetics he notes that the body is a heavy bond.[95] The same prioritizing of soul over body occurs in other texts, when Augustine either provides a rational exposition of our resurrection or seeks to comfort despair.[96] When responding to heretics in his *Exposition on the Book of Psalms,* Augustine contends that the body is just the garment of the soul.[97]

The same body-soul dualism, with a priority on humanity's spiritual "interior," is also evident when in his *Confessions* Augustine engages in apologetics or reflects on comfort the Gospel affords from despair.[98] A similar prioritizing is evident when he engages in polemics with false teachings in his *On the Soul and Its Origin.* In the same work, addressing a similar agenda, he deliberates on Biblical references to humanity as "spirit," contending that the spirit relates to the soul as the power of rational thought.[99] This stress on reason and spirituality as the core of nature is also evident in the *Confessions* and *On the Trinity* as he engages in apologetics or seeks to dialogue with the Manichees in *On the Morals of the Catholic Church.*[100] Elsewhere when engaging in apologetics with some exhortation, he also claims that the body cannot affect the soul.[101]

Despite these differences, Augustine clearly avoids extremes of dualism. In one of his polemical treatises concerned to explicate The Creed, Augustine speaks of humanity in three parts—as body, soul, and spirit. He defines "spirit" as humanity's rationality and "soul" as the life force uniting to our bodies. He notes that it is just as valid to speak of humanity in two parts.[102]

In the *City of God,* while extolling the blessings of God in our fallen world, he also extols the beauties of the human body.[103] While refuting the Manichees, he praises bodily senses and is willing to identify a human as soul and body.[104] While explaining his own life experiences, Augustine claims that every movement of the mind impacts the body, and that the mind can create habits. The soul quickens or animates the body.[105] While engaging in exhortation to faith in one of his sermons, he suggests that the body is like the soul's spouse.[106] The holism of body and soul in this image is readily apparent.

The Image of God

In apologetic contexts, in *On the Trinity* and elsewhere on occasion when dealing with how to live as a Christian, Augustine contends that we can find the image of God in the rational soul. He identifies it with reason or with the human mind when it contemplates truth.[107] When expositing the faith he refers to the image more in terms of an immediate tendency toward God, rendering humans capable of partaking of Him, or of humanity's triune character as creatures who are, know that they are, and delight in their existence.[108] Generally speaking, though, the African Father does not elaborate much further on what the image is.

The topic does receive some attention in connection with the question of what happens to the image of God in sin. When exhorting faith, Augustine claims that the image of God is said to be lost in sin.[109] But when sketching the eschatological vision (including a critique of those who deny the resurrection of the body), he contends that the capacity for receiving instruction from God is not lost.[110] When engaging in apologetics, with those concerned about the Biblical claim that unbelievers can do good, he expressly asserts that the image of God is not totally blotted out in sin. In the *Retractions* he claims that the image of God is only deformed.[111]

Other Characteristics of Human Nature

There is a sense in which human nature is a mystery, in Augustine's view. Thus he claims in his *Confessions* that there is something of humans that is in us that we do not know, that we are puzzles to ourselves. But God knows all of us, the African Father adds, for He made us. He is the life of our life.[112]

Nevertheless, we can know much about human nature, according to Augustine. Given his reliance on Greek philosophy when dialoguing with the Manichee heresy, it is hardly surprising that in such an early work he identifies humans as created rational, capable of wisdom. When doing apologetics he claims that reason is our best quality.[113] Elsewhere in one of those early treatises he elaborates on this commitment by asserting that when reason rules the emotions, then a person has perfect order. To this he adds that whoever wishes to live rightly, preferring that before all transient goods, attains that object.[114]

In this treatise he also reflects on the core of what makes people tick. All, he contends, desire happiness. He also makes this point when engaging in apologetics in *On the Usefulness of Believing* and in his *City of God*.[115]

Existence is so pleasant, Augustine adds, that even the wretched do not wish to die. And no rational creature can truly be happy apart from God, for lovely things are nothing if not from God.[116] True happiness has important behavioral consequences, Augustine contends. Those happy in their love of eternal things are obedient to eternal law, while unhappy people have the temporal law imposed on them.[117]

It is readily apparent how in Augustine's thinking human beings are clearly portrayed as theocentric (God-centered). Thus he contends that the light of such wisdom is common to all.[118] Awareness of this capacity in human beings for reason, a capacity for high goods, leads Augustine to praise the products of reason, like the arts, technology, and medicine.[119]

Another way Augustine has of describing the core of human nature is his contention that love is the root of all human action; he even claims in an apologetic treatise while exhorting Christian living that human beings naturally love themselves.[120] The supreme end of humanity, he asserts, is that good is sought for its sake.[121] His theocentric anthropology is again evident when he contends that one who knows how to love oneself loves God; love of self without this higher love is said to be hatred. (Augustine seems to posit a peculiar kind of self-serving character even to the love of God in these contexts, a commitment that does not surface in anti-Pelagian polemics.)[122]

He makes the point in a similar way in a later text. The object of the mind's self-love and self-knowledge is not changeless, he notes.[123] Truthful knowledge in ourselves is a kind of word. Nothing we do is not preceded by this inner word. This word owes its conception to love. Creatures are to be loved not for their own sake but for God. We are to enjoy ourselves and our fellows in the Lord, not to use them merely for our own gain.[124]

It is best when what we will rests in knowledge itself and does not love carnal things. In that case the conception of the word and what it brings forth are divided (for the word is spiritual). This leads to unhappiness. What makes a word is knowledge united with love. The mind possesses a certain likeness to the object known. So far as we know God we are like Him.[125] Thus human wisdom is being in accord with God.[126]

I have already noted some examples that Augustine provides in order to make the case for the trinitarian nature of human life. Among these are: (1) the trinitarian character of love (lover, object of love, love itself);[127] (2) the triad of mind, love, and self-knowledge—each is singly in the other, with love bringing the other two together;[128] and (3) the triadic comprehension of the mind knowing by means of memory, imprinted image, and agency combining the two.[129] About the second trinitarian characteristic Augustine adds that the mind has never ceased. In its act of turning on itself a trinity is presented in which it is possible to recognize a word. In this we recognize the image of God. It is the image of God because it has power to love God.[130]

Though he uses Greek philosophy in certain polemical and apologetic contexts, Augustine is guarded about the use of such concepts even in these contexts. Thus in *On Free Will* he advises that we not get tied down to just one philosopher's opinion about the origin of the soul, but proceed with the investigation on the basis of Scripture, with an openness to interpretations other than one's own. Elsewhere he also criticizes the claim of the great early theologian Origen that souls are imprisoned in the body.[131]

In addition to comments already noted, in other significant ways Augustine's reflections on human nature break with Platonic thought. For example, in a sermon exhorting faith he claims that the soul is capable of change (impossible for a Greek philosopher to believe). He makes a similar point in *On the Trinity* when he defines human nature in terms of the actions of memory, understanding, and will. For it we are what we remember, understand, and decide to do we are always different from what we were yesterday.[132]

In the *City of God,* while articulating the logic of faith, Augustine praises the human body as a revelation of God. The body is like a beast, he concedes. Yet human beings walk erect, not bent to the ground like animals. This posture reminds us to keep thoughts on things above. Other features of the body receive praise, like how the tongue makes speech possible.[133]

To be sure, the African Father concedes that bodily age is not a matter of the will. No one grows or is born when one wills.[134] Human beings and other creatures are intimately temporal. "For where there is no creature whose changing movements admit of succession, there cannot be time at all."[135] We are reminded here of the naturalness of death in the original divine plan.

Augustine distances himself from an unequivocal endorsement of Neo-Platonism in other ways. While explicating the logic of faith in his *City of God* and critiquing Manichee thinking in *On the Good of Marriage,* he asserts that human beings are essentially social.[136] God, he claims, created a sole individual so that the bond of humanity might mean more as kinship unites humans, not just common nature.[137] This bond of common humanity obliges affection for all, he asserts.[138]

At one point, while dealing with lifestyle issues, Augustine does rely on images more compatible with Neo-Platonism. When describing the idyllic existence in Eden he hypothesizes a passionless procreation as God's original plan.[139]

Nature and Grace

In connection with Augustine's manner of construing human nature before the Fall, in a work devoted both to exhorting the Christian life and to apologetics, as I have previously noted, the African Father often affirmed the continuities between reason and faith and also claimed that in Paradise humans were able to destroy themselves by an act of the will. However, he adds, to have maintained a life of righteousness would have required sustaining by the Creator.[140] In this context, the African Father also maintains that grace was required by humans even before the Fall.

With the exception of a work in which he did not "sharply debate and contend," the continuity between creation and redemption, between nature and grace, is largely rejected in texts addressing Pelagius. In this context, Augustine claims that as the Law is not of grace, neither is nature graced (1 Cor. 2:14; Gal. 3:10–11). For if righteousness came by nature, Christ died in vain.[141]

Elsewhere he draws the contrast in relation to the sort of grace that God gave Adam. According to the African Father it was a grace that could be forsaken, while the grace given in Christ does more. It makes man will to love.[142]

SUMMARY

As with the other doctrines covered thus far, the most unambiguous reliance on Greek philosophical suppositions occurs in polemical and apologetic contexts as well as frequently when exhorting to comfort from despair. More stress on the holism of human nature and the interactions of divine and human activity appears in other contexts: (1) where faith is exhorted; (2) where the logic of faith is outlined; (3) where the logic of his own coming to faith is explained; (4) when offering comfort on account of despair occasioned by an awareness of sin; and (5) when the Manichees are encountered, not in dialogue but in an attempt unequivocally to refute them. These patterns are characteristic of Augustine's treatment of other doctrines.

No less interesting is that another pattern of relating dualistic patterns of thought to the thrust toward unity is evident in the way Augustine relates nature and grace (Law [God's Word of mandate and judgment] and Gospel [God's Word of unconditional love]). He stresses the continuity of the two in contexts of exhortation, when comforting despair, and for apologetics. But he construes nature and grace in a more dialectical fashion in polemical contexts (especially when criticizing all forms of Pelagianism).

Chapter 5

Sin, Free Will, and Atonement

One's construal of Augustine's treatment of the doctrines of sin and free will say much about how one understands the African Father, whether as Catholic theologian or as the impetus for the Protestant Reformation. As in the case of the other doctrines we have considered, the various interpretations of Augustine's thought are all correct for certain texts of his (especially those which address concerns like the interpreter's own). As the framer of the doctrine of original sin, he of course rejects free will and affirms the total sinfulness of humanity, claims he makes particularly when dialoguing with Pelagianism (Rom. 7:14–23). In some of these contexts he also relates original sin to concupiscence. But this is not the whole story.

FREE WILL

We have already observed that when Augustine dialogues with the Manichees he endeavors to affirm free will and avoid all hints of determinism. Thus it is hardly surprising to find him asserting in these contexts that evil was the result of our own choice. Consequently, God is not author of sin. Of course, this "choice" is a swerving toward lower things, an emptiness or nothingness.[1] As he puts it elsewhere against the Manichees in *On Free Will*, there are two sources of sin: (1) a person's spontaneous thought; and (2) the persuasion of the neighbor.[2] When engaging in apologetics early in his career he also affirms the voluntary character of sin. But no less interesting is that he likewise affirms this later in his career when seeking to exhort Christian living along with the critique of Pelagianism. The very fact that sins are actions and that God admonishes us to do works testifies to sin's volitional character, he maintains.[3]

It is true that while reflecting on these earlier writings in his *Retractions* (426 or 427), the African Father qualifies these points. He claims that he had made these affirmations only in response to the Manichees and that this is why he had not dealt with grace, except in passing. He warns the Pelagians not to boast that he had pleaded their cause because "I have said many things in defense of free choice that the disputation required."[4] Augustine clearly concedes at this point the self-consciously contextual character of his theological approach.

At another point in this text he further qualifies the broad sense in which he intended to refer to sin as the result of the sinner's choice. He claims that sins are voluntary even when done in ignorance or unwillingly as overcome by lusts. In either case the sins are still being committed because the sins are still done voluntarily insofar as one performs them and consents to the lust.[5]

Even in these early works in this context there are indications that Augustine is taking positions compatible with his later anti-Pelagian works. Thus he makes some points that are certainly in harmony with comments about human bondage to sin and original sin. For example, even in *On Free Will*, before writing his *Retractions*, he claims that wrong things may be done of necessity when one wills the good and has no power to accomplish it due to ignorance or custom. It is a just penalty of sin that one has lost the power to do what is right for being unwilling to make use of that power.[6] He seems to endorse something like the bondage of the will to sin here.

Elsewhere in the treatise Augustine clarifies what he means when he contends that we have free will: Freedom of the will, he asserts, pertains to the freedom in which humans were created. He also seems to affirm something like original sin in the sense that Adam does not beget children better off than he is.[7]

Several comments in both this anti-Manichee text and one devoted to apologetics help us further define what the African Father means by "sin." Many of them are compatible with points he makes about sin when addressing other pastoral concerns throughout his career.

In *On Free Will* Augustine considers the question of what causes the will to turn in the direction from the unchanging good of God to private and inferior goods. The answer is nothing, the nothing which cannot be known. When good is taken away, when life turns toward temporal objects (as happens in sin), nothing is left.[8] In short, sin and evil are nothingness (a concept already encountered in the previous chapter).

Elsewhere in the treatise, Augustine notes that to raise these questions leads to an infinite regress, to a noetic avarice.[9] To ask why we sin is itself a manifestation of sin.

In an early apologetic work he makes a similar point about sin. It is defined as worship or love of the creature, not of God, as the perverse imitation of God. When engaging in apologetics later in his career in *On the Trinity* he makes a related point. By loving its own power, the soul slips from the whole to itself and in so doing becomes less than it is.[10]

ORIGINAL SIN

There has been a debate over whether Augustine's development of the doctrine of original sin is simply the result of the Pelagian controversy. Several recent interpreters have insisted that prior to the Pelagian controversy Augustine's references to something like this doctrine are not compatible with it.[11] They are correct up to a point. Augustine did not expressly identify a doctrine of original sin in his thought until the Pelagian controversy. But it is hard to see incompatibilities between his mature, post-Pelagian position and his comments in an earlier treatise like *To Simplician,* where, while responding to an exegetical question, he refers to the "inherited sin" and to Adam's original guilt and penalty, which then became our burden, or another early treatise *On Genesis Literally Interpreted,* where with a similar agenda he refers to subsequent creatures who no longer receive what Adam lost in sin.[12]

Similar statements can be identified in the anti-Donatist writings. While explicating the life-giving character of the Church and the Gospel, the African Father refers to how the seed of Adam are born to mortality and have received a nature that cannot be free from sin.[13] Likewise, he seems to describe something like infant sin in the *Confessions* (about which I shall subsequently elaborate).[14]

Analysis of the bulk of Augustine's writings, including his anti-Pelagian works, will indicate the comparability of these comments with his treatment of sin and original sin in contexts where exhorting Christian life or apologetics were not his primary agenda. Thus interpreters who have contended for a continuity between Augustine's pre-Pelagian treatment of sin and his later positions are also correct.[15] Once again we note that there is something correct about virtually all the major strands of Augustinian interpretation.

The Nature of Sin

I have already alluded to the references to the sins of infancy in the *Confessions.* Elaborating on this point while praising God (recounting the content of faith), the African Father refers in that work to how gluttonous and clamorous children are. In anti-Pelagian writings he expressly identifies such sin by infants as original sin.[16]

This same vision of sin also emerges in the *Confessions* when Augustine recounts his own faith pilgrimage (a context analogous to apologetics). He speaks of the meaninglessness of sinful existence, of how the idling of boys is not unlike business, that it is rather like the idling that grown men do on their jobs.[17] He uses the story of his own participation in stealing from a pear tree, noting the pleasure it gave him precisely because it was forbidden. The story illustrates how sinners love the evil that is in them, he contends.[18]

A powerful exposition follows of the temptations resulting from the appeal of beautiful things to the eye. Augustine observes how worldly success has its glory and how human friendship is admirable. In enjoyment of all these things we sin, he notes, if through immoderate inclination to them we forget the things higher and better (God).[19]

Two points made by Augustine in an earlier work on apologetics he reiterates in the *Confessions* while still describing his spiritual pilgrimage or when in dialogue with Pelagius or outlining the logic of faith. Sin, he asserts, is a perverse imitation of God. Human ambition seeks honor and glory, but God alone deserves these. Likewise when in dialogue with Pelagius or when outlining the logic of Christian faith he describes sin as he had in earlier apologetic contexts, as the desertion of a better good for a lesser one, or as the misdirection of love toward ourselves and not toward God. In *On the Truth,* Augustine adds that in failing to love God, in hating Him, human beings effectively practice self-hatred in sin.[20]

Augustine's *Confessions* and his anti-Pelagian writings offer other striking insights about sin. Making a point most suggestive of the doctrine of original sin as he continued to reflect on his life experience, the African Father notes how the companionship of others who sin encourages sin. In a manner reminiscent of the points made against the Manichees (in affirming the choice we had to avoid sin), Augustine comments that we must take responsibility for our own sin.[21]

While further reflecting on his faith pilgrimage, Augustine laments that the pursuit for honor, money, and marriage leads to disappointment. All aim for happiness, but are really miserable in their striving. Or, as he observes in a treatise directed against Pelagianism, sin is really a self-hatred. We are not truly happy, because we seek joy in bodily things and not in God.[22]

In view of these realities, it is evident that humans in sin are displeased with themselves, Augustine confesses. We are a race curious to know of others' lives, but slothful to correct our own.[23] Miserable as we are, we are never satisfied. Joy and sorrow always contend in our lives. Though enjoying to endure, humans would rather they had nothing to endure. In adversity they desire prosperity, and in prosperity they fear adversity.[24] Life since the Fall into sin is said to be filled with storms of pride, depths of curiosity, and a restless tossing of instability.[25]

We can identify more of the same descriptions of sin in Augustine's anti-Pelagian writings. Sin is self-love because such love shatters love's trinitarian character. The self focuses only on its own body to the exclusion of true love's commitment to reaching beyond its own being.[26]

Among the other points the African Father makes in these texts are how sin: (1) leads to a restless seeking after external things, so that the mind comes to be conformed to them; and (2) makes us victims of passion.[27] These texts endorse the familiar idea that sin is not a substance but a deprivation of it (of God), as abstaining from food can hurt the body. Consequently sin is not a new corrupt nature, but a corruption of what is created good.[28] As such, it is an emptiness, a nothing or a falling into nothing.[29]

Themes consistent with these construals of sin are also evident in some of Augustine's sermons and in the *City of God* when he either exhorts faith or outlines the logic of faith. Thus he identifies sinful existence as a long sickness, as a dying, as a life filled with all sorts of miseries as is evident insofar as life begins with (the newborn's) tears, and not with laughter.[30]

In connection with this last point, Augustine observes that nature falls away from God because it is made out of nothing. Thus in turning toward themselves, human beings become less than they are. We approach nothingness in sin.[31] But in making this point, Augustine is quick to affirm the goodness of the physical order in this context. "Things of flesh," he contends, refer to the whole of human nature. We ought not blame sins on the nature of flesh, for this disparages the Creator. What is not good is to abandon the goodness of the Creator in pursuit of a created good. Flesh itself is good. The punishment of the first sin is that humans are now totally flesh, even the soul. The self that we chose has become a tyrant.[32]

In a 397 Sermon, Augustine elaborates further on the hardships the life of sin imposes. To be born, he claims, is to enter a life of toil. The hard work we do to amass treasure is really madness, as it will not last and we will quickly pass away. The disquiet we feel, he notes, leads us to be creatures who would escape evil but are slow to do good.[33]

In the *City of God,* Augustine appeals to the familiar theme that love is the root of all human action. With that presupposition in hand he traces the direction of all human history, maintaining that humans have aligned themselves either with the earthly city or with the city of God, depending on what they have loved. The cities originate from two loves. Worldly society has flowed from selfish love. The communion of saints, by contrast, is rooted in the love of God, which will trample the self. In the earthly city, the rulers and the people they dominate are dominated by the lust for dominions. In the City of God, citizens serve one another in charity.[34] As we shall see, this distinction has rich implications for the African Father's social ethic.

Of course, Augustine concedes, in the earthly city and its governments there are goods. But the good we have on earth, the happiness it nurtures, is really misery, or, as he puts it elsewhere, as fleeting as smoke and wind. In fact, he adds, even good people deserve affliction because they wink at sin.[35]

None of these points made in these contexts about the nature of sin is inimical to the African Father's reflections on sin's character when dealing with the Christian life or in apologetics. We see this in his *Enchiridion,* a work addressing these concerns. In this work he claims, as he had in other contexts, that the cause of evil is the defection of the will of a being who is mutably good from the Good that is immutable.[36]

The depth of sin and its sinister character receive further elaboration in this work. We may look on even great and detestable sins as trivial the more we get accustomed to them.[37] If we observe in history a decline in moral standards, and wonder how it could transpire, Augustine would have us realize that the generation involved in allowing for more permissiveness never realized it was happening.

Another interesting point in this treatise is how he defines here and elsewhere the unforgivable sin, the sin against the Holy Spirit. He takes a position that has had an important impact on Western theology. He claims that this sin is the despising of God's mercy.[38]

I noted in the previous chapter how Augustine took different positions on whether the image of God remains in fallen human beings. Of course, the position one takes on this question has implications for concluding how thoroughly mired in sin we are. Consequently, as I noted, an insistence that the image is totally lost in sin, that we are fully mired in sin, is more typical of Augustine's thought when exhorting faith, but when apologetics or exhorting the Christian life is his agenda, then he only opts for its being defaced or deformed in sin.

The Bondage of the Will

The question of human free will is intimately related to the doctrine of Providence. But for Augustine, at least when criticizing Pelagius and when articulating the logic of Christian faith, belief in the bondage of the will is also related to our sinfulness.

I previously noted that even in his earlier writings on behalf of the apologetic agenda and in critiquing the Manichees, Augustine made some points that suggest that the will has been in bondage since the Fall. He makes these points in these treatises either to distance his affirmation of free will from a total compromise of grace or because his agenda moves from refuting Manichees and apologetics to critiquing Pelagius or expositing the faith.

Thus in the anti-Manichee treatise *On Free Will,* at one point the African Father seeks to clarify why all are not able to obtain the happy life since all desire it (merely articulating the logic of Christian beliefs). In that context, free will is denied. He claims that when people are unhappy this is voluntary, not that they want to be unhappy but that their wills are in such a state that unhappiness follows even against their will. In other dialogues with the Manichees he speaks of how sin becomes a habit that we cannot conquer.[39]

When the agenda shifts to polemics with Pelagians, Augustine makes a similar point by noting that nature and custom joined together render cupidity strong and unconquerable.[40] In an early work addressing this sort of context, he expressly affirms the bondage of the will. The African Father claims that actual willing is in our power, yet it has been lost as the penalty for our sin. Free will exists, he claims, but has no value for those sold under sin; it is only effective for sin.[41] Elsewhere Augustine feels the need to address how our once good will became evil in this way. It was caused, he claims, when the will turned itself to something lower.[42]

The bondage to sin is affirmed in other ways in Augustine's anti-Pelagian works or when just critiquing Pelagian views. He notes that no one in this life is found without sin, that free choice alone avails for nothing but sin.[43] He adds that the spring of free choice is in ourselves, a comment that suggests that we are curved in on ourselves in sin and cannot escape.[44]

Elaborating on these points elsewhere Augustine refers to a conflict within ourselves.[45] Since the Fall we cannot do good of ourselves, but only through the Spirit. Grace alone makes the will good. Since sin damages nature, we need grace to make us new.[46]

Other express affirmations of original sin and our bondage to sin appear when Augustine claims that all have sinned, that no one is without sin, and that we are born in sin. Our hearts and thoughts are not in our power, he observes. They recall us to worldly, voluptuous things. Only God can give power. Thus we are in His power.[47]

Perhaps the most famous, most historically important affirmation of our bondage emerges in the *Confessions* while Augustine addresses the miseries of human life (comforting despair). He prays that God would command what He will and give what he commands (the very remark that originally inspired the Pelagian controversy).[48] The logical outcome of this comment is that God commands some things that we cannot do in order that we might know what to ask of Him, so that faith obtains by prayer what the Law commands.[49] In short, God commands the impossible.

In many contexts, pride and lust (concupiscence) play major roles in Augustine's construal of sin and the bondage of the will. When expositing the faith early in his career, the African Father contends that we fall through pride, and elsewhere in such a context that pride is the beginning of all sin.[50]

Of course, Augustine never means to connote that every sin is pride. He does believe, though, that pride is the commencement of every sin, just as the devil used it to lure Adam to be like God. Pride begins when we depart from God. We are never free of pride, in Augustine's view, as it lies in our hearts even in deeds rightly done. Such a person takes pride in overcoming pride.[51]

Even when engaging in apologetics in one of his letters, the African Father contends that pride spoils even good actions by the desire for praise. The good works we do are spoiled by pride, as they become nothing more than means for congratulating ourselves.[52] Another way he puts it is in a dialogue with those contending that we can achieve virtues and happiness through philosophy. Such virtues, Augustine insists, are still marred by pride and so are vices.[53]

While explicating the logic of faith in the *City of God,* Augustine claims that pride commits one to an unreality tending us toward nothingness. For the pretensions of this life are pride, he asserts. People desire to vaunt themselves upon their honorable positions; they think themselves great because of their wealth or power.[54]

Another thoughtful way of describing our bondage emerges in the *Confessions* while he recounts his own spiritual pilgrimage and why he had not yet converted. Augustine claims that the enemy holds the will, enchains it. The perverse will changes to lust, which becomes a habit.[55] Making a point much like he did against the Manichees, Augustine asserts that the law of sin is the fierce force of habit by which the mind is held even against its will. The soul is said to be so weighted down by custom that it cannot rise.[56]

This theme of sin as lust or concupiscence, the inescapable habit, plays an important role for Augustine in many contexts. In writing *On Nature and Grace* and *On the Grace of Christ and Original Sin,* two anti-Pelagian treatises, Augustine observes that the penalty for sin is more sin, being given over to lust. We sin according to cupidity (strong desire, greed).[57] In another work devoted to articulating the logic of faith, Augustine notes that carnal concupiscence reigns and has made the human race one lump of sin from which God sanctifies some and lays others low.[58] There is no escape from this concupiscence. None fails to yield to its promptings, even though one might not want to submit to them.[59]

Augustine seeks to find ways of relating both his affirmation of free will against the Manichees and his denial of free will in sin. (This suggests that even in his strongest anti-Pelagian tendencies he never intended to deny that what happens to us happens through the will, that we are not robots. Thus in one anti-Pelagian work the African Father contends that free will does not perish in sin, for we still enjoy the sinning we do.)[60] In another similar treatise he observes that we have a free will in sin, but need a physician because we are sick, a vivifier because we are dead.[61]

In *On Nature and Grace* he expressly addresses this issue of the comparability of the necessity of sin and free will. It is rather like saying that we wish to be happy but cannot be, he claims. It is like having the ability to see, but not being able to because we have no light, or like losing the power to smell effectively when the only smell around is noxious. In another work he claims that free will does not perish in sin in the sense that we enjoy the sinning we do.[62]

Concupiscence and Sin

The idea of sin as concupiscence [*concupiscere* or *cupiditas,* translated as "lust" in some English translations of Augustine] was typically deployed in the same contexts in which he denied free will. Among the texts where this is identifiable is the *City of God,* where while explicating faith he contends that sin is concupiscence, that it prevents sinners from doing what they desire. The compulsion to sin is a bit like the sexual passion one experiences just before the moment of climax. The sinner and lover are out of control and cannot stop. When dealing with the Pelagian insistence on achieving perfection in *On Man's Perfection in Righteousness* Augustine expressly identified sin as concupiscence.[63] In a similar context in *On Marriage and Concupiscence,* parental sexual concupiscence is said to transmit original sin. The fruit of the lust of desire, what drives the sexual union, cannot but reflect this lust. Augustine does not exclusively describe the inherited character of original sin by appeal to the concept of concupiscence, but he does so often.[64]

It is hardly surprising to find Augustine identifying sin with lust, given his own pre-Christian lifestyle and sexual escapades.[65] In the *Confessions* he generalizes this to the human condition and refers to his longing to love and be loved. He says he was enslaved to lust.[66] Thus he claims that we are all weighed down by concupiscence; our passions, loves, and uncleanness of spirit press us down.[67]

Writing against the Pelagians also gave rise to two other profoundly significant insights about the nature of concupiscence as sin. Concupiscence increases and receives greater energies from prohibitions of the Law, Augustine maintains.[68] Reiterating a point made elsewhere, Augustine asserts that God commands some things that we cannot do in order that we might know what to ask of Him. God commands the impossible. But faith obtains by prayer what the Law commands, he adds.[69]

The African Father is concerned that concupiscence not be understood in a physical, bodily way, but in a spiritual sense to refer to unsatiated, uncontrolled desire for self-gratification and pleasure. Thus he claims that sin is not caused primarily by the flesh but by the soul, especially when it transgresses God's commandments, loses grace, and consequently lapses into a ruinous disharmony with itself and the body.[70]

When Augustine deals with the nature of the Christian life, concupiscence plays a less central role in his thinking about sin. He interprets it more as the result of the Fall, as he claimed that with the Fall crept in ignorance of right things and a lust for what is hurtful.[71]

In the analogous context of dealing with what to make of unbelievers who are outwardly moral or when dealing with the practice of the Christian life and the goodness of the created order even in sin (issues also related to behavior), as well as when exhorting Christian life and comforting despair, one finds the African Father distinguishing between venial and mortal sins. (He speaks of a difference between heinous and trivial sins in the *Enchiridion*.) Such a distinction has been scrupulously followed in subsequent Roman Catholic thought.[72]

Also, while addressing similar concerns in the *Enchiridion,* we find the African Father grading sins. He asserts that while every lie is a sin, intention makes a difference. The sin of one who lies to help another is not so great as that of one who tells a lie to injure another.[73]

When dealing with the Christian life along with trying to assert the power of Baptism, Augustine seems to distinguish two sorts of concupiscence. He contends that after regeneration concupiscence is no longer sin, but although inherited it is only called sin as it is stirred by the delight of sinning.[74] Such a perspective has significant implications for a too simple, unambiguous identification of sin with concupiscence in Augustine's thought.

In *On Marriage and Concupiscence,* a work both directed against Pelagius but also concerned to apologize for the validity of Christian marriage (a concern with sanctification and living the Christian life), Augustine claims that in the regenerate concupiscence is more like the means for sin and can produce sin.[75] The old comment about Augustine giving rise to both the Medieval Catholic heritage and to the Protestant Reformation seems evident in his diverse treatment of sin and the role of concupiscence in it. With regard to the question of which strand of thought predominates in Augustine himself, it is all a matter of context.

ATONEMENT

Similar contextual patterns are evident when Augustine reflects on the atonement. When merely explaining the logic of Christian faith, telling the story, or comforting despair, he opts for a view of Christ's redeeming Work as accomplished by conquering the forces of evil, death, and chaos (Col. 2:13–15).[76] But when addressing matters related to living or practicing the Christian life or when critiquing sinful pride or unbelief, the African Father portrays Christ's atoning work as a Sacrifice paid not to the devil but to God (the so-called Satisfaction Theory of the Atonement [Eph. 5:2; Heb. 10:12]). Sometimes when contexts are mixed with the concern about Christian life and with the logic of Christian faith, we discern some combination of these models for depicting the atonement.[77] A particularly intriguing image can be noted near the end of the *Confessions,* as the African Father seeks both to explicate the logic of the faith and to exhort Christian life. Augustine asserts that the Lord has destroyed all his acts that deserve ill in order that God might not punish him.[78]

When undertaking apologetics or exhorting Christian living, Augustine refers to a pedagogical role for Christ's atoning work, its influence on the believer's morality or piety that can then lead to salvation. (This is the so-called Moral Influence Theory of the Atonement [1 Cor. 11:1].)[79] Although this was his earliest view of the atonement, he remains consistent in using this image whenever addressing these concerns. The consistency of Augustine's contextuality is evident again.

Chapter 6

Salvation, the Christian Life, and Predestination

Augustine does not frequently expressly describe his positions pertaining to the doctrines of justification (*iustitiam*), sanctification (*sanctificatio*), and predestination (*praedestinatio*). However, much that he writes has implications for positions on these doctrines, and so they warrant detailed consideration regardless of how frequently he expressly addresses them.

One finds in Augustine's thought the viewpoints of virtually every major Christian denomination on these three topics. The Protestant Reformers' version of salvation by grace though faith, that God is righteous in making us righteous (Rom. 3:21–28; Gal. 2:15; Eph. 2:8–9), is clearly evident in contexts where Augustine dialogues with Pelagianism or merely proclaims the faith. Along with this line of thought, other commitments of the Protestant Reformation heritage appear, even with regard to the doctrine of predestination. On the other hand, in many cases when the African Father addresses living the Christian life or comforting despair (particularly when combined with critiques of Pelagianism), we can also discern ways of describing sanctification most suggestive of Reformed, Baptist, Pentecostal, and even Methodist heritages (1 Pet. 5:5–6; 2 Thess. 2:13). In contexts where predestination is under fire or he has to refute the Manichee heresy (and occasionally just when exhorting readers to live the Christian life), Augustine takes positions suggesting that election is based on divine foreknowledge and deals with justification in ways compatible with historic Roman Catholic and even Eastern Orthodox conceptions. The African Father has clear lessons to teach us about ecumenism and pastoral sensitivity in the way in which he deals with these doctrines pertaining to Soteriology (the doctrine of Christian salvation).

JUSTIFICATION: PROTESTANT-LIKE THEMES

The Protestant Reformers' readings of Augustine regarding his commitment to affirm that salvation is by grace alone are on target in many of the anti-Pelagian writings. In *On the Spirit and the Letter,* devoted to addressing this context, his very definition of both justification and sanctification bespeak this commitment. Justification, he claims, means to be "deemed or reckoned as righteous, as it is predicated of a certain man in the Gospel." (In another text in the treatise he defines it as being "made righteous" [Rom. 4:6; Gen. 15:6].) Similarly, he defines sanctification "to mean that He makes those to be saints who were not saints before."[1]

Both definitions (particularly the one pertaining to justification) imply a forensic understanding of the doctrines. That is, justification is not the result of a change in the believer, something that we do, but is a consequence of God looking at the believer in a new way, as righteous and holy. A stronger emphasis on God's action in redeeming us is also construed in these definitions—the belief that we are justified by grace alone.

The numerous express affirmations of justification by grace through faith, not works, emerge especially not just in anti-Pelagian contexts, but also when he is merely explicating the faith, sometimes along with some attention to exhorting Christian living.[2] He makes the same point in another way in similar contexts, including exhorting Christian life and exhorting comfort from despair, by contending that grace is not given on account of our merits, that we have been saved by grace.[3] As he puts it against the Pelagians in *On Grace and Free Will,* if righteousness came by nature, Christ died in vain.[4]

As Augustine elaborates in a similar context and also when outlining the logic of faith, to be justified, then, entails that the Law is no longer of use. God justifies the ungodly not because they are upright, but in order that they may become upright in heart. Similarly, when engaging in apologetics and polemics over the Trinity, he claims that the Father loves us not as we are but as we shall be.[5] When confessing his faith, he says that confession entails that when I am wicked it means being displeased with myself, and when I am good it means not attributing my goodness to myself but to God.[6] Expositing the faith, he notes that we are freed from our wretchedness in ourselves to come to happiness in God. Our weakness is swallowed up in God's strength.[7] God sought us when we did not seek Him. He does not forget us when we forget Him, the African Father asserts. Or as he puts it in his anti-Pelagian works: God's grace is prevenient.[8]

Augustine's explanation of the righteousness of God has been enormously influential in the development of Protestantism (Rom. 3:21–28). When critiquing Pelagianism or when preaching, he claims that the righteousness of God is "not that where He is Himself righteous, but that with which He endows man when He justifies the ungodly."[9] Along with this insight, which Martin Luther contended was the turning point of the Reformation, Augustine also taught Luther, not only in anti-Pelagian contexts but also when exhorting Christian life along with an apologetic concern, that the righteousness given is not our own but God's.[10]

In other ways, Augustine's reflections when articulating the logic of faith and when polemicizing against Pelagianism are most suggestive of Luther's appropriation of him. While articulating the logic of faith in the *City of God,* the African Father claims, in a manner most akin to Luther's Theology of the Cross, that there is a kind of lowliness that lifts up. In bowing to God we are exalted. Grace helps us not to escape suffering but to bear with it.[11]

In the same vein, while responding to Pelagius, Augustine asserts in *On Grace and Free Will* that God commands some things that we cannot do, in order that we might know what to ask of Him. Faith obtains by prayer what the Law commands.[12] Citing a theme we observed in the previous chapter in his *Confessions,* Augustine here effectively asserts that God commands the impossible. However, in a different context, one in which he was concerned not just to dialogue with Pelagius but also to consider issues pertaining to Christian responsibility, he claims that perfect righteousness may have no examples in this life, and yet not be impossible. Such righteousness could become realized, he contends, if we became sufficiently committed to use the grace of God that has been given for that purpose. That it does not happen, Augustine concludes, is due not to its impossibility but to the judgment of God.[13] Again we can see how the diversity in Augustine's thought is not necessarily in contradiction, as in each case he denies that anyone has kept the Law perfectly and affirms our need for grace. But the different contexts lead to different assessments regarding the possibility of achieving such perfection.

Regarding the impossibility of perfection, Augustine argues in a sermon exhorting faith and in a letter comforting despair written in 400 that perfect love would entail the abolition of fear. But without fear, which is the preparation for love and justification, there is no justification. On this side of the eschaton, then, he believes that we cannot have perfect love.[14]

Related to the denial of the possibility of perfection is the African Father's belief that justification does not remove sin, that justified Christians are simultaneously saint and sinner (*simul iustus et peccator*). Writing against the Donatists he claimed that Christians continue to drag along with them the traces of our mortal nature. Or as Augustine puts it in his *Confessions* while articulating his faith pilgrimage, the new will and old will of sin are in conflict. We need to humble human beings by comforting them with these new insights, he says in *On the Predestination of the Saints,* so that God may be exalted.[15]

Justification, Grace, and Faith

Great theological debates have been fought through the centuries over the question of how these three concepts relate. Generally speaking, especially in contexts not directly concerned with exhorting to Christian life, Augustine makes clear that the faith which justifies is in fact a work of grace. However, on several occasions, especially when writing against the Manichees and concerning himself with exhorting Christian living, he implies that faith is something we must do in order to earn grace and salvation.[16] In fact, while critiquing Pelagianism at one point (but only in that context), the African Father claims it is wrong to deny, as he had, that faith is preceded by grace.[17]

We receive hints about Augustine's preferences for describing faith as subordinate to God's grace in some passages from his *Confessions* as he either offers praise (outlining the logic of faith) or recounts his own spiritual pilgrimage. He refers to how God excites humans so that to praise God is our joy, and how God is fragrant to us and draws us to His loveliness.[18] In both of these texts, God is portrayed as active in bringing us to faith. Augustine makes this point even more clearly in describing the essence of conversion, not just in this document, but also when merely explicating the logic of faith: By God's gift we come totally not to will what we willed, he claims, but to will what God willed.[19] God works through our wills.

In the anti-Pelagian literature, Augustine makes his points more sharply. In one case, where he is also concerned about exhorting Christian living, he does insist that freedom of choice is not made void through grace, just as the Law of God is not made void by grace. Grace establishes freedom. Faith is not then placed in our power, he insists, for willing is one thing, ability another.[20]

Augustine had made a similar distinction in an earlier work that had a certain anti-Pelagian tone as he exposited the faith and also urged Christian responses. He distinguishes in this context between the power to will and the thing actually willed. God has willed that the power to will should be both His and ours—His because He calls us and ours because we follow when called. But what we actually will, God alone gives (the power to do it right). Good will, the African Father asserts, is wrought in us by God. Because good will is preceded by calling, the fact that we have a good will is rightly attributed to God. Or as he puts it elsewhere in the treatise, one receives grace the moment one begins to believe.[21]

Elsewhere in the later anti-Pelagian treatise the African Father makes the point more concisely. He contends that the love of God is shed in our hearts not by free choice, whose spring is in ourselves, but through the Holy Spirit given to us.[22] This love, he asserts, is not God's love for us, but that by which He makes us His lovers.[23]

Other examples in texts of this genre include the African Father's claim in his anti-Pelagian treatise *On the Predestination of the Saints* that faith is received as a gift of God.[24] In other treatises characterized by such polemics, as well as in polemics against the Donatists and when exhorting Christian life along with exhorting faith, he claims that faith is of God, is a gift of God.[25] In all of these contexts he often declares that the beginning of faith is of God. He even claims at these points that God can take a will averse to faith and make it a good will, that God makes willing people out of the unwilling.[26]

The introduction of the human will in faith alongside the Work of God in bringing it about raises a perennial problem for Western theology. Although Augustine is sometimes blamed for this problem, he offers reflections for resolving it. His point in these cases is essentially that God works through the human will.

While laying out the logic of faith, Augustine claims that we are drawn to faith by the Spirit, but not against our will. He makes virtually the same claim when he deals with both a concern for holiness and refuting Pelagianism in *On the Spirit and the Letter*.[27] Against Pelagius he claims that God works in us to will.[28] Both the beginning and end of faith are of God, he concludes.[29] It is all God's Work, and yet the work is done through us. We do the willing, but God makes us will what is good. Believers have the ultimate freedom when God works on them in this way, for they are free not to sin. This is evident insofar as the freedom of heaven will be more potent than anything we can now imagine, for sin is impossible in heaven, Augustine notes. Such freedom approximates the freedom of God, Who cannot sin but is still free.[30]

At some points, especially when endeavoring to refute the Pelagian heresy, Augustine carries this theme of faith as God's Work in us to its logical outcome and advocates predestination. For example, in *On the Predestination of the Saints* he writes:

> And He [Jesus] says that a man is justified by faith and not by works, because faith itself is first given, from which may be obtained other things. . . . Faith, then, as well in its beginning as in its completion, is God's gift; and let no one have any doubt whatever, unless he desires to resist the plainest sacred writings, that this gift is given to some, while to some it is not given.[31]

Several texts in the Augustinian corpus do not clearly indicate whether they advocate the position of faith as God's Work or might be indications of his advocacy of faith as an act of the free will that characterizes much of his polemic with the Manichees. One example is in his *On the Spirit and the Letter*, as he criticizes Pelagianism, though with some concern to exhort Christian living. In a context in which he had stressed the Work of the Holy Spirit and noted that the act of the will to believe is attributable to the divine bounty, he still affirms that this gift comes through the freedom of choice. Freedom could produce no act of belief were there no inducement or invitation to belief, he claims. It is God Who brings about the will to believe in humans. In all things His mercy anticipates us.

These comments are most characteristic of Augustine's manner of construing faith in such anti-Pelagian contexts. But then he adds, somewhat uncharacteristically, that to consent to the calling of God or to refuse it belongs to our will.[32] Is he advocating here that we will to believe independently after the offer of grace (a Semi-Pelagianism)? Or is he contending that grace brings about our willing action, in line with predestination? More likely the latter, he seems to conclude, as he reflects on and construes as a mystery the question of why some yield to God's persuasion and others do not.[33] Given this lack of clarity, it is no wonder that Protestant denominations embedded in the thought of the Reformers and Catholics still quibble about this matter and about the heritage of Augustine.

Elsewhere in the same treatise Augustine offers another remark about faith whose meaning is ambiguous. He begins by noting that even our believing is a gift of God. But then he adds that this does not entail there is no will save God's, for then God would be the author of sin. Freedom is not taken away because help is given, he points out in a 414 letter concerned with Christian responsibility.[34] This remark could be reconciled with both the Protestant understandings of justification by grace and the characteristic Roman Catholic conception of faith and justification as the cooperation of human work and grace.[35] A similar point is evident in another anti-Pelagian treatise. While offering such a polemic and also pointing out disagreement with earlier positions on faith as what we do, Augustine claimed that faith is of God, but is only brought about with our good will.[36]

Augustine speaks of faith in at least two ways, distinguishing (in what has become a classic distinction) between what is believed (the Rule of Faith, or thinking with assent) and the way in which one believes.[37] When focusing on human nature and behavior (or apologetics), he identifies faith with the way in which one believes. In one case when dealing with such contexts, he even specifies faith's Trinitarian character, equating it with a remembering, a beholding, and a loving of the object of faith.[38] He also speaks of faith as thinking with assent or refers to the Rule of Faith (as a credal formula) in polemics or when presenting the logic of faith.[39]

The Augustinian bias (though not exclusivism) toward prioritizing grace over faith in the event of justification leaves open the question of what actually happens when we are justified. In Protestant theology two historic construals have emerged. As I shall note, both have precedents in Augustine's thought: (1) Justification is understood as Conformity to Christ, as a kind of marriage between the believer and Christ that is manifest in their total sharing of all that belongs to each other. There are interesting similarities between this image and the mysticism of the great Neo-Platonic philosopher Plotinus.[40] Such a conception emphasizes the life-transforming character of justification. (2) Forensic justification presents the doctrine primarily in terms of a declaration by God of the faithful's righteousness in spite of sin. In addition to these two models, Augustine also relies on images for describing justification most suggestive of the characteristic Roman Catholic and Eastern Orthodox conceptions.

Justification as Conformity to Christ

In contexts where faith is exhorted or comfort is offered to those in despair over the challenge of living the Christian life, we find Augustine employing images suggesting the Pauline concept of the blessed exchange between Christ and the believer (1 Cor. 6:16b, 17). For example, in his *Confessions* as he exhorts or confesses his faith, he claims that our souls are too small to receive God and instead prays that God would expand our souls so that He might be received in them. God must remake us, he contends, or we are not saved. Augustine urges God to enter our souls and fit them for Himself. A similar point about God fashioning us as good human beings is made in the *Enchiridion* in response to concerns of work righteousness. These images certainly entail that Christ lives in believers, and in so doing transforms them, a point actually asserted while offering comfort and exhorting faith in one of Augustine's 417 Sermons.[41]

Other examples of the African Father depicting justification as Conformity to Christ are evident as he exhorts faith in several early fifth-century sermons. He speaks there of God dwelling in us or of receiving a blessed exchange from Christ of all His goods for our sin. In one of his letters written in 416 both to exhort faith and to combat Pelagian tendencies, he even expressly invokes the image of the believer being Christ's spouse.[42]

In the dual context of exhorting faith and the Christian life, Augustine speaks of being conformed to the Son's image. While depicting the faith in a context concerned with refuting Antinomianism and Pelagianism, he contends that we are made truly free when God fashions us as good human beings.[43] In a similar context in at least two anti-Pelagian texts and also when explicating the faith in another treatise he claims that we are given a new heart through grace, and the stony one is taken away.[44]

Two other texts could be cited to exemplify Augustine's endorsement of this manner of construing justification. While seeking to console despair in a 408 letter, he claims that we shall become more like Christ as we advance in knowledge of Him. In his *Confessions,* while explicating the logic of faith, he claims that we cannot support our own good until God heals our weakness, crowning us with loving-kindness and compassion.[45] There is a bit of ambiguity in these remarks. The first might just refer to sanctification, not to a Christlikeness given in justification. And the text from the *Confessions* might refer merely to a divine declaration. Nevertheless, it is readily apparent that at times in his career when he refers to justification while exhorting faith, tracing out its logic (even if also in polemical contexts), and comforting despair, the African Father employs conceptions that stress that in redeeming us God has intimately bound Himself to us. Of course, that is not the whole story.

Forensic Justification

I have already noted one example of Augustine's propensity to refer to justification in a forensic manner (the idea that God *declares* us righteous) in an anti-Pelagian context. Another example includes his claim in another anti-Pelagian work that sin remains after Baptism but is no longer imputed. We find the theme evident again in his claim when exhorting Christian life with an apologetic concern that the righteousness received in justification is alien, not our own but God's. This view or at least the claim that God covers up our sin also appears in his *Confessions* at a point when he reflects on how one comes to belief (a more apologetic or evangelistic concern).[46]

JUSTIFICATION: CATHOLIC AND ORTHODOX-LIKE THEMES

There has been general scholarly consensus that the characteristic Eastern church concept of *theosis* (the idea that God became man so man could become like God, as per 2 Pet. 1:4) is not typically advocated by Augustine. In a 408 letter criticizing false teachers he even expressly rejects this view.[47] However, at least on one occasion, while exhorting the Christian life in *On the Trinity*, he employs images affirming either this concept or the idea of Conformity to Christ (the idea that the believer has been united to Christ, like a bride to the groom, sharing all things in common, so that every spiritual gift that the believer has derives from Christ, the groom):

> And we must understand it to be said on account of this perfection [our renewal in Christ], that "we shall be like Him, for we shall see Him as He is. . . ."
> . . . "He that is joined to the Lord is one spirit." The mind will be raised to the participation of His being, truth, and bliss which is His own. In the being, joined to it is perfect happiness, it will live a changeless life and enjoy the changeless vision of all that it will behold.[48]

Remarks in his 416 *Lectures of the Gospel of John,* while explaining the logic of faith, also suggest the African Father's endorsement of *theosis,* though he is probably portraying justification as Conformity to Christ and the Church as the Body of Christ. As he puts it: "Let us rejoice, then, and give thanks that we are not only made Christians, but Christ. . . . For if He is the head, we are the members: the whole man is He and we."[49]

Another image that is at least compatible with the concept of *theosis* is evident in the *Confessions* as Augustine deals with the despair that comes with being dragged down by concupiscence. He claims that the Holy Spirit *lifts us up* above our concupiscence, our passions, loves, and uncleanness of spirit (presumably lifting us up to the spiritual realm, to God). In one of his earliest apologetic treatises, also concerned with expositing how humans are to live, Augustine made a similar point while relying on Mystical notions of the soul's seven-stage ascent to full union with God. And in his *Confessions* while recounting his spiritual pilgrimage he likewise reports how in entering into his own self he was lifted above his mind to God.[50]

Alongside these affirmations, though, one can also identify texts in which Augustine speaks of salvation as a process involving the cooperation of grace and good works, and others in which he expressly affirms free will (Jas. 2:14–17). Correlated with such affirmations is a construal of Providence and election in relation to divine foreknowledge. These affirmations tend to emerge in situations when he addresses moral laxity, the general refusal of the Manichees to acknowledge human responsibility, or the importance of preaching. It is no accident that on these occasions, when his remarks seem almost Pelagian, the African Father addresses concerns not unlike those that motivate his British opponent.[51] Among examples are his comments while exhorting Christian living in the *City of God* about the reward in heaven for faith, and his claim in a 390 letter devoted to this concern that the merciful providence of God cannot permit a person of God's will to be an alien from Christ.[52]

Augustine's use of divine-human cooperation language is even carried so far as to imply a semi-Pelagianism in some contexts when dealing with the Manichees. In *On Free Will* and *Concerning the Nature of the Good*, he claims that one must be willing or converted (respectively) in order to receive grace.[53] As he puts it elsewhere in *On Free Will*, as well as in a later work while exhorting Christian living, the soul returns to its position of superiority "by imitating His [Christ's] visible humility." He also claims that the justice of God is preserved in punishing sin, but that we are "aided" in recovering salvation because we sinned less than the devil.

While concerned with issues of morality in his *Our Lord's Sermon on the Mount* and at one point in *City of God*, the African Father claims that one's status in the Kingdom is determined by God's Law, even contending that if we wish God to forgive our sins or hope to have Him hear our prayers we must forgive sins committed against us. Likewise in an anti-Pelagian work, *On Grace and Free Will*, while exhorting Christian life, Augustine claims that we have a good will if we merely desire to do God's Commandment but are unable. He adds that we are made able by grace, but it is unclear if the initial good will is a work apart from grace.[54] Not only is the Pelagian emphasis on human works evident here, but likewise divine righteousness is defined in terms of judgment, rather than defined as in the anti-Pelagian works as God's Work of making the faithful righteous.

The same sort of construal of the human contribution to salvation is evident in an apologetic context also concerned about holy living in the treatise *On True Religion*. Augustine there seems to affirm something like the Medieval theological concept of a preparation for grace, but like the late Medieval Nominalists construes this preparation as an autonomous act that merits grace. Indeed, he asserts, through reason we turn to God in order to *deserve* illumination by the Word.[55] He also claims that when one believes God's dispensation in prophetic history, then a way of life agreeable to divine commands will purge the mind and make it fit to perceive spiritual things, for God has given all the possibility to be good.[56]

In the same apologetic treatise Augustine also states in a similar manner that if the soul serves God, if it overcomes the desire to enjoy mortal things and believes it has the aid of God's grace to enable it, then the soul will be restored. The language here is clearly Pelagian. In *Retractions*, however, the African Father seems to amend his thinking, as he insists, with Pelagianism in view, that God does not just "aid" the diligent and pious.[57] Again it is evident how the African Father takes different positions when addressing different concerns.

At a number of other points Augustine's use of the language of divine-human cooperation in salvation is confused regarding whether Pelagianism with its prioritizing of the human action is endorsed. This confusion emerges in the apologetic work, *On the Usefulness of Believing*. He claims that humans may excel in reason, but unless God be with them they merely crawl. This clearly entails a prioritizing of God's grace over human activity. But then he adds that God is only with those who have care for human society, a remark that seems to make divine action dependent on human action. Even less clear in this regard are his remarks in other apologetic works, *On True Religion* and *The Happy Life*, as well as in an anti-Manichee treatise, *On Free Will*. He asserts that we must turn to God in order to deserve illumination, that we must hold to Christ with faith.[58] It is not made clear in these cases whether faith is God's Work or something we must do.

As previously noted, Augustine's soteriology has been validly claimed by Roman Catholic theology. On some occasions, the African Father endorses the characteristic Catholic affirmation of justification as the result of the cooperation of grace and works—with an anti-Pelagian prioritizing of grace. Typically he affirms this concept in his writings when he addresses concerns about sloth in the Christian life or responds to the charge that grace might reduce us to mere robots. For example, in *On Grace and Free Will* he writes:

> He operates, therefore without us, in order that we may will; but when we will, and so will that we may act, He co-operates with us. We can, however, ourselves do nothing to effect good works of piety without Him either working that we may will, or co-working when we will.[59]

Elaborating further he states that our merits are God's gifts, that God does not crown our merits but is really crowning his own gifts in us.[60] Another example of Augustine prefiguring the dominant Catholic treatment of justification is evident in his attempt to justify the value of the Law of God while still contending with Pelagian elements in *To Simplician*. He speaks, as later Medieval Scholastic theologians do, of the infusion of God's grace and charity, a grace infused through the Sacraments. In sermons exhorting Christian living, the African Father prefigures Medieval Scholastic interpreters by contending that there is no true faith without love and in another sermon refers to merits that spring from grace.[61]

We even find the language of divine-human *cooperatio* in some of Augustine's anti-Pelagian writings when he deals with exhorting Christian life, comforting despair, or refuting links to Manichee determinism with Pelagianism in view. In *On the Merits and Forgiveness of Sins* and *On the Baptism of Infants* he construes salvation as a process, much as authoritative documents of the Catholic Church do. In *On Grace and Free Will, On Nature and Grace, Against Two Letters of the Pelagians,* and in some of his letters during the time he was writing these treatises, the role of both grace and works in saving us is affirmed, with even our preparation construed on at least one occasion as God's action on us.[62] These latter affirmations entail what Augustine says explicitly while addressing contexts of exhortation to Christian living, that faith without works is dead and does not save.[63]

The growing ecumenical consensus among scholars is that this sort of preoccupation with sanctification seems to underlie Catholic theology.[64] Thus it is hardly surprising that in instances when Augustine addressed this concern, his Roman Catholic interpreters most correctly represent him. (Another context in which such a Catholic-like construal of justification as the cooperation of grace and works, correlated with a notion of God's "permissive will," appears is in works of apologetics like *On True Religion.*)[65] I have noted that this tradition's version of the African Father is a bit less accurate in instances when he addresses other concerns (especially the Pelagian heresy or the narrative logic of the Christian faith). Thus the classical interpreters of Augustine all seem to have some validity. They seem most correct about his thought in contexts when the African Father addresses concerns like those of the interpreter in question.

Because he often embraces the characteristic Catholic formulation of the doctrine of justification, it is not surprising to find in such contexts the endorsement of a number of other characteristic contemporary Catholic construals of grace and Christian practice in order to facilitate grace. There are also some texts, notably in Augustine's *Enchiridion* and in his anti-Pelagian works, which might be read either as embodying the classical Catholic vision of divine-human cooperation in justification or as being more akin to the characteristic Protestant stress on salvation by grace alone.

In the *Enchiridion,* he contends at one point, using images adopted in Medieval Catholic theology, that God prepares the will and assists it. Then he proceeds to refer to how God has made the unwilling willing. The whole work, he insists, belongs to God.[66] The last two affirmations are compatible with Protestant renderings, though the Catholic heritage that rejects Pelagius can also account for and claim these Augustinian reflections too. In the same vein he remarks that the mercy of God is necessary not only when a person repents, but even to lead to repentance.[67]

Similarly, several interpretive traditions can claim the African Father's remark in the anti-Pelagian treatise *On the Spirit and the Letter.* While also concerned about renewal of the inward person (questions pertaining to living the Christian life), he speaks of how the love of God shed abroad in our hearts is not God's love for us, but that by which He makes us His lovers.[68] This remark could suggest the Catholic view of infused grace, but the point is not clear.

Especially at certain points in the *Enchiridion* while grappling with the concern to exhort and enhance Christian living, we discern Augustine's apparent endorsement of several classical Catholic construals of grace and Christian practice in order to facilitate grace. At one point he claims that we need to be born again to be freed from the sin in which we are born. Sins committed afterward can be cured by repentance, he claims. Elsewhere he expands this point by observing that those who repent need never despair of the mercy of God.[69] These remarks seem to open the door to the Catholic emphasis on Confession as an essential ingredient in the Christian walk of faith.

Elsewhere in the *Enchiridion,* responding to advocates of sloth in the Christian life, Augustine reiterates a point I have previously noted, that faith without works will not save.[70] From this point he proceeds to make several characteristically Roman Catholic–like observations about the role of works in salvation. These include his claim that many kinds of alms and performance of the Sacrifice of the Eucharist can assist to procure pardon of sins, not just by supplying the wants of the needy but also by rebuking or correcting sinners and forgiving those who have done evil.[71] Of course, he adds, alms do not make clean without faith.[72]

In these remarks Augustine even expresses an openness to the need for purgatorial fire. In his *City of God,* still concerned with the practice of Christian living in the broader context of articulating the logic of faith, he speaks only of such purgatorial fires as "possibly true."[73] In the *City of God,* while praising the faith of the martyrs (concerned with issues of Christian life), he notes that these martyrs can make intercession for the faithful.[74]

Final Thoughts on Justification

There is an interesting insight about Augustine's overall theology that his view of justification entails. It has to do with how he sees the doctrine as entailing a communal orientation to one's theology, a Confessionalism or veneration of Tradition, not typical of most Protestant denominations. Thus after affirming that the just shall live by faith, he adds that faith imposes the duty of confession on us.[75] Such a confession is for and on behalf of the whole community; it is a way of orienting the faith of that community and of seeking the salvation of others by professing faith. This is the role of Confessional documents in the oldest Protestant denominations and also demonstrates how Augustine saw an evangelistic role for the Church growing out of the *sola gratia.*

I have previously noted how Augustine's Protestant-like (and even some of his Catholic-like) images for depicting justification entail predestination insofar as faith is construed not as something we do, but as God's act. Once again we find a rich, contextually patterned diversity in his thought.

PREDESTINATION

Augustine's reflections on the relationship between grace and faith have already been noted; his tendency in most, but not in all, contexts (especially not when dealing with Christian responsibility) is to subordinate faith to grace. This commitment has direct implications for his views on predestination.

Some maintain that Augustine taught predestination only with the beginning of the Pelagian controversy, since prior to that he affirmed free will. Granted, as a description of the tendencies, there is some validity to this comment. But it is not the whole story.

For example, contrary to the contention of some previously noted interpreters who see a total discontinuity in Augustine's thought before and after this controversy, we find the African Father arguing for the opposite conclusion. In his pre-Pelagian-era *To Simplician,* while explicating the faith (as portrayed by Rom. 9), and so critiquing works righteousness, he claims that God has mercy on whom He wills. He proceeds to add that even our motivation toward the good things of God is kindled by God.[76] In his *Confessions,* while confessing his faith in face of despair, he claims that we love God because He has stricken our heart with His Word.[77] Subsequently he adds that all hope is naught save in God's mercy, and then continues to pray that God would grant what He commands and command what He will.[78] While not expressly endorsing predestination in these texts, he so emphasizes the priority of God's action to anything we can do as to create a conceptual context in which an affirmation of predestination logically fits the scheme. The eventual affirmation of predestination is not really anything radically new for the African Father in comparison to his earlier writings.

In his anti-Pelagian works, Augustine offers some provocative reflections on what is at stake in the affirmation of predestination. In one case he marvels why some would rather entrust themselves to their own weakness rather than to God's strength.[79] In *On the Gift of Perseverance,* he claims that preaching predestination and preaching the Gospel go together insofar as one who is living faithfully will not be lifted up if it is clear that the obedience is God's gift. And although obedience is a gift of God, it is good to exhort because this is how the gift is given.[80]

As we shall see, predestination is most unambiguously, though not exclusively, taught in contexts where Augustine grapples with Pelagianism. At those points he characteristically assumes the position of double predestination (the belief that in eternity God made two decisions, sending some to damnation and electing others to salvation) (Rom. 9:6ff.; Exod. 7:33). Even in these contexts, though, he urges that care be taken when preaching predestination so as not to confuse the multitudes. He cautions that references to reprobation never be made in the second person, but that preachers should merely refer to those (the third person) who are rejected.[81]

Augustine does not always affirm unconditional election. Quite frequently when dealing with the logic of faith, exhorting it or Christian responsibility, or when defending faith from the Manichees, he is totally silent about predestination or occasionally teaches something more like single predestination (1 Cor. 5:19; Eph. 1). In fact, in contexts where predestination is under fire or in seeking to refute Manichee determinism or insisting on Christian responsibility, he even takes positions suggesting that election is based on divine foreknowledge (1 Pet. 1:2; Rom 8:29), positions that he expressly repudiates elsewhere when expositing faith or replying to Pelagianism.[82] His insistence that election is not based on divine foreknowledge is also evident in such contexts, as he claims that we are not chosen because we chose God, but that we chose God because we were first chosen. God's grace is prevenient (preceding our actions). We are elect not because we believe, but elect in order to believe; we are elect to make us holy, not elect because we are holy.[83]

The apparent contradiction between these disparate views has troubled Western theology since Augustine. However, he offers us some possible resolutions. We find some in the *City of God,* a work whose overall agenda involves articulating the logic of faith (a world history), but in specific texts in which he is engaged in dialogue with the Stoics or teaching Christian responsibility against false ideas about the sin that remains in us when we give alms. In that context Augustine teaches predestination with free will and divine foreknowledge. However, he hastens to add, God's Will is affirmed to be the supreme power. He makes a similar affirmation in an anti-Pelagian work also devoted to the need to exhort Christian living.[84]

In *On the Gift of Perseverance* and *On the Trinity,* the African Father offers other observations that have great potential for resolving disputes between proponents of unconditional predestination and those who would reject it or claim that it is based on God's foreknowledge of what we will do in the future. In the first text, Augustine claims that predestination is the ordering of God's future in His foreknowledge. In fact, he adds, the Bible sometimes signifies predestination under the name of foreknowledge.[85] Perhaps we should not take Augustine's references to foreknowledge in his corpus as implying that we are elect on the basis of foreseen faith.

The preceding comments seem to resolve the tension over predestination in favor of unconditional election. Augustine's apologetic remarks in *On the Trinity* may be a more fruitful resource for overcoming the dispute over predestination. God knows all things, he says, in a way that what is past does not pass, and the future is present. This is impossible to comprehend, he contends.[86] Trading on the previously noted concept of eternity, this passage seems to entail that there is no tension between predestination in light of divine foreknowledge and the insistence on the irrelevancy of foreknowledge for salvation. For given this conceptuality, God's election and His foreknowledge are simultaneous.

Double Predestination

As we would expect, Augustine's affirmation of the doctrine of double predestination is apparent in his anti-Pelagian works. If the agenda is to refute the belief that we can save ourselves by our works, it is quite obvious that the Christian could best accomplish this agenda by crediting God with agency in all that happens regarding soteriology, both salvation and damnation. Consequently in a number of these texts he speaks of God both showing mercy through election and blinding others. He refers to God's hardening the reprobates' hearts.[87]

However, double predestination is affirmed in other contexts. Among these is a Sermon on John's Gospel explaining why heretics do not return to the Catholic Church and why those returning will not lapse. A softer version of this emerges in another sermon in this treatise, as Augustine, while critiquing pride in his exhortation, refers to how God hardens simply by letting alone and withdrawing His aid. Also, in the *Enchiridion,* at a point where he sought to undercut the claims of reason, unconditional double predestination is implied, along with the insistence that there is no injustice in this.[88] Even in his *City of God,* while exhorting Christian life though with an anti-Pelagian concern alongside or when critiquing false claims of reason, Augustine's remarks imply unconditional double predestination.[89]

Even in his earlier work, *To Simplician,* as he refuted Pelagian-like ideals, we find a clear endorsement of double predestination. Many are called, but only a few are effectually called, he asserts. God has mercy on whom He will and hardens whom He will. This belongs to a hidden equity that cannot be searched out by any human standard of measurement.[90]

Augustine is quick to note in the treatise that God hates nothing in human beings but sin; He does not hate the person, but the sinner. In making vessels of iniquity for damnation God does not hate them for themselves but for their iniquity. In fact, they are good insofar as they provide correction for others.[91] In this context Augustine also adds that God did not call all Jews, but only some of them.[92]

In *On the Gift of Perseverance* the African Father reflects on why double predestination needs to be taught. He noted that it is a matter of God's inscrutable judgment.[93] In so doing God Wills that His grace is gratuitous. By not giving to all, Augustine contends, God shows what all deserve. Those not delivered get what they deserve. God's decision is not for us to question.[94] Double predestination gets us on our knees and helps us to realize that we do not deserve salvation, for what we deserve is the gallows of hell.

In other anti-Pelagian treatises Augustine addresses Biblical references to the universal thrust of the Gospel. He proceeds to assert that God wills all to be saved in the sense of having every kind of person among the elect. All are said to come to Christ in the sense that none comes to God in any other way except through Him.[95] In a sermon on the Gospel of John dealing with sanctification along with a concern to refute works righteousness, Augustine claims that references in John to the world being saved really mean that all in the Church are saved.[96]

Single Predestination

Although in polemical contexts, as noted above, Augustine clearly reinterprets (explains away) Biblical references to the universal thrust of the Gospel, one finds this theme endorsed with remarks that suggest something like single predestination (the belief that God only elects to salvation and that damnation is caused by our own falling away) when the African Father is expounding the logic of faith. Thus in the *City of God* he offers an analogy to divine election. The human situation, he claims, is like that of the body. Like the relationship of human beings to God, the body does not live by choice, but only with nourishment. The choice not to live is a negative act.[97]

In a sermon exhorting faith, Christ is said to quicken whom he will. Humans do their own will only when they do not do what God commands. A similar point is made while trying to defend God's goodness and still critique Pelagianism.[98]

Another apparent example of single predestination is evident at one point in the *Enchiridion* when describing the logic of faith, as Augustine claims that all things are gathered up in one in Christ. In *On the Trinity* in a similar context and also in his *Exposition on the Psalms* while seeming to comfort despair over sin, Augustine refers only to election—to the elect, who in perfect goodness enjoy truth in eternity.[99]

Another related image that emerges in Augustine's thought when he is articulating the logic of faith is the concept of being elect in Christ. While explicating the faith in his *Confessions,* he claims that Christ was predestined in eternity.[100] Elsewhere when laying out the logic of faith and in one case sanctification, he speaks of an election in Christ.[101] Images suggesting single predestination seem to be especially appropriate on Augustine's grounds in these contexts.

In a sermon explicating the logic of faith, Augustine invokes an image that is at least compatible with single predestination. He claims that hearts are hardened only in the sense of God not offering aid or withdrawing it. God did not compel anyone to sin. In fact, God acts righteously in withholding aid. It may well be that the African Father is endorsing single predestination at this point.[102]

Points made by Augustine in his anti-Pelagian treatise *On the Spirit and the Letter* warrant attention in this connection because of their ambiguity. The act of the will to believe is attributable to the divine bounty, he asserts, not only because it comes from the freedom of choice. In fact, freedom could produce no act of belief were there no inducement or invitation to belief. It must be God Who brings about the will to believe in human beings. In all things the divine mercy anticipates us. Yet Augustine still insists that to consent to the calling of God or to refuse it belongs to our will.[103]

Written along with a certain concern about the nature of the Christian life (sanctification), this discussion could make it appear that Augustine is conceding that we independently exercise our will after the offer of grace. But the text might also be read as teaching, in accord with the concept of single predestination, that grace brings about our willing action and that all we can do is resist or remain passive. Again it becomes obvious why Catholics and heirs of the Protestant Reformers are still quibbling about justification, predestination, and the heritage of Augustine. Some of it has to do with certain texts difficult to interpret like this one.

Another text pertaining to predestination that is difficult to interpret emerges in the *City of God* as he both expounds the logic of faith but also dialogues with the Manichees. Referring to the Fall of the evil angels, he mentions their refusing God's grace (single predestination), but also contends that the evil angels' happiness in Paradise "was destined to end."[104]

We have already observed that generally Augustine emphatically rejects the possibility of the salvation of all, especially in polemical contexts. This trend is also evident in at least one passage in the *City of God* as Augustine, concerned to defend the authority of Scripture and the mercy of God, expressly rejects the salvation of the devil and his angels.[105] Likewise, in the *Enchiridion,* a work devoted to exhorting Christian living, he claims that not all are saved, because not all are willing. All are saved, he claims, in the sense that no one is saved unless God wills one's salvation, and every human group will receive salvation.[106]

On the other hand, in at least one passage, in a 409 letter addressing the despair occasioned by theodicy questions, Augustine hints at universal salvation or at least the chance for all to be saved. He notes that there may be a divine purpose in God not revealing Christ to all, for He knew who would believe.[107] Of course, the text may also instead entail that we, and not God, determine who will be saved.

In a 414 letter, while explicating the Bible's literal sense (1 Pet. 3:18–21), the African Father does concede that at least some in hell who had not believed, though not all as his correspondent Evodius alleged, might have been saved by Christ's descent in hell after His death. While exhorting Christian life in a context mindful of avoiding Pelagianism, we can discern an even more vigorous affirmation of the universal thrust of the Gospel. Augustine claims that God commands us to will that all to whom we preach may be saved.[108]

Integrating the Diversity

As in the case of some of the other doctrines thus far considered, Augustine offers reflections about how to reconcile the diversity in his thought about predestination, which as we have seen runs the gamut from a kind of absolute determinism evidenced in an affirmation of double predestination to an affirmation of free will in texts in the anti-Manichee writings like *On Free Will* that are concerned to exhort Christian responsibility.[109]

As previously noted, Augustine explains in his *Retractions* his reasons for making such affirmations. He contends that it had to do with the context he was addressing, the Manichees, which gave less occasion for teaching grace.[110] The self-consciously contextual character of Augustine's theology is again in evidence.

The same spirit is evident in other pastoral advice given elsewhere about preaching predestination. Predestination must be preached with sensitivity to when hearers are prepared for it, he says. It must be preached with sensitivity to people of slower understanding.[111] He also advises that when dealing with those who do not persevere, it is better to speak of others, not of those in the congregation.[112]

In *On the Spirit and the Letter,* while addressing the dual context of anti-Pelagianism and a concern with exhorting Christian responsibility, Augustine acknowledges the theological diversity in his thought in a profound way. He concedes that both grace and free will must be taught, as he had. The Bible mandates this, he concludes, for both have their proper voices in Scripture.[113] It seems that we need a conceptually diverse, contextual theology because the Bible has that character. This is a potentially rich insight not just for appreciating Augustine's thought, but also for understanding the rich diversity that has characterized Christianity over the centuries. Likewise Augustine's previously noted observations about how in eternity all events in the universe, including the exercise of human free will and divine election, might be deemed simultaneous offer a promising way to integrate the diversity in Augustine and the Bible.

SANCTIFICATION

As in the case of other doctrines considered, the African Father's treatment of sanctification (the character and shape of the Christian life) is also a conceptually rich but contextually organized pattern. Sanctification belongs together with justification. Consequently, what Augustine says in a given context about sanctification is characteristically related logically to his construal of justification in that context.

Simultaneously Saint and Sinner: Freedom from the Law

We have already observed that when the African Father deals with polemics, describes his faith pilgrimage, and exhorts faith, he describes the Christian life as *simul iustus et peccator* (as *totally* sinful and *totally* saint).[114] Even virtues, when inflated with pride, are vices.[115] This entails that since even good deeds are marred by sin, a situational ethic is appropriate, a point Augustine makes in a context when engaged in apologetics (or speculation). Sometimes even sins like lies can serve the neighbor. Thus it follows in these contexts that Augustine can assert that as long as Christians love they may do what they will.[116] This follows from being free from the Law, from its disposition as well as its condemnation.[117] Christians experience freedom, he claims, as the willing delight in God's Law (Gal. 3:10–13; 5:1ff.).[118]

Given these suppositions, it follows that good works, love, and other Christian virtues come from grace, not grace from human initiative. When expositing the faith as well as when polemicizing against Pelagianism, the African Father clearly affirms the spontaneity of works, as he notes that a soul that feels itself loved becomes inflated with love or inebriated with the plenty of the divine house.[119] Elsewhere Augustine makes this point claiming that God is the source of even the desire to do good. Consequently, good works attend greater delight for Christians in proportion to God being more and more loved as author of the good.[120] We love ourselves by hating ourselves in the right way. In other contexts, when exhorting Christian living or comforting despair, Augustine refers to this lifestyle as a life of sacrifice, inflamed by God's love or as a life of subjection easy to live because we are already in subjection to God.[121]

Happiness and enjoyment are the outcomes of such faith, Augustine writes, as the mind goes beyond itself and earthly transient things to Wisdom. The love of God and true love of self are said to be identical. In apologetic contexts he notes that to know and love God is the blessed life.[122]

Likewise when expositing faith, Augustine asserts that the only legitimate cause of self-love must be one's righteousness. Otherwise self-love is evil.[123] God has brought our passions under control. We are poor and needy, yet better when with anguish of the soul we see ourselves as hateful and see God's mercy until what is damaged is repaired. When this happens we may be freed by God as we cease to be miserable in ourselves and come to happiness in Him. Along the same lines, while exhorting faith in the context of polemics with Pelagianism, the African Father adds that sin and death remain among the faithful in order to continue to exercise them in righteousness.[124] The temptations that faithful followers endure are good for us, Augustine adds elsewhere, as they send us seeking more abundantly for heavenly peace. The good we have on earth, the happiness it nurtures, is really misery.[125]

Life then comes to be seen as a wayside inn. Christians are people who are never captive to money and the world, but use them like travelers in an inn use tables, cups, and couches for the purpose of not remaining but of leaving them behind.[126] We should use the things of the world but not enjoy them, he claims while explaining the logic of faith. Only God is to be enjoyed, and other human beings can only be enjoyed in God.[127] Likewise creatures may be loved, but only as long as they are loved in the Creator, and not for themselves.[128] Christian life as portrayed by Augustine when exhorting faith or polemicizing against Pelagianism is a joyous, liberated way of life. (Note here again how when Augustine describes the Christian life in this way it is still intermingled with a self-seeking that can be interpreted as sin. Even in the practice of love and faith, Christians on Augustine's grounds in these contexts are driven by selfish aims of using people and by the quest for happiness.)

A similar vision of sanctification and the Christian life appears in those texts by Augustine like *On True Religion* where his main attention is devoted to apologetics (albeit with some recognition of links between this agenda and the character of the Christian life).[129] Addressing the consequences of persecution he makes clear that the nature of the Christian life, because it is mired in sin, is not visible. Thus, he contends, if people hold fast to the Catholic faith, even if they leave the Church, they may still be crowned in secret.[130]

Growth in Grace

Some dimensions about the Christian life, insofar as it is not out of harmony with the Law of God, are affirmed by Augustine in all contexts. Thus when exhorting the practice of the Christian life or comforting the despairing, he makes points compatible with the vision of sanctification observed when he exhorts faith. For example, when his concern in *On True Religion* shifts expressly to exhorting Christian living, he urges readers to keep quiet if the mind pants for mutable things, to strive only not to be accustomed to them.[131] A Platonic orientation typical of his apologetic efforts seems evident in these remarks.

Elsewhere in the treatise, the African Father makes a related point. Whoever has overcome vices cannot be overcome by other human beings, he contends, for such a person loves only what cannot be taken away. If ablaze with love for eternity, such a person will hate temporal relationships, only loving the image of God in them.[132]

On the other hand, when Augustine exhorts the practice of the Christian life or comforting the despairing, we can discern a different vision of the Christian life in other respects in his thought. The African Father taught the possibility of making progress in the Christian life, of becoming better Christians (Eph. 4:14–15; Phil. 3:14). There is need for discipline to live such a life, he claims. A Use of the Law of God to guide Christian living is indicated in these cases, as well as when he calls on the faithful to imitate Christ.

The imitation theme is especially evident in the anti-Manichee writings concerned to assert human responsibility, as well as in his *Confessions* when exhorting Christian living and in his *Commentary on Galatians* when comforting anxiety.[133] A text in the *Enchiridion* may also endorse this theme. Focusing concern on the nature of the Christian life, the African Father observes that the Christian life is modeled on Christ's death and Resurrection.[134] This remark may refer to the Christian's responsibility to imitate Christ, or it could refer to the Christian being conformed to Christ when justified.

In the *Confessions* another theme emerges that is characteristic of Augustine's treatment of sanctification when exhorting the Christian life or engaged in apologetics. He refers to mounting beyond the power of human nature, "rising by degrees" toward God, of his mind's ascent toward God. There is an apparent affirmation of the possibility of growth in the Christian life here. This is language that might also suggest the African Father's possible dependence on Plotinus's mysticism.[135]

Elsewhere in the same work his reflections on his spiritual pilgrimage imply this theme of growth in the Christian life. Lamenting his remaining lusts and other temptations like eating and drinking, pleasures of sight, scent, and ear, he notes how God has changed him and curbed his pride.[136]

There are many other examples of believing that the Christian grows in grace and can make progress in the Christian life. The idea that we can make progress in the Christian life is reiterated on many occasions by Augustine, but, with one exception, only when addressing contexts where there is some concern about exhorting the Christian life. In that case, while outlining the logic of faith, the reference to progress is a mere affirmation of a reality that Christians are given in virtue of being sanctified in (conformed to) Christ.[137]

I have already noted Augustine's affirmation that the Christian always remains a sinner as well as a saint by virtue of being justified by God. However, although in contexts of exhorting faith, polemicizing with Pelagius, and even when doing apologetics, the *simul iustus et peccator* was regarded as *totus-totus,* the Christian being totally saint and sinner. When exhorting Christian life, Augustine claims that we are only partly saint and partly sinner.[138]

The same way of construing the saint-sinner character of the Christian life, coupled with a belief that we can become less sinful as we make progress in the Christian life, is evident as Augustine recounts in the *Confessions* his faith pilgrimage, with special attention to the divine demands or to the despair sin occasions. For example, he claims to have been commanded by God to abstain from lust and fornication and was given the power to do so. Yet consent to such lust still lives in his memory, he concedes. Nevertheless, he believes that God will increase His gifts in him that he may be freed from the hold of concupiscence. In fact, he adds, though still tempted by the pleasure in the fear and love that people have for him, God resists the proud and gives grace to the humble. Even in this context, the African Father's commitment to the primacy of grace is evident. He insists that all good things are wholly of God's grace.[139]

In his earlier writings, when dealing with apologetics, but with special attention to exhorting the Christian life, Augustine also spoke of the partial character of our saintliness and the partial character of our sinfulness. Thus he claims that though no one can live a new life without associating with one's "old" sinful being, Christians are constantly making progress till death. Although we cannot be without sins, he claims, yet it makes a difference what kind of sins we commit.[140]

Some texts that seem to teach progress in the Christian life are easily confused with images implying the Roman Catholic view of justification. Thus, for example, in one of his pre–418 sermons, Augustine claims that we have been justified, but justice grows as we progress. It is hard to discern whether this is an advocacy of progress in the Christian life or an assertion that we become more justified.[141]

Other problematic texts that are relevant to sanctification but whose meaning is difficult to ascertain include a reference to divine-human cooperation in *On the Spirit and the Letter* and some remarks about faith in two of the *Ten Homilies on the Epistle of John to the Parthians.* In the first text, the African Father notes that the human will is divinely assisted to do the right in such a manner that, besides being created with the endowment of freedom to choose, the believer receives the Holy Spirit. Then there arises in the believer's soul the delight and love of God.[142]

The problem with these remarks is that it is not clear if all that the believer does is God's Work. Such an emphasis on God's Work would fit the generally anti-Pelagian character of this treatise, which seeks to refute all assertions giving human beings credit for salvation. However, the ambiguity of the African Father's thinking in texts like these in part accounts for disputes from the sixteenth century to now between Protestants and Catholics, with Protestants stressing an anti-Pelagian reading and Catholics insisting on the need for divine-human cooperation. Reading Augustine in context (understanding this text in relation to his position in other anti-Pelagian treatises) may contribute to adjudicating this long-term debate about his heritage.

In one of the aforementioned 1 John sermons, apparently concerned to offer exhortation to Christian living, Augustine first claims that knowledge without charity cannot save. In another sermon in the same series he makes a similar point contending, as I have noted elsewhere he did in such contexts, that faith without works cannot save.[143] The language here implies that the African Father was a forerunner of the Medieval Scholastic idea that faith must be formed by love.[144] The agreement in these contexts is hardly surprising, as a preoccupation with sanctification and the Christian life was the primary agenda for medieval Catholic thought.[145]

In the sermon from which Augustine's references to faith without works is taken, he subsequently moves from exhorting Christian life to expositing faith. He elaborates on the previous remarks in a way as to take positions less compatible with Catholic thinking and more in line with that of his Protestant Reformation interpreters. When addressing this new agenda he asserts again that love must be added to faith. But here he clearly affirms that such love is love directed to God in Christ.[146]

One other set of remarks, interspersed in a number of Augustine's writings when he exhorted the Christian life, gives further witness to his inclination to speak of growth in the Christian life when addressing such pastoral contexts. In both the *Enchiridion* and in *On True Religion* he speaks of different stages in the Christian life. He counts the number of stages differently in the two works, but is consistent in his analysis of how the Christian moves from the shadows of ignorance taught by the stories of history, through a knowledge of sin, to faith and the struggle against sin, on to a perfection ready to endure the trials of the world with love, culminating in heavenly peace and beatification.[147] In a similar context, concerned with exhorting Christian life, he likewise identifies three eras (dispensations) of world history: (1) before the Law; (2) under the Law; (3) under grace.[148] When the concern is to challenge people to practice the Christian life, the African Father sets definite goals for which the people of God are to strive.

Perseverance

Another manifestation of Augustine's affirmation of how becoming a Christian changes our lives is evident in his view that perseverance provides certainty about one's salvation. He makes this point in a significant number of texts throughout his career when exhorting Christian life or when comforting despair (especially despair over whether one is elect), including his *City of God, On Grace and Free Will, On Rebuke and Grace,* and *On the Gift of Perseverance.* His point in these cases is that perseverance provides certainty of salvation since it is a mark of being of God.[149]

Even though preoccupied with exhorting Christian life, at least when this concern is combined with the anti-Pelagian critique, the African Father insists that perseverance is God's gift and that it does not cease.[150] The irresistible character of grace seems affirmed in these contexts.

There is an apparent contradiction in Augustine's thought regarding how much certainty perseverance offers the believer regarding his or her election. Thus at one point in *On Rebuke and Grace* he claims that none can be certain of one's own predestination. At another point in the same treatise he claims that the elect can never lapse.[151] The apparent contradiction can be explained with reference to the distinct contexts addressed. Though the overall agenda of the treatise is a dispute with the Pelagians, in the case of his affirmation of the certainty of election he was exhorting faith, while the reference to our uncertainty emerges when he was preoccupied with exhorting the Christian life.

This pattern makes obvious sense. When the preacher is seeking to exhort faith, the certainty of salvation is a message that needs to be delivered. But when the concern is to stimulate and encourage the Christian lifestyle (works), then it makes sense to prod such behavior with some degree of uncertainty in order to stimulate desired behavior. Such discourse presents God's Word as the Law (as a divine command). A Use of the Law of God to guide Christian living characterizes Augustine's efforts to encourage his hearers and readers to make progress in the Christian life (Matt. 22:37–40; Jas. 2:25).

The Role of the Law in Christian Life

Exhorting Christians to practice the Christian life presupposes that a standard has been set, that the Law of God is to function as the norm for guiding behavior. In a sense Augustine is inconsistent about this point regarding the role of the Law in Christian life. Often, especially when exhorting Christian living or comforting despair, he opts for using the Law as a guideline to behavior. In other contexts, however, he neglects and even rejects such a Use of the Law. In these texts he refers to the Law of God primarily in its capacity of condemning sin.

We have already observed a number of occasions when, especially while criticizing Pelagianism or exhorting the faith, Augustine contends that the Law of God condemns our sin, that God commands the impossible.[152] Such points are made more explicitly elsewhere, not just in polemics but also when explicating the logic of faith and exhorting belief.

In all contexts, Augustine is concerned to extol the goodness of the Law. Thus in his *City of God* while expositing the logic of faith he notes that God's Work in providing peace is facilitated by His giving the commandments to love Him and one's neighbor. The Law, Augustine adds, also entails loving oneself. In exercising this sort of love for God and neighbor, one hopes to be helped by one's fellows when needing assistance. Out of this love a peace will be established.[153]

In another, earlier treatise Augustine expressly asserts the goodness of the Law of God. Such an affirmation is presupposed by his endorsement of the concept of natural law in one of his anti-Pelagian works.[154] For if the Law of God is written on our hearts as part of God's good creation, the Law must be good.

In *To Simplician,* while defending the Law of God and explicating the faith, he elaborates on the goodness of the Law, noting that it was given to make sin known by heightening a sense of guilt.[155] In that context and also while describing his faith pilgrimage in the *Confessions* (a sort of apologetic context), he claims that the Law makes us sin, makes sin sweeter, because it is more attractive to do what is forbidden.[156] He also makes similar points when exhorting faith, depicting the logic of faith, and even when exhorting Christian life (since, as we shall see, in the latter context the Law does not just guide Christian living, but may also function to condemn sin). He speaks in these contexts of the Law discovering sin and then increasing and working concupiscence in us.[157]

Augustine illustrates the accusatory function of the Law in other ways. Again when describing his faith pilgrimage in his *Confessions,* he claims that we are poor and needy, yet better when with anguish of the soul we see ourselves as hateful and see God's mercy until what is damaged is repaired. When this happens we are freed by God as we cease to be miserable in ourselves and come to happiness in God.[158]

In these contexts (especially in polemics with the Pelagians, in some cases combined with exhortation to faith or to Christian living), he speaks of the Law giving knowledge of sin but not being able to destroy it.[159] Yet the Law is still said to kill or slay sin by giving us this knowledge.[160] This censuring of sin has the purpose of having sinners flee for refuge to grace and divine mercy. As he puts it in another anti-Pelagian treatise, the Law is written outside humans to be an external terror, while the Gospel is written in humans to justify them from within.[161] Augustine adds to this point in *On the Spirit and the Letter,* while also concerned about living the Christian life, that although the Law sets the stage for hearing the Gospel by discovering the weakness of the will so that grace may restore the will and the restored will may fulfill the Law, nevertheless we are not justified by the Law.[162]

Augustine makes this point regarding the Law's inability to contribute directly to our salvation even more sharply in one of his letters devoted to Pelagian propensity. One cannot become righteous, he claims, simply by knowing the Law.[163] Indeed, he insists elsewhere when writing against this heresy, the Law is not grace, as Pelagians taught. For apart from love, knowledge of the Law puffs us up.[164]

Next the African Father turns to why the Law is necessary in order to make sin known. It seems to have to do with the insidious character of sin. The rebuke of those who do not do God's Commands is needed, he claims in another anti-Pelagian treatise, for those who do not want to be rebuked would then see no need for the Redeemer.[165] However, as he puts it even when exhorting Christian life, without the Holy Spirit through Whom love is shed abroad in our hearts, the Law only commands. It cannot assist.[166]

In other works addressing Pelagianism, Augustine makes this point by drawing on something like the Pauline distinction between the letter and the spirit (Rom. 2:29; 2 Cor. 3:6). The Law of God, he claims, is the letter to those who do not fulfill it in spirit. Indeed, the Law kills if the Spirit is not present.[167] In another way of making the point in *On the Spirit and the Letter*, he claims that the divine aid given the faithful to work righteousness is not a giving of the Law, good as it is. But the divine aid is an uplifting of our will by the imparting of the Holy Spirit. Thus one is justified not by the law of works but by the law of faith, not by the letter but by the spirit, not by deserts of actions but by grace.[168]

In such anti-Pelagian contexts the African Father also makes a provocative comment with important implications for his view of sanctification. He claims that the Christian is free from the Law in the sense of being set free from its disposition and condemnation.[169] The Christian need not take guidance from the Law according to Augustine at these points. But as we have observed to be the case in every doctrine, what he says against Pelagius is not the whole story.

The Law as Guide to Christian Life

In contexts at least somewhat preoccupied with exhorting Christian life, Augustine actually relies heavily on the divine commands to guide Christian behavior. Rebuke and discipline must not be neglected, he claims.[170] In these contexts he offers specific directives about behaviors Christians should avoid, like drunkenness. While describing the Christian life in his *Confessions* he claims that passions are brought under control by chastity, fasting, and pious thought.[171]

As previously noted, when Augustine addresses heretics like the Donatists who had rejected all overtures of love and reconciliation, the African Father contends that though we cannot be without sins, it makes a difference what kind of sins we commit.[172] While trying to defend the value of God's Law and Christian responsibility, he argues, even in contexts in which a dialogue with Pelagius is somewhat involved, in contrast to his claims in strictly anti-Pelagian contexts, that with the aid of grace we can fulfill the Law.[173] God, it seems, is not said to command the impossible in these contexts.

Even in the *City of God,* when dealing with issues related to behavior the African Father observes the need for guidance in living. A commandment to love is posited. Even peace is ordered, in accord with God's eternal law.[174]

Reliance on the divine command to guide Christian living in contexts of exhortation to Christian life or when engaging in apologetics leads Augustine to believe that we can grow in grace and enhance the quality of Christian life. Thus when addressing a dual agenda in *On True Religion* he claims that pride quenches charity and humility strengthens it.[175] Elsewhere, while dealing with the question of how others are evangelized, Augustine claims that holiness leads Christians to greater effectiveness as teachers.[176]

Such commitments entail that the Christian life is visible, that people can tell Christians by their attitudes and behavior. Consequently it is in line with this visible character of the Christian life and its correlated endorsement of the Law used to guide Christian life to find Augustine advocate Christians crossing themselves as a comfort from despair.[177]

Perhaps a remark in the *Ten Homilies on the Epistle of John to the Parthians* best sums up the African Father's view of the Law of God and Christian life when his pastoral focus deals with sanctification. He observes that we know God if we keep His Commandments.[178] The Law is indeed seen here as a measure of the Christian life.

The passage just cited also refers to a mandate to strive for perfection, a topic that I need to address in closing. First, however, I would have us note again the apparent contradiction between insisting on a role for the Law of God in mandating good works when exhorting to Christian living or engaging in apologetics and the denial of such a role or even of guidelines for Christian living when exhorting faith or engaging in polemics.

How can we relate the different approaches to the Law-Gospel relation? Augustine again illustrates the self-consciously contextual character of his thought. When dealing with issues of Christian responsibility he claims that there is no tension between James and Paul. Paul, he contends, spoke of works that precede faith, and James spoke of those that follow faith.[179] This seems to be a valuable insight for appreciating the need to articulate a conceptually rich theology. The Bible exhibits such conceptual richness.

The Bible also teaches perfection as a goal for which to strive (2 Cor. 7:1; Heb. 6:1; 1 John 4:17–18). Although I have identified rejections of the concept of perfection when dialoguing with Pelagius or when exhorting faith, Augustine is not systematically negative toward the concept.[180]

Striving for Perfection

In view of the fact that, as noted, when exhorting Christian living Augustine believes that we can make progress in our practice of Christianity, it is not surprising that in these contexts he also expresses the hope of achieving perfection, not unlike earlier African Fathers and modern Methodists have.[181] When writing against the Manichees, Augustine also claims that the faithful burn with a perfect love when sanctified. When dealing with despair occasioned by sin, Augustine speaks of the hope of being made perfect.[182]

Historically the theme of perfection has been associated with the Eastern church's affirmation of deification, as becoming like God entails becoming perfect. Thus in the anti-Pelagian work *On Nature and Grace,* at a point where the African Father is exhorting good works, he claims that we can become like God through God's love, and then speaks of perfection—a perfection defined only with regard to its impossibility except through Christ.[183]

One interesting remark in this connection is evident in Augustine's *On Man's*

Perfection in Righteousness, as he claims that God wants us to be perfect, and that we are being healed of sin daily by being renewed from day to day.[184] The question is whether this is an endorsement of perfection or more in line with the idea of Martin Luther that "the entire life of believers [is] to be one of repentance."[185]

It is important, though, to reiterate that these endorsements of perfection are more atypical than typical. His openness to achieving perfection is apparently contradicted by Augustine when he addresses other contexts, notably in polemics with Pelagianism. In one instance in such a context he claims that perfection is not possible until death because of concupiscence.[186] The possibility of perfection is also rejected in a letter, when comforting despair over suffering.[187]

When dealing with Christian life (the goodness of marriage) while still polemicizing with Pelagius, Augustine does concede that perfection can be reached in future immortality, and that in the meantime we should make progress.[188] In the same treatise he elaborates further on this point, assuming a kind of *simul iustus et peccator* position (but only in the sense of being *partially* saint and *partially* sinner). Typical of his perspective in contexts with any specter of Pelagianism in view, he claims that though concupiscence is remitted in Baptism, it remains until our entire infirmity is healed. Of course, he adds, in harmony with other comments made when exhorting the Christian life, concupiscence in the regenerate to which they do not consent is not sin. (Such concupiscence is called "sin" only in the sense of producing sin.)[189] In another anti-Pelagian work he elaborates on this point. He argues that perfection is not possible in the present state of existence, that even as the Christian progresses and approaches heaven on the way to perfection, concupiscence never diminishes. In the same spirit, Augustine argues in *On the Spirit and the Letter,* a similar anti-Pelagian work with a concern about sanctification, that perfection is not impossible, though it is not found on earth.[190]

These conflicts regarding perfection may also be addressed in *On Nature and Grace* when polemicizing with Pelagians. He claims not to care to express a definite position.[191] There are rich ecumenical implications in these remarks for overcoming tensions between the Methodist-Holiness heritages that advocate perfection and the rest of the Church catholic.

Regardless of one's assessment of Augustine's views on perfection and his reliance on exhortation to live the Christian life, any reader can admire a number of his insights when he engages in such exhortation. In a letter on the Christian life Augustine claims that people are not made good by the possession of good things, but that they make these things good by using the goods well.[192] In a previously noted sermon from the *Ten Homilies on the Epistle of John to the Parthians,* while exhorting the logic of faith, he claims that it is not for preaching to work the enlargement of hearts. We are to ask God that we may love one another, and He will grant it. We are to love all people, even our enemies, not because they are our brothers and sisters but in order that they become so.[193] This last point suggests that good works happen spontaneously through the love of God, a theme that is very common in such contexts and in anti-Pelagian texts.

The Spontaneity of Works

When merely testifying to the Gospel, Augustine clearly asserts the spontaneity of Christian living (without need for the Law to exhort Christian response). Even in these contexts, however, the African Father does not always stress the distinction between Law and Gospel. The more polemical the context, the more concerned he is to assert our sinfulness, and the more he stresses the distinction between these two forms of the Word of God.

In a sense we have already observed the African Father's endorsement of this manner of depicting the Law-Gospel relationship and the Christian life in his references to our freedom from the Law.[194] In a sermon on the Christian life, Augustine turns to expositing the faith. He then claims that to love God is to love His Commandments, one of which is to love the neighbor. He also adds that to love the Son and Father is to love the children of God. One who loves them becomes a member, and if one does not love the members one does not love the Head. In fact, he adds, Christian love is like a flame fusing all pieces together. It is a lump of gold fused in a furnace, and a single object comes to be made of it.[195] Faith entails good works, and the way in which Christian love fuses diverse people together is said to happen as spontaneously as gold comes to be fused in a furnace.

The same sort of affirmation is evident elsewhere in the anti-Pelagian work *On Nature and Grace:* All things are easy to love for the Christian, Augustine claims. In another work of this genre he asserts that grace makes us lovers of the Law, which we would otherwise break.[196]

We previously observed Augustine's endorsement of something like a situational ethic, either when doing apologetics or expositing the faith, as he claims that you can "act as you desire, so long as you are acting with love."[197] Along the same lines, while engaged in expositing the faith in the *Confessions* he observes that some things that are very much like sins are not sins since they do not offend God and the bond of society. Many actions that to humans seem blameworthy are approved by God. God may order something formerly forbidden.[198] Freedom from the Law and even a sort of situational ethic seem taught here. Elsewhere in this treatise when describing his spiritual pilgrimage and the comfort he received, the African Father elaborates further on the freedom grace has provided. He claims that in Christ the mind is free from cares that gnawed at it, from aspiring for lust.[199]

We have also previously noted Augustine's reference to the hidden character of the Christian life. Something like such an affirmation appears in one of his sermons on 1 John while he is explicating the faith. Pride and love are no different in the works they do, he claims. The deeds of the loving Christian, then, are in principle no different from those of the unbeliever. Then Augustine proceeds to reflect in more depth about the nature of Christian love. We love in the neighbor not what he or she is, but what we wish he or she may be.[200]

The spontaneity of Christian life and love receives further testimony from

Augustine when explicating the logic of faith at points in *On the Trinity*. The trinitarian character of love (the lover, the object of love, love itself) entails that love needs an object. Thus, Augustine claims, God causes us to love our brothers and sisters by filling us with love. We receive love from God's grace. Or as he puts it in another passage in the treatise, when the mind loves God, love for neighbor follows.[201]

At a point where faith is exposited in the anti-Pelagian work *On Grace and Free Will*, Augustine claims that we are given a new heart by grace, and that the stony one is taken away. Justification as Conformity to Christ is affirmed here. As a result we are caused to walk in God's statutes.[202] This construal of justification entails the spontaneity of works.

All of these passages presuppose that we need God's grace for every good work. This point is expressly made in an anti-Pelagian work. Augustine asserts that God never forsakes us, just as the physician who heals turns the sick over to God's good care, and as the eye of the body still needs brightness of light, so we need assistance even when healed.[203]

Elsewhere in the treatise he claims that grace is a kind of medicine to fight sin. We work, Augustine claims, but are fellow workers with God, Who does the work because His mercy anticipates us.[204]

While explicating the logic of faith in *On the Trinity*, Augustine makes a related point by explaining the Holy Spirit's role in our spontaneous reactions to divine love. When given to the faithful, the Spirit kindles us with the love of God. We have no means of loving God unless it comes from God.[205]

While exhorting faith in confession (in the famed treatise of that name), the African Father claims that our good deeds are God's acts and deeds. We move toward doing good because our hearts are so conceived by the Holy Spirit; that is, the Spirit has provided us with hearts that want to do good. Elsewhere he claims that we do no good things that God does not cause.[206]

In his anti-Pelagian writings Augustine makes these points with equal clarity. Thus he claims that grace does not just avail to remission of past sins. In contrast to what the Pelagians teach, he insists that grace also helps us avoid future sins.[207] Elsewhere the African Father asserts that God makes the elect do good works, do what He commands. This is Good News. For saints with grace are said to have a greater freedom in face of all temptations.[208]

Confessing the agency of God in these contexts is indeed a freeing Word, for the believer is no longer alone in struggles with evil. Of course, even in these contexts, Augustine does not diminish the point that the righteousness of God and grace have no implications for sanctification and good works. Thus he writes that in the freedom of love, the Law is a companion.[209]

How are we to relate these passages that make God the agent of our good works and faith to those affirmations of free will (some of which imply at least a Semi-Pelagianism), made especially against the Manichees and to a lesser extent when exhorting Christian life? A previously noted observation by Augustine in his *Retractions* both answers this question and also provides another indication of the self-conscious character of his contextual approach to theology. In these reflections he claims that in the earlier anti-Manichee works no mention was made of grace because it was not under discussion in that context. It was the Manichees who needed to be addressed.[210] Such a viewpoint accounts for the diversity in Augustine's thought on the range of issues covered in this chapter.

ECUMENICAL-PASTORAL IMPLICATIONS

The pattern we observe in Augustine's contextually sensitive treatment of these doctrines has rich pastoral implications. It makes common sense. In contexts where the threat is a compromise of the grace of God, and too much attention is paid to our works, grace and its dialectical relation to human beings and behavior are stressed. When exhorting faith or simply teaching the logic of faith, the dialectic between God and humanity, between nature and grace, may be relaxed a bit, as long as it is still clear that grace is prior to human action. By contrast, when doing apologetics or when exhorting Christian living, the dialectic is almost completely replaced by a stress on the continuity and cooperation of nature and grace. In short, the more it is believed necessary to highlight Christian responsibilities, the more the conceptuality used to depict grace will be related to human behavior and the more expressly will "proper" Christian behavior be demarcated.

Wise parish pastors may already be aware of these patterns, deploying classical theological conceptions (in the West most of these have been adopted from Augustine, at least indirectly). But these patterns suggest that the themes denominations share with Augustine may indicate their respective strengths and weaknesses. Traditions borrowing mostly from the African Father's anti-Pelagian writings may be best equipped to deal with modern Pelagian abuses. By contrast, those theological heritages more indebted to Augustine's earlier anti-Manichee works and treatises addressing how to live the Christian life are likely those traditions which are themselves inclined to stress sanctification.

Chapter 7

Church and Ministry

The struggle between Catholics and Protestants for Augustine's soul has implications for what one makes of his view of Church and Ministry. Generally speaking we can designate him as a man of the Church, who finds the Church, its Ministry, and its heritage more important and prior to the experience of the individual Christian. This is characteristic of the thinking of premodern Christians. As we shall observe, however, in some contexts that is not the whole story.

Augustine's view of himself and his flock as people of the Church is nowhere more evident than in his designation of the Church as Mother and Virgin, as the Mother of all Christians. He makes this assertion in a variety of contexts, particularly, though not exclusively, when endeavoring to refute perceived heresies.[1] Another image Augustine uses in order to communicate how the Church is greater than the sum of its members, how the Church nurtures Christians, is his idea of the Church as a society that is the only means by which one comes to faith. As he puts it in *On Faith and the Creed,* "Christian faith gather[s] men into a society in which brotherly love can operate."[2] These images are core commitments reflecting Augustine's Catholic and (perhaps) African ethos. The latter is

113

particularly evident when Augustine addresses questions about how we are saved or how Christian nurture takes place.

A related theme emerges when, while exhorting faith or doing apologetics, the African Father identifies the Church as the Body of Christ (Eph. 1:22–23). Indeed, as he puts it in a 416 lecture series, "we are made not only Christians, but Christ. . . . For if He is the head, we are the members." In one of his sermons he presses this point so far as to claim that whatever is attributed to Christ may be attributed to the Church and vice versa, as they are one.[3]

This commitment to asserting the objective character of the Church, to make clear that it is not marked by what the faithful do, is evident in a 408 epistle, as Scripture, not our own righteousness, is identified as the Church's mark (Eph. 5:25–27).[4] In some of his writings against the Donatists, Augustine makes comments implying that there are external activities that mark the Church. These include: (1) forgiveness of sins; (2) the reading of Scripture; (3) the preaching of repentance and remission of sin; and (4) the spreading of charity abroad. About the first mark, the African Father notes, when comforting despair and in response to the Donatists, forgiveness of sins may be granted only by the Church, for it does not happen outside the Church.[5]

So committed is Augustine to these objective realities of the Church and its authority that he goes so far as to claim in his polemics that he would not believe the Gospel except on the authority of the Catholic Church, that there is no salvation outside the Church. For only through the Church and Sacraments can one become a Christian.[6] Like the Church, the Christian life is a Work of God.

In the context of his polemics with the Donatists and even when explicating the logic of faith, he stresses the universal character of the Church, its openness to diversities of customs, laws, and traditions. Thus he remarks in such writings that while on earth the heavenly city invites citizens of all nations and tongues to unity. It takes no issue with diversity of customs, laws, or traditions. It appropriates whatever in distinct races aims at human peace, as long as they do not stand in the way of faith. The City of God does not care, he adds, what kind of dress or social manners a person of faith has as long as it gives no offense to divine law. Believers can live a life of faith in any of the modes of life. In one of his epistles he expressly advocates conforming to the customs of the church in which one is participating.[7] Augustine in these texts gives an unambiguous testimony to an inclusive Church.

In one of his homilies on 1 John, against the Donatists, Augustine also stresses that the Body is found where repentance and remission of sin are preached, and where charity is spread abroad. Note here how he returns to emphasizing the objective nature of the Church. But these points, especially the Catholic Church's forgiveness of sins, were important to make against the Donatists, whose rigor allowed for little practice of forgiveness. Augustine then proceeds to emphasize the point further. Some Donatists, he claims, would set the boundary of charity in

Africa. Love cannot be for only part of the Body.[8] Further to undergird his accusations of their sectarianism, Augustine adds that Donatists limit Christ to two languages—Latin and Punic or African.[9] Donatists were largely located only in Africa.

In response to such Donatist sectarianism Augustine strongly emphasizes the universal character of the Church. Thus against such heretics he claims that deserters of the Church cannot be in Christ, for they are not among Christ's members. In one who loves the brother or sister there is no offense, for the love of the brother or sister endures all things for unity's sake. By finding cause for stumbling in Africa, Donatists have cut themselves off from the world (the unity of the Church).[10]

Those who have gone out of Church (heretics) were never of the Church, Augustine claims. But those who have gone out and return are not Antichrists.[11]

Augustine's commitment to the Church's universality led him to assert that Donatists confess Christ. But they have withdrawn from the Church, not Catholics from them. Indeed, Catholics hold Christ's inheritance, he insists. Donatists do not, for they will not have communion with the world.[12] Augustine is willing to grant the salvific character of Donatist Sacraments and ecclesiology, but only in the sense that they reflect elements of the true Church.[13]

In these polemical contexts and when exhorting faith, the African Father stresses the objective character of the Church in other ways. The wholeness of the Body is constituted by all the members together.[14] The authority of the Church is confirmed by consensus of agreement among many nations, supported by Apostolic Succession and the Councils.[15]

Likewise a strong affirmation of Apostolic Succession is offered as an additional way of asserting ecclesiastical authority. In his view Succession is not negated by wicked officeholders, for the stability of hope is fixed not on human beings but on God.[16]

The theme of basing hope not on human beings but on God is applied to ecclesiology in other writings against the Donatists. In such contexts, Augustine also observes that fervent and cold Christians, good people and bad, are mixed in the Church.[17] Against the Donatists he even claims that the Church is the fixed number of predestined saints, but that this includes some presently in heresy or vice. Yet none belongs to God outside communion with the Church.[18] Even the Church's holiness is understood in this objective manner in such anti-Donatist contexts, not interpreted in terms of its members' holiness but in terms of the holiness of the Sacraments (or when merely reflecting autobiographically as involved in a progression toward holiness).[19]

We observe this appreciation of the objective character of the Church in other writings against the Pelagians, as there too Augustine asserts that the Church includes a mixture of evil people with the good.[20] He makes a similar affirmation when exhorting the faith in the *City of God* and elsewhere.[21] In all of these contexts the objective character of the Church as a Work of God is stressed.

THE CHURCH AS THE PEOPLE

When focusing on the nature of the Christian life, on Christian responsibility, and on the eschaton, Augustine suggests that the Church may be portrayed in a different way. He hints that it may be construed as a community built on its members' faith and constituted by them (Titus 2:14; Rom. 9:25–26).[22]

In one of his *Ten Homilies on the Epistle of John to the Parthians* concerned to exhort Christian responsibility, Augustine offers a thoughtful Trinitarian image. The end of the love of the Son leading to loving the children of God entails that there is one Christ, loving Himself, for the love of the members for one another is the love of the Body for itself.[23]

When dealing with problems of Christian living and heresies Augustine pre-occupies himself with the mandate to enforce church discipline.[24] Along the same lines, in these contexts he rejects the idea that mere membership in the Church saves, no matter how one lives.[25]

When turning to the eschatological vision (describing the logic of faith), but with a certain concern about how Christians live, the African Father sketches a majestic vision of the Church, one that may stress its objectivity more than the description of the Church as a people. In these contexts Augustine defines the Church's membership as including not just those on earth, but also the loyal angels. Even the souls of the pious dead are not separated from the Church. In that sense the Church is even now the Kingdom of Christ.[26]

MINISTRY

Augustine's view of Ministry is very much in line with the polity that had emerged in his lifetime. When reflecting on polity he embraces the early church's commitment to a threefold Ministry—as Bishop, Presbyter, and Deacon.[27]

A proponent of episcopal polity and of Apostolic Succession, Augustine particularly focuses on this set of commitments when dialoguing with or refuting heretics. In these contexts he posits a high view of ministry as he deems the rite of Ordination as a Sacrament alongside Baptism and even claims that the succession of Bishops was not disrupted by some unfaithful Bishops.[28] Elsewhere, when addressing heretics, Augustine refers to Apostolic Succession as the highest pinnacle of authority.[29] He even strongly affirms episcopal authority in the midst of a controversy with the Donatists and when expositing the mysteries of the faith (Eph. 2:20; Acts 13:3–4; Matt. 16:18–19; 28:16–20).[30]

This very Catholic polity when in dialogue with the heretics further manifests itself on several occasions when Augustine speaks of the primacy of Peter. In fact, when not engaged in such polemics, Augustine says that Peter is the unity of all pastors.[31]

There are only a few references to the priesthood of all believers in the Augustinian corpus. They emerge only when exhorting or describing the Christian life (1 Cor. 12:14–31; 1 Pet. 2:5, 9).[32]

Augustine engages in discussions of the tasks of ordained ministry, especially when exhorting faith or laying out its logic. Proclamation, he states at one point, is a work of the Holy Spirit. In another treatise he asserts that the Holy Spirit fills ministers for their tasks.[33] These tasks are defined primarily as the preaching of God's Word and the administering of his Sacraments.[34]

When exhorting faith to the ordained, he seems to define the ordained ministry in terms of these tasks. This fits the more objective treatment of the Church that Augustine offers in such contexts. For when we recall that the Holy Spirit is working through the pastor, it follows that these tasks are ultimately not the work of the minister but God's Work, just as in these pastoral contexts it is God Who is said to create the Church. The whole point of the Donatist Controversy from Augustine's Catholic viewpoint was to assert that the Power of Christ can work through a sinful priest.[35]

In other contexts, when addressing issues of lifestyle, Augustine does define the ordained ministry in terms of the behavior of the officeholder (1 Tim. 3:1–13; 2 Tim. 2:14ff.). Thus he posits lifestyle standards when contending that one could be degraded from the priesthood for lifestyle reasons. Even against the Pelagians, while insisting that no priest can be sinless, he did concede with a view toward everyday church life that a legitimate qualification for Ordination be that the candidate be "blameless."[36] In a mixed context of laying out the logic of faith with an effort to exposit principles of sermon preparation, he claims that while preachers can often teach many things that they themselves do not practice, their teaching might be to even greater effect if they lived in harmony with this teaching.[37]

Pastoral Advice

In several of his works, especially when concerned with laying out principles of Biblical interpretation, Augustine offers some advice about how to preach and teach. In one case he claims that the techniques of teaching and communication (i.e., rhetoric) are advantageous only when God uses them. For God could give the Gospel to humankind without human agency.[38]

Augustine also provides some valuable advice about Christian education. The teachers or priests should be like a hen covering her brood, he says, and be willing to descend to the people's level of understanding.[39]

Other advice about doing ministry is offered by Augustine in response to various matters of discipline or turmoil in the churches. He claims that it is best to honor local customs when there are no prescriptions by Scripture and Tradition.[40] When addressing congregational sloth, Augustine asserts that it is good if pastors receive honor, but they ought not exult in it. Similarly in two of his sermons he urges preachers to seek God's glory, not their own, to avoid the temptation to seek human applause.[41]

WORSHIP

Since worship is so clearly related to the Church and Ministry, a brief closing analysis of Augustine's views on the subject seems appropriate. For the African Father, worship also happens outside the sanctuary. We are to worship God in faith, hope, and love. Worship is the love of God.[42]

Eastern churches had been the first to sing Psalms and canticles, and this had begun prior to Augustine's lifetime. He was exposed to it in Milan with Ambrose. Reflecting on this practice, he notes in his *Confessions* that hymns overcome our anxiety. Indeed, Augustine reports, he weeps at the hymns, for their sound streams truth in his heart resulting in a joyful feeling of devotion.[43] On the whole, then, he approves the custom of singing in church, for by pleasure of the ear weaker minds may be aroused to feelings of devotion. But we sin when we are moved more by the singing than by the thing sung.[44]

In the context of a criticism of Donatists in one of his letters in the year 400, Augustine offers an interesting insight about the worship style in his own diocese. He notes that the Donatists had criticized Catholics for not being passionate enough in their singing.[45] Apparently Augustine and his diocese advocated more restrained, not so spontaneous and enthusiastic worship as characterized the Donatists. It is tempting to reflect on whether this less "African" sort of worship might indicate Augustine's identification with Roman ways.

This is not to say that the Bishop of Hippo totally disowns African ways in worship. He provides indications that a call-and-response style of worship (not unlike African American and Holiness models of worship) characterizes his own North African ethos. One of his congregations is reported to have offered enthusiastic responses to points made during the course of homilies.[46]

Other dimensions of worship in Augustine's contexts are evident in one of his *Lectures on the Gospel of St. John*. The African Father reports that the Eucharist is celebrated daily in some African parishes, and only at intervals of days in others.[47] Regarding prayer, he notes in one of his anti-Pelagian works that the prayers of the Church give testimony to the fact that the good that happens is God's doing. Augustine himself was in general a proponent of long prayer, rather than the short ejaculatory (exclamatory) prayers he claimed to characterize Egypt. The longer prayer, embodied by his great autobiography (the *Confessions,* which is nothing but a prayer), makes the heart throb.[48]

SUMMARY

The study of Augustine's views on Church and Ministry reveals another common pattern in his theology and perhaps in the history of Christian thought. In essence we see that in cases where exhorting Christian life is at stake it is common to define these doctrines primarily in terms of the faith or behavior of their members or officeholders. But when dealing with heretics or when exhorting faith, both Church and Ministry are described more objectively, with more emphasis on God's action through these institutions and their members.

Chapter 8

Sacraments

Catholic that he was, one would expect to find Augustine endorsing a Sacramentology that the Vatican would approve of today. But that is not the whole story. Indeed, it would be anachronistic to expect to find in his thought a full endorsement of transubstantiation and other post-Medieval Sacramental affirmations. Likewise it is not reasonable to expect him to have provided a self-conscious listing of all the Sacraments (whether the historic seven or the more Protestant enumeration of two or three). He addressed the number of Sacraments once, in *Replies to Questions of Januaris*. Augustine claimed in that letter that the number of Sacraments are few, naming only Baptism, the Lord's Supper, and "such other things as are prescribed in the canonical Scriptures."[1]

There is not much in the way of specific general reflections about the nature of the Sacraments in general in the Augustinian corpus. He usually devotes attention to particular Sacraments, rather than generalizing about them as a genre. Where he does, one finds a bias toward language suggesting the Real Presence of Christ in the rites. Of course, this may be the result of the specific contexts he is addressing in these instances.

Augustine defines the Sacrament in one of his sermons in such a way as to entail the Real Presence of Christ: the Sacrament, he claims, is the Word added to an element. Other ways in which he makes this affirmation are evident when, while endeavoring to quash any tendencies to Pelagian-like thinking in *To Simplician,* he contends that grace is infused through Sacramental rites.[2] In an expressly anti-Manichee context, in defense of the unique character of Christian Sacraments, he describes the Sacraments as "Visible Words."[3] In all these cases Augustine implies that grace (and Christ) is actually given *in* the Sacraments, that He is Really Present.

The objective character of grace in the Sacraments receives further attestation in much of Augustine's writings against the Donatists. The whole point of the conflict is, from his Catholic vantage, to affirm that the Sacraments work and are holy no matter who administers them. They are done by the whole Church, though even in these contexts as well as when exhorting faith he added that without faith the Sacraments do not affect what they signify.[4]

With regard to the number of Sacraments, in addition to the two rites about which there is catholic consensus regarding their Sacramental status (Baptism and the Eucharist), I observed in the previous chapter how the African Father expressly attributes Sacramental status to Ordination. He does the same, when writing against the Donatists, with regard to Confirmation (anointing of Catechumens).[5] Likewise when defending Marriage against heretics critiquing the goodness of the institution, Augustine identifies it as a Sacrament. In his view, its status rules out remarriage after divorce, even if the divorce was occasioned by unchastity. He contends that the marriage to just one partner, which is the new custom of his era, signifies the unity of all made subject to God in the one heavenly city.[6]

I have been unable to identify any reference to the rite of Extreme Unction (Last Rites) in the Augustinian corpus. Penance or Confession seems to have been practiced in the African Father's church, but only for "heinous" sins where the exercise of church discipline including excommunication might be imposed. He refers in these contexts, devoted to exhorting Christian life, to the washing in prayer available to the penitent for light sins and to the curing of sins after Baptism by repentance.[7] He also refers to a rite of exorcism held prior to Baptism that was intended to release those to be baptized from Satan's power.[8]

BAPTISM

With regard to Baptism, Augustine does claim, while explaining the core beliefs of faith or polemicizing against the Donatists and Pelagianism, that in the Sacrament we are given a new will and are born again.[9] While expositing the logic of faith in the *Enchiridion* (a work that also has a concern about exhorting Christian life), the African Father speaks of the meaning of Baptism as dying to sin, as dying and rising with Christ (Rom. 6:3–6). This happens to infants as well as to adults.[10]

Augustine also elaborates on the lifelong consequences of Baptism. While engaging in apologetics in *On the Trinity* he claims that the baptized must be renewed daily, as the outward person is put to death and the inner person (the image of God) is daily made anew.[11]

Augustine elaborates further on what Baptism accomplishes in other works, while expounding on the logic of faith. Past sins are said to be done away in all who are baptized. In grown-ups the will itself is healed.[12] There is a more qualified affirmation of the sense in which Baptism has overcome our sins in contexts where Augustine addresses Pelagianism. In those contexts he claims only that Baptism washes away all sins, but does not take away our weaknesses. Against Donatism, Augustine added that the grace of Baptism remains, even among recipients who have denied it in their lives.[13] In works also devoted to refuting Pelagianism, but at points where he is especially concerned to assert the effects of Baptism for living the Christian life, the African Father reiterates that sins are remitted in Baptism. In language most reminiscent of Medieval Catholicism, he concedes that lust remains after Baptism, but it is no more sin.[14]

Not surprisingly in light of the forensic view of justification's endorsement in contexts where Augustine addresses the Pelagian heresy, the African Father also associates this construal with Baptism in a treatise against Pelagianism. He claims here that sin remains after Baptism, but is no longer imputed.[15]

Given the objective view of the Sacraments and of Baptism that he posits, it is also not surprising that Augustine advocates recognition of the Baptism of heretics. He makes this point by appealing to Tradition and also with an argument referring to the unity of the Church to which the sanctity of the Sacraments witnesses.[16] As I have noted, it is the Church's action that counts, not who administers the rite.[17]

We have not discerned any occasion in which Augustine addresses Baptism merely while exhorting Christian life. It is interesting to speculate whether another vision of the rite (perhaps understanding it as a mere symbol) might have emerged, as it has in the case of other more modern traditions (Baptists, Anabaptists, etc.).

Infant Baptism

Generally speaking, infant baptism was a new development in African Christianity in Augustine's career. His own baptism, as was typical of the church in Africa in this era, had been postponed for fear that a child baptized might subsequently sin, and then not be forgiven for such postbaptismal sins.[18] The African Father did come to advocate the practice, however, especially in contexts in which he disputed Pelagianism. In one of these treatises he notes that infant baptism is a clear exemplification of salvation by grace. In another he seems to address Pelagian critiques of original sin by contending that the Church classes baptized infants as believers.[19] Even outside anti-Pelagian contexts, while explicating the faith with a concern to exhort Christian life in view, the African Father insists that infants are baptized because of (as a remedy to) original sin.[20]

Augustine offers several other arguments on behalf of infant baptism. The practice was handed down by Tradition, he claims in several works.[21] He also notes, while critiquing Pelagius, that even children are reckoned among believers through the power of the Sacrament and the faith of the sponsors. In addition, he refers to infant faith, for infants in Baptism receive the Sacrament of faith, while seeking to witness to the power of the Sacrament.[22] Likewise, when criticizing the Manichees, and so with some concern about Christian responsibility, Augustine claims that Baptism benefits infants because their parents' faith is imputed to them.[23]

Another intriguing observation about infant baptism emerges in one of the African Father's 413 sermons. While explicating the faith, he claims that the crying of infants at their baptism is a sign of the inner yearning for liberation.[24]

The endorsement of infant baptism did not lead Augustine to give up all hope for the salvation of the unbaptized. While explicating the faith in the *City of God* and elsewhere in dialogue with Donatists, he points out that the unbaptized who confess Christ can still be saved, and we previously noted his openness to the salvation of some in hell whom Christ saved during His descent into hell. However, when disputing with Jerome over the origin of the soul (Augustine contends that each soul is not merely created at birth), in other disputes about the state of the soul since the Fall, or when refuting Pelagianism, the African Father claims that unbaptized infants born in sin cannot be saved.[25] Yet he does hold out hope for the salvation of aborted infants, while responding to critics of belief in the resurrection or in response to those who despise forgiveness of sin. In a treatise against the Donatists he claims that we need not despair of the salvation of those who have aligned themselves with the Church but were never baptized.[26]

THE LORD'S SUPPER

Augustine's treatment of this Sacrament exhibits the same diversity we have observed with regard to other loci. He makes points that aré characteristically Catholic, but also some that are more compatible with Protestantism. In Roman Catholic fashion he refers to the Lord's Supper as a Sacrifice, even to the point of referring to the Church sacrificing herself in the Sacrament or of this sacrifice benefitting those who died in faith. He makes these points especially when dealing with issues of Christian living.[27] When more concerned with exhorting faith in the *City of God,* however, he describes the Sacrifice as such in the sense that Christ the one true Sacrifice is present in it. Such a view is compatible with Martin Luther's thinking, as it is quite clear on such grounds that we do not need the Lord's Supper in order to complete Christ's Sacrifice on the Cross.[28] But when the concern shifts back to exhorting the Christian life, the African Father makes a more characteristically Catholic point in contending that the Sacrifice involved in the Sacraments along with the giving of alms benefit the dead.[29] He was also open to daily reception of the Sacrament, though he did not insist upon it.[30]

We would expect Augustine to have endorsed the idea that Christ is Really Present in the Communion elements. He does this, though not in the mode of the Catholic view of transubstantiation, when describing what the Church is doing in worship and how it relates to Christ's Work.[31] Likewise in the same contexts he speaks of Christ's Presence in the Lord's Supper, even when partaken of by unbelievers, and of receiving Christ through the eating and drinking of the elements.[32]

But in other contexts, when defending faith from the onslaughts of reason or when urging the practice of Christian living in face of confrontation with evil, Augustine takes a different position. He employs language suggesting that the Sacraments had the status of "signs," perhaps more like what John Calvin taught. Thus in his *Expositions on the Book of Psalms,* he describes the evil that David and Jesus confronted with forbearance:

> by that so great and so wonderful forbearance of our Lord; in that He bore so long with him [Judas] as if good, when He was not ignorant of his thoughts; in that He admitted him to the Supper in which He committed and delivered to His disciples the figure of His Body and Blood.[33]

In one of his sermons, while dealing with misunderstandings about the Sacrament due to the flesh (a dialogue with reason), Augustine speaks only of "mystical words" about eating Christ's Body in the Lord's Supper.[34] Is this an effective endorsement of a view of the Sacrament as a mere symbol?

CONCLUSION

Another set of patterns in Augustine's thought that may have catholic implications for explaining the diversity in the Christian tradition is evidenced again in his treatment of the Sacraments (especially the Lord's Supper). When focused especially on exhorting or inspiring Christian living, Augustine shows less concern to affirm Christ's Real Presence in the Sacraments. In most other contexts, he affirms the Real Presence (though not necessarily transubstantiation) in the elements. Could this suggest that the differences among denominational traditions over the Sacramental rites are largely functions of different traditions concentrating more on some pastoral issues than others (the traditions espousing symbolic conceptions being more preoccupied with sanctification than traditions endorsing the Real Presence)?

Chapter 9

Eschatology

Generally speaking, most of Augustine's writings about eschatology pertain to future eschatology. In one Epistle, written somewhere around 419 to a fellow bishop, Hesychius, the African Father offers some reflections that imply his endorsement of a realized eschatology and the urgency of living in the present (Mark 1:14–15). Apparently, according to Augustine, Hesychius had engaged in a good bit of speculation about the End Times. In response, Augustine contended that we must always be prepared for an immanent End, for the Last Days began with Jesus' Ascension.[1] Another dimension of realized eschatology related to the prefiguring that the faithful have of the End in the present by the experience of the hope they have. When dialoguing with philosophical worldviews the African Father affirms in the *City of God* how human life can be happy because of the hope of heaven. While seeking to comfort despair in that work, he claims that only Christians can feel joy in face of death of loved ones, knowing they are freed of evil.[2]

The urgency associated with realized eschatology also surfaces in his *Expositions on the Book of Psalms*. While exposing the text of Psalm 101, though with heretics in view, he claims that our days are short in comparison to eternity.

Nothing is stationary in time, while God's everlasting years are unchanged. Elsewhere, while also preoccupied with the Day of Judgment, he asserts that "now" is the time for conversion.[3]

A CATHOLIC ESCHATOLOGY

When dealing with questions about our responsibility to live Christianly (especially with what to make of those unbelievers who live in outward obedience to the Law of God), when he also distinguishes venial and mortal sins, Augustine refers to different levels of glory in heaven for the saints, albeit with no envy among the lower to the higher.[4] In a 426/427 Letter addressed to monks and exhorting Christian living, Augustine claims that we will be judged by our works, by the merits earned when working with grace. Similarly, in *On Grace and Free Will* while both affirming free will and a polemic against Pelagianism he asserts that eternal life is both a gift of grace and a reward, but since the works were done by grace even the reward is a gift.[5]

When dealing with despair along with apologetics, along these same lines the African Father speaks of a reward in heaven for faith.[6] Sometimes in these contexts, when also concerned to assert our responsibility as Christians, he even refers to a kind of purgatory where the dead can benefit from acts of faith by the living.[7] In other works while concerned about how it helps to bury Christians near the memorial of a saint, he claims that sacrifices of prayer, of alms, and of the altar are good for the dead.[8] With an apologetic agenda in view or when concerned with exhorting Christian faith, the African Father observes that the Martyrs can make intercession, that the souls are benefited by Sacraments and the alms of the living.[9]

AN ESCHATOLOGY FOR PROTESTANTS

A more Protestant-like image appears in the *City of God* and elsewhere when Augustine responds to Pelagian views. In theses contexts he articulates a view most compatible with Protestant readings of him, claiming that we are saved by faith.[10] As I noted in chapter 6, when explicating the logic of faith the African Father on occasion even offers the hope that some, if not all, who had not confessed Christ might be saved.

When he preaches, other Protestant-like themes appear in Augustine's thought. He claims that all the dead sleep, but that the dreams of the damned are frightful, while those of the righteous are pleasant.[11] When recounting his faith pilgrimage, he also asserts that when united to God there will be no more grief and toil, for in eternity we will be totally filled with God.[12]

In the *City of God* Augustine elaborates further on this point while comforting despair and engaging in apologetics. We will be most free, have the ultimate freedom, in eternity, he claims, for we will then be free of sin, will not be able to sin.

Such freedom approximates the freedom of God, Who cannot sin but is still free.[13] In the *Enchiridion,* while extrapolating on the End Times but always with a concern about living the Christian life, the African Father likewise claims that in the future it will not be possible for the redeemed to will evil.[14] In a similar vein, while expounding the faith in a polemical context, Augustine claims that the right hand of the Father is not a place, but a supreme blessedness where righteousness is.[15]

In heaven, the human spirit will be without passion, Augustine adds while comforting despair the individual might feel. Those who have risen will have peace, calm, and repose, a peace beyond the understanding that the angels have.[16] They will have an uninterrupted vision of God. Indeed, happiness in heaven is one long praise of God. In another treatise, against the Manichees, Augustine adds that this occupation of praise will be undertaken in the spirit of leisure and rest.[17] Elsewhere in his *City of God* he claims that the memory of our previous miseries will be purely mental. Contemplation of these miseries will have none of the feelings associated with them. We will consider such memories in the sort of mode of thought that doctors know bodily maladies.[18]

Other characteristics of eternal life, which Augustine articulates while reflecting in grief in his *Confessions* over his friend's death, imply that we will remember the past in heaven, though intoxicated with God. This will be in the memory. Likewise, in a variety of contexts he also claims that in heaven all our thoughts will be visible to all the saints, that we will bear nothing alone.[19] When engaged in apologetics earlier in his career, Augustine also claims that in eternity there is neither past not future. For in eternity there is no changeableness and so no time, which is characterized by movement. He makes a similar point while preaching, as he contends that eternity is an everlasting day, for the Father is said to be light.[20]

Elsewhere, while extrapolating on the faith, Augustine claims that the virtues which make life good will not change in eternity. Justice will be the sole virtue to continue. But the activities of the virtues will be accounted as things past. Yet there will be a trinity of memory, true recognition, and union of both by the will.[21] The African Father has painted us a glorious vision of eternal life, one that seems fairly consistent in all contexts.

Other topics on which the conceptual richness of Augustine's thought is evident pertain to his views on the millennium and the distinct, apparently contradictory positions he takes on whether the dead have bodies in heaven (the more Platonic position emerging in discourses when he is especially concerned with issues related to comforting despair or engaging in apologetics) (1 Cor. 15: 35–49; Matt. 22:23–33).

Resurrection of the Body?

Augustine's affirmation of the resurrection of the body is a fairly consistent theme in his thought, especially when explicating the faith.[22] When addressing a variety of contexts he claims that in heaven the faithful have bodies.[23]

The resurrected body, as Augustine portrays it, will not be identical with our earthly bodies. They will be like the Body of Christ, not affected by gravity when ascending into heaven. The health of the body will render it easier to move. As perfect, the heavenly body is readily moved.[24]

Such resurrected bodies will retain gender, but be rid of imperfections (like being overweight). The movements of these bodies will be of unimaginable beauty.[25] Indeed, the deformed shall have perfect bodies at the Resurrection. Each body may retain its own peculiarities, yet all shall be equal as their defects are supplied.[26]

Although disowning it when reflecting on the logic of faith in his *Retractions,* a different perspective on the resurrection from the dead appears in Augustine's thought in contexts when he concerns himself with critics of the faith. Thus in his *On Faith and the Creed,* he claims that at the resurrection the bodies of the faithful will no longer be flesh and blood, but be changed into angelic realities.[27] In one of his epistles, while exhorting Christian life and comforting despair, he claims in a similar manner that earthly bodies become spiritual bodies, a point he makes elsewhere in related contexts.[28]

Millennial Speculations

As noted, Augustine also takes different positions on millennialism. In one of his *Sermons,* while concerned to exhort Christian living, and elsewhere when refuting the Manichees, he embraces this sort of speculation and affirms that the faithful would rule with Christ for a millennium. Yet he renounces such speculation when merely recounting the logic of faith in his *City of God,* claiming that the thousand years to which Revelation 20 refers is a figure pertaining to the history of the Church.[29]

Other millennial-related reflections include Augustine's claim in a work devoted to exhorting the Christian life that, though deserving punishment, humankind will have a portion restored by God to fill the loss of fallen angels. At the resurrection the saints will become equal to angels.[30] The lost will be raised in order to be punished.[31] Christ is to be the judge of both parties at the Last Judgment.[32] In his *Exposition of Genesis According to the Letter,* while engaging in apologetics and also critiquing speculation, Augustine even affirms something like the Rapture (the transmigration of believers through ecstasy into Christ's heavenly Presence prior to the Second Coming [Matt. 24:36–44; 1 Thess. 4:15–17]).[33]

SUMMARY

Most of what Augustine has to say about the End Times relates to future eschatology. One finds the full range of Christian images to describe the End (save no reference to the Rapture). Both Protestant and Catholic ways of viewing the End are embedded in his literature—more Protestant elements in his preaching and exposition of the faith, and more Catholic elements when his concern shifts to questions about our responsibility to live as Christians. This insight may help offer Protestants a new appreciation of the significance and pastoral strengths of purgatory and belief gradations in heaven.

Chapter 10

Social Ethics: The Two Cities

Even Augustine's views of church-state relations and his social ethic reflect conceptual richness in different contexts. Thus he can sound so much like Martin Luther's Two-Kingdom Ethic and the American Constitutional system in the *City of God*, particularly when articulating the history of humankind from a Christian outlook (Mark 12:17; Rom. 2:14–15). A different construal of church-state relations emerges in the Augustinian corpus in other contexts, when the African Father undertakes apologetics, defends Christianity from charges of being detrimental to society, or finds himself in the midst of ecclesiastical disruptions. In those contexts, as later in the traditions of Calvin, Puritanism, and medieval Catholicism, he advocates that Christianity helps make good citizens, that the state may be used to spread Christianity, and that the state is well governed when it reflects Christian principles (Eph. 1:20–22; 1 Tim. 2:1-2).

TWO CITIES IN PARADOX

With regard to the strand in his thought that Martin Luther and the American Constitution have accurately portrayed, segments of the *City of God*, particularly

133

when Augustine articulates the history of humankind from a Christian outlook, most clearly endorse these commitments. In those contexts he claims that government is the embodiment of self-love and the quest for power. Consequently, it cannot legislate love. The best that can be done politically, he argues, is to ensure that all citizens have an equal opportunity to pursue their own interests, to receive their due.[1]

Augustine develops this view of government especially in the context of his work in the *City of God* as he offers there his version of world history (with the ultimate aim of accounting for the fall of the Roman Empire). For all the differences among people, there are two kinds of societies, he contends—the "city of men," who are those who live according to the flesh, and the "City of God," comprised of those who live according to the spirit.[2]

The two cities originate from two loves, the African Father maintains. Worldly society flows from selfish love. But the communion of saints is rooted in the love of God, which will trample the self. By contrast, in the earthly city, rulers and their subjects are both dominated by lust for dominion. In the City of God, citizens serve one another in charity. Of course, God populates that City only by undeserved grace. But the earthly city lusts to dominate the world.[3]

When pointing out Christianity's superiority to the pagan gods, when explicating the logic of Christian faith, and even when critiquing Pelagianism, Augustine posits something like a natural law—the idea that God has given all people a sense of right and wrong that has not been eradicated by sin.[4] God is deemed to be involved in the affairs of state in this way. Thus Augustine claims that God alone has the power to give people an empire. God never permits the human race to be without His wisdom and power. In fact, the African Father adds, God even granted this to the Roman people.[5] There is no such thing as a purely secular government on Augustine's grounds.

The African Father does concede that in a qualified sense good things can happen in the earthly city and so in civic government. The original Romans were honorable people, he contends. But eventually their desire for domination overcame their love for liberty. Thus temporal glory was granted to the Romans by God as a reward for their virtues.[6] God's mercy continued to be manifest to the Romans even during the Fall of Rome, Augustine contends. As evidence he points out that the barbarians spared many Roman citizens at that time.[7]

Not just the Romans, but all people are in Augustine's view able to do by nature the things in the Law. They can do civilly good deeds, not outwardly obeying lusts. The African Father even makes this claim, affirming something like a civic righteousness distinct from the righteousness of God that saves, while critiquing Pelagianism. All human beings, he asserts, can perceive and do what is lawful.[8]

Elsewhere in the *City of God* Augustine trades more on this distinction, as he notes that even the wise in the earthly city live according to humankind and have as their goal the goods of mind and body. Nevertheless, he hastens to add, the mercies of God are still available to those paying the price of Law and discipline.[9]

In one his anti-Pelagian works he even goes so far as to make the distinction explicitly, distinguishing between righteousness "in" the Law (a civic righteousness) and righteousness "of" the Law (righteousness before God).[10]

Augustinian Realism about Governmental Affairs

The African Father applied these insights expressly to his theory of social relations even early in his career when concerned to assert the goodness of the Law against the Manichees. All temporal law, he claimed, must derive from the eternal law based on reason.[11] In other periods of his career, when addressing analogous concerns, Augustine made a similar point. Thus in his *Confessions* he claimed that when God orders something against the custom or covenant of a state, it must be done.[12]

The need for rigorous adherence to such norms is apparent in view of the sinful character of human nature and the earthly city of which the state and other social institutions are a part. For as Augustine notes, apart from justice, sovereignty is groups of men dividing booty.[13] In the earthly city, though the bond of common nature makes all one, each individual, Christian and non-Christian, is driven by passions to pursue private purposes. None is ever satisfied. Thus the earthly city is characterized by a perpetual civil war. Those who succeed always oppress those who fail.[14]

Along the same lines Augustine also observes that peace presupposes that there is a removal of tension through the subordination of some to others, a relationship which presupposes good order.[15] An unambiguously just peace seems impossible to achieve in the earthly city, for we will always seek to impose our own version of peace on others.[16] Resonances are readily apparent with the American system of government's suspicions of how power if unchecked always corrupts.[17]

Even when a city has peace, Augustine adds, some must judge others. This inevitably causes misery. None can judge another's conscience, and so many times the innocent are tortured.[18]

While presenting the logic of faith, the African Father notes that true justice is not realized on earth (for even Christians are not virtuous).[19] While describing world history he makes the point another way. He claims that true justice has no existence in the earthly city.[20] In fact, he adds, there never was a true Roman republic, because there was never in Rome a mutual cooperation, a recognition of rights and justice.[21]

Augustine's realism surfaces in his willingness to have Christians participate in and obey the laws of the civil realm. Thus in the *City of God* he contends that as long as the denizens of the divine city remain alien the Church has no hesitation about keeping in step with civil law. As long as the two cities are mingled, Christians can make use of the world's peace and are to pray for the world's kings. To this point, Augustine adds, it does not matter what government we obey, as long as it does not compel us to act against God. After all, he adds elsewhere, the quest for peace in society is a response to the law of nature accessible to all human beings.[22]

The Christian's responsibility for the institutions of society surfaces in other works, in subtle ways such as when Augustine criticizes heresy. Thus he notes in one of his sermons that Donatists claim to have nothing to do with Catholic Christians, because these heretics will have no communion with the city where Christ was slain. The African Father argues in response that Christ loved that city.[23]

That he opts only for the use of the natural law known by all through reason, not the Gospel, as the norm for Christian interactions with society is evident at several other points in the Augustinian corpus. While critiquing Pelagianism and articulating the faith, or when critiquing Donatist harassment, the African Father claims that human society is knit together by transactions of giving and receiving, and things are given and received sometimes as debts, sometimes not.[24] In these contexts Augustine clearly viewed human society as predicated on the transactions of law. The Gospel does not have direct bearing on the affairs of state.

This same propensity on Augustine's part not to identify the Gospel of Jesus Christ with the affairs of state was even apparent while the Roman Empire and its establishment of Christianity as the official religion was still in place. In the heat of the Donatist Controversy, the African Father still did not advocate that the state coerce membership in the Church.[25]

That the Law and not the Gospel is the proper norm for the affairs of state in Augustine's view is also evident in his reflections on political leadership. While dealing with temptation in his *Confessions,* he notes that many of society's institutions demand that the officeholder seek love and praise. Thus the institutions of society are governed by pride.[26] They will not be transformed simply by doses of humility. Besides, as Augustine notes while simply describing the history of the two cities, on this side of the End Times the earthly city is always governed by the praise of our peers and pays homage to their rulers as symbols of the populace's own strength.[27] If one does not use power in this context one will not be able to rule effectively, it seems.

The Gospel's message of salvation is not able to provide the sort of authorization for effective rule that the just and fair administration of their power can. The best that distinct Christian teachings can provide, it seems, are inward dispositions for rulers and citizens. Thus Augustine claims that, unlike church leaders, Christian emperors rule best when they govern with justice and instill fear, seeing their rule as a ministry of God. And without the institutions of such justice, kingdoms become, in Augustine's view, nothing more than a band of robbers.[28] This idea of governing with justice connotes Augustine's advocacy of political rule conducted under the auspices of the moral law, rather than on grounds of unique Christian insights (the Gospel). As I have noted, though, this model of Christian social ethics that the Lutheran heritage and the American Constitutional system have found amenable is not the whole story with regard to the African Father's thought.

TRANSFORMING THE EARTHLY CITY

A different construal of church-state relations emerges in the Augustinian corpus in other contexts, when the African Father defends Christianity from charges of being detrimental to society, finds himself in the midst of ecclesiastical disruptions, or deals with lifestyle issues. In those contexts, he advocates, like the later traditions of Calvinism, Puritanism, and Medieval Catholicism, that the state may be used to spread Christianity and that the state is well governed when it reflects Christian principles.[29]

In part this interpenetration of church and political realm was the result of Constantine's decision in 318 to grant legal status to Bishops' tribunals. Thus civil cases were brought before Augustine, and he was expected to make legally binding judgments.[30] Of course judgments were to be rendered according to the canons of Roman civil law, which could suggest that effectively, like in the first model, the Law and not the Gospel was governing Christian political judgments.

Augustine contradicted his earlier rejection of the use of force to coerce membership in the Church, when contending with Greek and Roman religion and when responding to Donatist rigorism. In these contexts he argued that governments should intervene against cults.[31]

Augustine develops this viewpoint elsewhere in his *City of God.* At one point he reiterates his definition of justice as the virtue that accords to each one's due. But then he adds that there can be no justice in unbelievers, because they cannot properly exercise dominion over their bodies inasmuch as they themselves are not properly subject to God. Thus there is no justice in an assembly comprised of such persons.[32] For there is no justice if the soul is not subordinate to God or the republic is not founded on Christ.[33]

The context for these commitments is a concern with sanctification and apologetics (or at least a dialogue with classical philosophers).[34] These passages became the basis for the development of Medieval "Political Augustinianism," the insistence that only in the state of grace has one the authority to rule and own property.[35]

ECONOMICS, SLAVERY, AND FAMILY

Clearly Augustine understood economics, an activity of the earthly city, in relation to his pessimistic, realistic view of human nature as mired in sin.

> Whither does worldly covetousness lead thee? And to what point does it conduct thee at the last? Thou didst at first desire a farm; then thou wouldest possess an estate; thou wouldest shut out thy neighbours; having shut them out thou didst set thy heart on the possessions of other neighbours; and didst extend thy covetous desires till thou hadst reached the shore: arriving at the shore, thou covetest the islands: having made the earth thine own, thou wouldest haply seize upon heaven.[36]

In a more irenic tone the African Father notes in the *City of God,* while describing the ends of the two cities, that in the earthly city the purpose of temporal goods is to enjoy earthly peace. While expositing the faith in one of his sermons on the Gospel of John, he contends that property is held by human right.[37]

Though open to private ownership, in accord with the Christian consensus that emerged in the early church and continued until the Middle Ages, Augustine rejects all usury.[38] The only acceptable usury in his view is to give to the poor, for then Christ repays more than we give.[39]

Regarding material goods, the African Father contends in the same spirit that their purpose is to meet the basic needs of human beings. When they become superfluous they are no longer rightly owned. Thus in his view not sharing this superfluity with the poor is equivalent to fraud.[40] In addition, Augustine advocates continuing the policy of offering sanctuary, especially for those in debt.[41]

Although the African Father does not advocate a government safety net for the poor, he does not reject a role for government in redistributing property that is possessed wrongfully. In one of his letters he writes:

> He who uses his wealth badly possesses it wrongfully, and wrongful possession means that it is another's property. . . . Yet, even here, we do not intercede to prevent restitution from being made according to earthly customs and laws.[42]

This commitment fits the African Father's general concern for the poor that he expresses from time to time, especially when exhorting the practice of the Christian life.[43]

In addition to these expressions of concern for the welfare of the poor, the African Father also decries rulers who are more concerned with magnificent mansions and provisions for actors than with the poor.[44] He is always lured by the monastic ideal of Christians sharing common property.[45]

Along similar lines, Augustine decries slavery, observing that it is full of bitterness.[46] The institution is not natural, he contends, but is a consequence of sin. Yet while asserting that sin is the primary cause of slavery, he insists that it does not befall humanity except by God's decree.[47]

Given the divine sanction he perceives, the African Father never condemns slavery. He even notes that the fathers in the faith had slaves, though he hastens to add that they dealt with their slaves as they did their own children. This point is in line with Augustine's consistent insistence on the gentle treatment of slaves.[48] In fact, he adds, in this context, it is better to be a slave of a person than a slave of passion.

To be sure, slavery is penal in character and imposed by the law that commands preservation of the natural order, Augustine observes. Noting that there would be no slavery had the Law of God not been broken, the African Father cites St. Paul's admonition to the slaves to obey their masters.[49] However, his final judgment on the evil institution is still that slavery is an ill befalling humankind.[50]

From this perspective it is noteworthy that the African Father laments the slave trade in Africa, in particular that many citizens were being kidnapped into slavery. Though not involved in the action himself, in a letter written in the 420s he notes with approval a raid of a slave ship led by several Christians in Hippo that liberated almost 120 of the enslaved.[51]

DOMESTIC LIFE

Augustine believes that the life of virtue is social or else the City of God could not make progress. Yet he also believes that due to sin, life in society has enormous drawbacks.[52] This cynicism leads him, when dialoguing with optimistic assessments of human capability by various philosophers, to a very realistic, almost pessimistic view of domestic life, an insight that can offer a healthy dose of realism as an antidote to naive expectations about marriage and one's partner. He writes:

> But who can enumerate all the great grievances with which human society abounds in the misery of this mortal state? Who can weigh them? . . . I am married; this is one misery. Children are born to me; they are additional cares. . . . Who ought to be, or who are more friendly than those who live in the same family? And yet who can rely even upon this friendship, seeing that secret treachery has often broken it up, and produced enmity?[53]

This realistic assessment of family life is typical of Augustine's views on marriage. As we would expect, there is some contextually conditioned variation in his thinking. Early in his career when engaged in apologetic dialogue with Greek philosophy he speaks of it as a barrier to spirituality.[54] He was still somewhat committed to the critical viewpoint in a controversy with the heretic Jovinian who had minimized celibacy. Augustine responded by arguing for the superiority of celibacy to marriage, contending that marriage is established only for those lacking the self-control needed for celibacy. For even in marriage, he asserts, lust and concupiscence characterize the relationship.

A somewhat different tone is evident in Augustine's dialogue with the Manichees. He offers Biblical and Apostolic authorization for the institution. Even in response to the Pelagians he refers to marriage as a natural good. In these contexts, though, he still deems marriage a lesser good.[55]

If the home offers no solid security, the city is full of legal battles, never secure from fear.[56] The family is the basis of society, Augustine contends. This leads him to conclude that in the family the father must apply certain principles of civil law to govern the home.[57]

We can observe some of these sentiments in Augustine's claim that it is a fundamental duty to look out for one's own family or home. The family arrangement, not domination, is what nature prescribes, he contends.[58]

For Augustine, procreation is the purpose of sexuality. (It is significant that he makes these points in dialogue with Pelagians, who sought to assert that there was no sin in sex and also when concerned to uphold the value of virginity along-side the married state.) Thus he opposes nonvaginal sexual activity, a stricture with broad consequences for subsequent sexual attitudes in Western society.[59]

This view of sexual expression leads the African Father to condemn abortion and even birth control in all circumstances.[60] When undertaken for its proper purpose prior to the Fall, sex was part of God's good creation, he contends. What is sinful about sex in Postlapsarian times is that it is undertaken without control.[61]

This stress on the social purpose of procreation is related to the African Father's contention that marriage has a social purpose. It leads to his view of marriage as the natural bond of human society.[62]

Augustine's relation to women has been a neuralgic subject. On one hand his youthful sexual proclivities, his relationship with a concubine, and his eventual dismissal of her in favor of the possibilities of arranging a "better" marriage, as well as his express denial of the validity of attributing female gender to God, seem to bespeak a rampant patriarchy. When instructing how to do catechesis he speaks of women's subordinate role to men in creation, as they are to imitate men in holiness.[63] Likewise while doing apologetics early in his career, the African Father identifies sexual lust as female and claims that because in Christ there is neither male nor female women also have some virile qualities with which they can subdue such feminine pleasures. In fact, in a sermon devoted to Christian living Augustine rails against double standards in favor of men regarding sexual promiscuity.[64] At other points too, the impact of his mother, Monica, on his life suggests a sensitivity to matriarchy, if not egalitarianism.

Some of the African Father's theological reflections are certainly women-friendly. Women, not just men, he insists, are created in the image of God. He makes this point in a context where the "image" refers to the rational mind wherein God can exist. And although at one point when engaged in polemics in his *Exposition of Genesis according to the Letter* he seems to posit women's intellectual inferiority to men (he did not do so in an earlier passing reference in the *Exposition* made while citing the logic of faith with apologetics in view), there are other clear indications that in Augustine's thinking women are rational, at least in principle as much as men are. This is also evident in his affirmations in several apologetic contexts that women, especially his mother, Monica, have a legitimate place in philosophical discussions.[65]

A similar commitment to sexual egalitarianism surfaces in *On Faith and the Creed* when he is expositing the faith. That Christ had Mary as His mother did honor to both sexes, Augustine asserted. Both had a part in God's care, not only that which He assumed but also the one through whom He assumed it. In his earlier treatise, *The Christian Combat*, while expositing faith's logic in response to heretics, he made a similar point in contending that Mary's role in giving birth to Jesus entailed that we were liberated through the agency of both sexes.[66]

Another example of Augustine's concern about women surfaces in his attitudes regarding rape. Women are still chaste if raped, he insists; chastity is not identical with bodily integrity. Perhaps with his own former lover in mind, he was willing to exonerate concubines who kept faith with their lover and remained celibate if left by the lover for another woman. And in a sermon on marriage he claims that women have equal rights as men concerning if and when to have sex.[67]

WAR AND PEACE

Given his realism about human life, it is hardly surprising that Augustine was no champion of pacifism, but instead the formulator of the Just War Theory in a Christian context. Consequently in the *City of God* the African Father refers to the fact that killing is not forbidden when waging war since the agent of authority is but a sword in the hand. (However, in his view suicide is forbidden.)[68] He refers to a just law to make the point about killing during war.[69] The Just War Theory seems to be in the background of these remarks.[70]

Augustine's Just War Theory is in fact indebted to the Roman philosopher Cicero. From him Augustine came to believe that war was justifiable only "when a people neglected either to punish wrongs done by its members or to restore what it had wrongly seized."[71]

There is a vagueness here about which Western society has debated ever since. Some have contended that this definition allowed for a war only to redress grievances by the injured party so that the status before the war could be restored. This interpretation would seem to allow for a war initiated in order to enhance the moral order of the international community as long as such a war were not found to serve selfish national interests. Elsewhere in the *City of God,* Augustine notes that a just war is necessitated only against the injustice of the aggressor, by the wrongdoing of the enemy. Yet even this war of self-defense is still a reality to lament. In that sense, and because exploitation or anxiety inevitably follow war, no war in Augustine's view can be entirely just.[72]

CONCLUSION

Some of Augustine's concrete social-ethical positions are clearly time bound and so of only historical interest. However, his economics may offer some useful perspectives on our present market dynamics. More relevant, the categories that modern theologians employ when trying to understand church-state relations and the theological suppositions for social ethics are all embedded in the African Father's thought, even though he himself never actually articulated fully blown reflections on the relationship between church and state. As in the case of the other classical doctrinal loci, the pattern in his thought for using each of the major alternatives may teach us some practical, pastoral lessons. From this pattern we might learn for which pastoral contexts each of the classical church-state formulations works best.

Conclusion

Toward an Ecumenical and Pastorally Sensitive Augustinianism

The diversity I have identified in Augustine's thought is not in itself a new insight. In 1886 the great Church Historian Philip Schaff noted the impact Augustine has had on a number of diverse movements—notably Roman Catholicism and Evangelical Protestantism. Then he wrote (referring to the African Father):

> In great men, and only in great men, great opposites and apparently antagonistic truths live together. Small minds cannot hold them. . . . Such a personage as Augustine, still holding a mediating place between the two great divisions of Christendom, revered alike by both, and of equal influence with both is furthermore a welcome pledge of the elevating prospect of a future reconciliation of Catholicism and Protestantism in a higher unity, conserving all the truths, losing all the errors, forgiving all the sins, forgetting all the enmities of both.[1]

There are exciting ecumenical implications in appreciating the richness of Augustine's thought.

I pointed out in chapter 2 that Augustine himself concedes this rich diversity in his thought. His comments noted there suggest a way of accounting for this diversity in a manner consistent with the findings and observations I have made on every one of the doctrines considered here. In *On the Spirit and the Letter,* he indicates that the rich diversity in his thought is Biblically rooted:

> Accordingly, as the Law is not made void, but is established through faith, since faith procures grace whereby the Law is fulfilled; so free will is not made void through grace, but is established, since grace cures the will whereby righteousness is freely loved. Now all the stages which I have here connected together in their successive links, have severally their proper voices in the sacred Scriptures.[2]

The great theologians who can hold together the great opposites and apparently antagonistic truths seem able to do this because of their superior insight into the Biblical witness, which holds these apparent contradictions together.

In his treatise *On the Gift of Perseverance,* as he tries to explain why he is emphasizing predestination against the Pelagians more than he had previously, the African Father provides a direct testimony to the contextual character of his thought:

> This is the manifest and assured predestination of the saints, which subsequently necessity compelled me more carefully and laboriously to defend when I was already disputing against the Pelagians. For I learnt that each special heresy introduced its own peculiar questions into the Church—against which the sacred Scripture might be more carefully defended than if no such necessity compelled their defence.[3]

Augustine clearly asserts here that new contexts led him to emphasize different points theologically. It is this point, the appreciation of the contextual character of his thought, that makes the analysis of his theology that you have been reading unique. What is particularly important is the identification of the pattern to his contextual approach.

Rereading the conclusion of each of the preceding chapters provides the best detailed summary of the patterns of Augustine's contextual approach. In this context, however, it is appropriate to offer some general comments on these patterns.

In examining these general characterizations of the patterns in Augustine's thought, one would do well to consider how Augustine treats two pastoral contexts in very different ways. The points he tends to make against Pelagianism or other times when he is defending the faith from legalistic distortions are almost the inverse of his characteristic construal of the classical doctrines when he is exhorting Christian living in face of sloth, comforting despair, or engaging in apologetics with the "cultured despisers" of the faith. In between these agendas is when he exhorts faith or merely lays out the logic of faith.

In other words, when engaged against legalism he is more concerned to stress dialectical relationships between the polar terms. For example, he stresses the dichotomy between divine work and human work in these contexts (so that it is clear that all good is God's Work, even to the point of denying human free will), he emphasizes the dialectical tension between divine wrath and divine love (manifest at times even in the affirmation of double predestination), and he endorses a corresponding view of the Atonement (the Satisfaction Theory, which posits the need for satisfaction of divine wrath). Other dialectical affirmations made in these contexts include: (1) the distinction between Law and Gospel (which entails that the Christian life is not guided by the Law) or nature and grace; (2) the distinction between the two cities (and so of church and state).

By contrast, when exhorting the practice of Christian living against sloth or engaging in apologetics, the African Father is less dialectical in his reflections, but is more inclined to present polar terms in harmony. Thus he gives more attention to the way in which God works through human beings, even to the point of affirming human freedom activated by grace at some points. Consequently, he never teaches unconditional predestination in these contexts (though occasionally when dealing with exhorting the Christian life he will teach a predestination contingent on divine foreknowledge, or when doing apologetics he suggests that divine election and the exercise of our freedom are simultaneous). He makes a more unambiguous affirmation of the loving nature of God (except in contexts of exhorting the practice of the Christian life, or when some concern for defending faith from Pelagian abuses is mixed with these other agendas, in which case the dialectical tension between divine wrath and divine love remains in place). He also endorses a corresponding view of the Atonement in these contexts: (1) the Satisfaction Theory, which posits the need for satisfaction of divine wrath, again appears when the divine essence is portrayed with wrath and grace in dialectical tension; and (2) the Moral Influence Theory is affirmed especially in contexts where he exhorts the Christian life and the distinction between divine work and human work is blurred.

When exhorting the Christian life especially preoccupies the African Father, he levels the dialectical tensions between Law and Gospel as well as the distinction between the two cities (and so of church and state). This entails that because the Law always accompanies the Gospel the Christian life is to be guided by the Law (the Third Use of the Law is embraced). Also this entails that the Gospel has direct influence on the affairs of state.

Note how in contexts that are somehow in between these extremes (when exhorting faith, merely describing the logic of faith, or undertaking these tasks with some concern about defending faith from legalistic propensities), Augustine presents these dialectical pairs in a mediating way, neither stressing their tensions nor diluting the dialectic. Thus we find him continuing clearly to distinguish divine work and human work—even denying free will, though not to the point of teaching double predestination. He would affirm something like single predestination (of God's electing responsibility only for salvation) in these contexts. Correspondingly he affirms more unambiguously the loving nature of God in these contexts, and endorses a related view of the Atonement (the classic view, which posits that a loving God is engaged in a struggle with the forces of evil that aim to work death and destruction to humanity). The dialectical construals of the Law-Gospel relationship and of the relations between the two cities (and so of church and state) are affirmed in these contexts.

I have noted that the African Father's approach to Biblical interpretation and Theological Method was contextually patterned, not just a consequence of development in his thought. When engaged in apologetics and when exhorting the Christian life in face of sloth he tends to interpret the Bible allegorically and to posit a synthesis of reason and faith. (Given the predominance of Greek philosophy in his lifetime, it is not surprising that Augustine's Anthropology and Eschatology have their clearest reliance on dualistic assumptions in these apologetic contexts.) But when exhorting faith or dealing with heresies, Augustine reads the Bible literally (even emphasizing the absolute truth of the Bible on all matters in polemical contexts). In these contexts the African Father poses a dialectic between reason and faith. By contrast he stresses the reason-faith synthesis more, to the point of claiming that even the Bible's literal sense was polysemous, when these concerns also include an apologetic agenda.

Regarding Augustine's position on the authority of Tradition, this too is a contextually patterned matter. Most of the time he consistently affirms its authority (especially the Rule of Faith) as an authoritative guide to Biblical interpretation. When dealing with heresy, however, the African Father tends to bypass Tradition in favor of appeals to Scripture alone.

With regard to the doctrines of Sin, Justification, Sanctification, Church, Ministry, Christology, and the Sacraments, Augustine's various construals follow the patterns previously noted. Those construals of these doctrines that most unambiguously assert the priority of divine action over human action appear when the African Father is refuting legalisms and when exhorting faith or describing the logic of faith. Consequently in these contexts the African Father affirms: (1) Justification by grace alone (a forensic view when refuting heresy, but also sometimes when exhorting Christian living, yet a construal of the doctrine in terms of a Union with Christ when exhorting faith); (2) Sanctification or Christian life is described as a gift, but still in terms of the Christian being mired in sin, with sin usually described as concupiscence; (3) Church and Ministry defined as God's act through human activities, with a high view of episcopal and priestly authority; and (4) the Sacraments construed as embodying the Real Bodily Presence of Christ. This entails the affirmation of an Alexandrian Christology in these contexts.

In contexts when Christian life is exhorted, by contrast we find the opposing construals of these doctrines. Thus he is sometimes inclined to regard concupiscence only as the means of sin, not sin itself, and in these contexts he even differentiates grades or kinds of sin. Likewise when addressing these concerns, the African Father is more inclined to refer to our salvation as a function of some form of divine-human cooperation, either referring to infused grace in the characteristic Roman Catholic mode or even hinting at the concept of salvation as *theosis*. He often teaches the possibility of growth in grace in these contexts.

Likewise, when exhorting Christian life is his preoccupation, Augustine defines the Church and Ministry more in terms of the behavior of the members and the officeholders, and minimizes the importance of affirming Christ's Real Presence in the Sacraments. Augustine typically characterizes Christ in Antiochene terms in these contexts, stressing the distinction between Jesus' Natures more than their unity.

AN ECUMENICAL PATTERN FOR PARISH MINISTRY?

It is my belief that these patterns of Christian thought do not just characterize Augustine's thought. We have already seen indications that characteristically Augustine's most famous interpreters lifted themes in his thought from documents when he himself was addressing issues akin to the contexts that preoccupied the interpreter. This indicates that the pattern in Augustine's thought for using Christian contexts may embody a truly catholic pattern.[4]

I previously noted my belief that this approach to interpreting Augustine can offer a new model for doing theology, not just in the Augustinian mode, but for ecumenical theology. The problem with much theology today is that it is perceived as irrelevant to the demands of everyday ministry. Pastors must address a wide variety of pastoral issues, and the dominant Systematic model of theology offers proposals geared to just one or two issues preoccupying the Systematician. Thus much contemporary theology, due to its dependence on Systematic models, is not flexible enough to address the full range of pastoral concerns that emerge from everyday life. Also the Systematic model does not offer guidance regarding when given doctrinal formulations are most helpful. The model I am proposing aims to overcome this deficiency. Not only does my way of reading Augustine provide today's church leaders with the wide range of diversity necessary to have options for every sort of pastoral concern that might emerge on their watch. In addition, this new paradigm for reading Augustine and other prominent leaders of the Church who like him employed an occasional, contextual theological approach provides today's pastors with guidance regarding when (for what pastoral purposes) each of the various theological formulations made available by the Augustinian heritage is best employed.[5]

The foregoing summary of the patterns in Augustine's thought also opens the way to another project, to determine whether this pattern can be of use in ministry today. Christian readers are invited to apply their common sense. Does it not make more sense to stress the Bible's literal sense in face of heresy, but to seek to bring Biblical insights into dialogue with reason (through an allegorical Method of Correlation) when engaging in apologetics? Likewise, does it not make more sense to stress individual responsibility, to affirm free will in some qualified sense and to exhort specific behaviors (the Law functioning as a guideline to Christian living) when encountering sloth? By contrast, would not a stronger emphasis on grace alone (to the point of teaching predestination) along with a stubborn unwillingness to prescribe specific works be the wisest way to respond to modern versions of Pelagianism? It is my suspicion that the viability of these ways of construing the Gospel for these particular contexts may be mandated or made normative by the way these conceptions were originally used in the Bible. After all, Augustine himself contended that some of the diversity in his thought was a function of the Bible giving voice to many distinct alternatives.[6]

This insight relates to an additional issue to tackle in the future, the question of whether there is a unity in the midst of this contextual diversity. Besides referring us to the Bible's own conceptual richness, the African Father provides another compelling suggestion in his treatise *On Christian Doctrine*:

> Of all, then, that has been said since we entered upon the discussion about things, this is the sum: That we should clearly understand that the fulfillment and the end of the Law, and of all Holy Scripture, is the love of an object which is to be enjoyed, and the love of an object which can enjoy that other in fellowship with ourselves. . . . Whoever, then, thinks that he understands the Holy Scriptures, or any part of them, but puts such an interpretation upon them as does not tend to build up this two-fold love of God and our neighbour, does not understand them as he ought.[7]

The diversity of the Biblical witness forms a unity in testifying to the love of God. If we consider the narratives of the loves in our lives, they are not always consistent, sometimes marked by apparent contradictions of birth and death, youth and age, tenderness and toughness, even of like and dislike. Yet these contradictions make sense in the context of the love of our loved ones and their love for us. Should we expect it to be any different when the story is about the divine lover? Among its other contributions, its celebration of diversity notwithstanding, my interpretation of Augustine as offering a pastorally sensitive, ecumenical, contextual approach to theology can also offer a model for Systematic Theology today.

APPENDIX
Charts Depicting the Patterns
in Augustine's Contextual Use
of Christian Concepts

CHAPTER TWO

Bible and Theological Method

Doctrinal Construal	Context of Use
*Allegorical Interpretation (seeking to relate the Word of God to a prior analysis of reality [often employing the concepts of Greek philosophy]) Modern theology's Method of Correlation	Apologetics Exhortation to Christian living Polemics against Manichees
*Dogmatic Method/literal interpretation 1. Insistence on the infallibility of Scripture Modern theology's Fundamentalism	Explaining the logic of Christian faith, while polemicizing against criticisms of Christianity Describing how one becomes a Christian while polemicizing against criticisms of Christianity
2. Merely concerned to subordinate reason, philosophy, and experience to the Word of God Must believe in order to understand Figural interpretation Modern theology's Narrative Theology	Exhorting faith Explaining the logic of Christian faith
*Literal interpretation, but with insistence on its polysemous meaning such that the Word transforms experience and is in turn interpreted in light of our experience Modern theology's Method of Critical Correlation	Exposition of the logic of faith, with some apologetic agenda

Chapter 2 (cont.)

Authority

Doctrinal Construal	*Context of Use*
*Scripture alone	Polemicizing against heretics
*Scripture and Tradition	When making ecclesiastical decisions
	Describing the logic of Christian faith
	Polemicizing against heretics like the Manichees who claim no value in Tradition

Relating Reason and Faith

Doctrinal Construal	*Context of Use*
*Continuity	Apologetics
	Exhortation to Christian living
*Dialectical Relationship	Polemics with heretics and critics of Christianity

CHAPTER THREE

God/Trinity/Christology

Doctrinal Construal	Context of Use
*Divine wrath and divine love in dialectical tension	Exhortation to Christian living
	Polemics with Pelagianism
*Divine wrath and love are only functions of how we perceive the unchanging God	Apologetics and eschatological inquiries
	Comforting despair
*Unambiguously loving in nature (subordinating divine wrath to love)	Exhorting faith and explaining the logic of Christian faith
	Describing the Christian life
	Comforting despair

Proofs of God's Existence

Doctrinal Construal	Context of Use
*Cosmological Argument	Apologetics
*Ontological Argument	Response to Manichee attacks on Biblical authority

Chapter 3 (cont.)

Christology

Doctrinal Construal	*Context of Use*
*Alexandrian Christology (stressing unity of the Two Natures)	Expositing the logic of faith
	Dialogue with Arians and Manichees
*Antiochene Christology (stressing the distinction of the Christ's Two Natures)	Apologetics
	Polemics
	Exhortation to Christian living
	Considering the Last Judgment

Holy Spirit

Doctrinal Construal	*Context of Use*
*Spirit cooperates with us in doing good	Exhortation to Christian living
*All good is the work of the Spirit	Refuting Pelagianism
	Explicating the logic of faith

CHAPTER FOUR

Creation and Providence

Doctrinal Construal	Context of Use
*All that happens in the world is the Work of God	Critiquing sloth and Pelagianism
	Comforting despair coupled with polemics
	Reflection on own spiritual pilgrimage and history of the world
*God does not compel all that happens. Humans or the devil responsible for evil (God may permit the evil)	Exhorting Christian living
	Critiquing Manichee (though determinism)
	Apologetics
	Comforting despair
	Critiquing Pelagianism, with some exhortation to faith
*God sets all in motion. Reality proceeds according to its own beat, but nothing proceeds without ongoing divine regulation	Exposition of faith, apologetics, and response to Pelagian-like critiques
*God creates all that is good, but human beings or the devil have distorted some of this goodness. God works through us in creating good	Depicting the logic of faith or exhorting faith
	Exhorting Christian living with Pelagianism in view

Chapter 4 (cont.)

Anthropology

Doctrinal Construal	Context of Use
*Dualistic view of human nature	Apologetics
	Exhortation combined with apologetics
	Comforting despair
*Holistic view of human nature	Explicating the logic of Christian faith
	Exhorting faith
	Criticizing the Manichee devaluation of the body

Creation-Redemption Relationship

Doctrinal Construal	Context of Use
*Posits a continuity between creation and redemption (between Law and Gospel, nature and grace)	Outlining the logic of faith from an eschatological viewpoint
	Comforting despair
	Exhorting faith
	Softer polemics
*Posits a dialectical relation between creation and redemption	Engaging in polemics (esp. against all forms of legalism)

CHAPTER FIVE

Sin, Free Will, and Atonement

Doctrinal Construal	Context of Use
*Image of God in humanity lost in sin	Exhortation to faith
*Image of God only damaged by sin	Apologetics

Free Will

Doctrinal Construal	Context of Use
*Affirms free will; sin said to be voluntary	Polemics with Manichee determinism
	Apologetics
	Exhortation to Christian living
*Humans in bondage to sin (though still responsible for it)	Polemics against Pelagianism
	Articulating the logic of faith

Chapter 5 (cont.)

Sin

Doctrinal Construal	Context of Use
*Sin identified as concupiscence	Explicating the logic of faith
	Polemics against Pelagianism
*Concupiscence only a root of sin or a consequence of the Fall	Exhorting Christian living
*Concupiscence no longer sin after regeneration	Exhorting Christian living
*Distinguishes venial and mortal	Exhorting Christian living
sins	Comforting despair

Atonement

Doctrinal Construal	Context of Use
*Christ redeems by conquering forces of evil and death	Explicating the logic of faith Comforting despair
*Christ satisfies wrath of God	Exhorting Christian living
*Christ offers a model for influencing the life of faith	Exhorting Christian living Critiquing works righteousness
	Apologetics

CHAPTER SIX

Salvation, the Christian Life, and Predestination

Doctrinal Construal	Context of Use
*Justification as the declaration of the believer's righteousness, by grace alone (forensic justification)	Polemics with Pelagian works righteousness
	Exhorting Christian life with Apologetics, polemics, and eschatology in view
*Justification as Conformity to Christ	Exhortation to faith
	Depicting the logic of faith
	Critiquing Pelagian works righteousness combined with the above
	Comforting the despairing
*Justification as deification/*theosis*	Exhortation to Christian living, sometimes along with an apologetic agenda
	Perhaps when comforting despair or even when explaining the logic of faith
*Justification as the result of grace and the good works it inspires	Exhortation to Christian living in face of moral laxity and Manichee determinism
	Apologetics
*Believers must prepare themselves for the grace they receive	Apologetics and some anti-Manichee contexts, when defending God from charges of covering evil

Chapter 6 (cont.)

Faith

Doctrinal Construal	Context of Use
*Faith as a human work	Polemics with Manichee determinism
	Exhortation to Christian life
*Faith as God's Work (working through the human will)	Almost every other context

Predestination

Doctrinal Construal	Context of Use
*Based on divine foreknowledge	Exhorting Christian responsibility
	Polemics with Manichees and Stoic determinism
	Apologetics
*Unconditional double predestination	Polemics with Pelagianism
	Addressing the unwarranted claims of reason
*Unconditional single predestination	Explicating the logic of faith
	Polemics with Pelagianism while still defending God's goodness
	Comforting despair
*Possibility of salvation of all	Rejected in all contexts except the explication of faith and polemics with Pelagianism
*Neglect of predestination	Exhortation to faith
	Exhortation to Christian living

Chapter 6 (cont.)

Sanctification and the Christian Life

Doctrinal Construal	Context of Use
*Christian as simultaneously saint and sinner (*totus-totus*)	Exhorting faith (often with Pelagianism in view)
	Polemics with Donatism
*Christian life is hidden (not clearly observable)	Apologetics
	Exhorting Christian living
	Explicating the logic of faith
*Situational ethic, with no reference to the Law as a guide to Christian life	Apologetics
	Expositing the faith
	Comforting anxiety and despair
*Spontaneity of good works	Expositing the logic of faith
	Polemics with Pelagianism, Donatism, and Manicheism
*Law of God to be preached in order to guide Christian living	Exhortation to Christian living (sometimes with apologetics)
	Comforting despair
	Defending the value of God's Law
*Posits the possibility of growth in grace (albeit while still partly a a sinner). Perseverance deemed a mark of certainty of one's salvation	Exhorting Christian living (sometimes with apologetics in view)
	Critiquing Manichee determinism
	Describing the spiritual pilgrimage
	Concerned with evangelism
*Posits the possibility of perfection	Exhorting Christian living
	Polemics with Manichee determinism
*Does not care to express a definite position on perfection. Other times in this context, rejects the possibility of perfection	Polemics with Pelagian works righteousness

CHAPTER SEVEN

Church and Ministry

Doctrinal Construal	Context of Use
*Church as a Work of God, defined objectively (as Mother of all Christians, Body of Christ, etc.) rather than in terms of members and their faith	Exhorting faith
	Explicating the logic of faith and Christian nurture
	Polemics (esp. with Donatism) Apologetics
	Comforting despair
*Church defined as the people (its members) —Posits the exercise of discipline on the membership	Explicating the Christian life or eschatology

Ministry

Doctrinal Construal	Context of Use
*Objective view of the office Authority not a function of the clergy's spirituality Minister exercises authority over the laity	Polemics against heresies Exhortation to faith
*Ministry defined in terms of behavior or spirituality of the officeholder	Exhortation to Christian living or dispensing advice to ministers
*Supports Apostolic Succession and episcopal authority	Polemics against Donatism
*Authority of papacy affirmed	Polemics against heresies
*Priesthood of all believers	Exhortation to Christian living

CHAPTER EIGHT

Sacraments

Doctrinal Construal	Context of Use
*Baptismal regeneration	Polemics with Donatism
	Expositing the logic of faith
*Sin cleansed in Baptism	Exhorting Christian living
*Though regenerated in Baptism, sin remains	Polemics with Pelagianism
*Must be baptized in order to be saved	Polemics with those engaged in rational speculation
*Open to the hope of salvation for the unbaptized	Explicating the logic of faith
	Polemics with Pelagians and Donatists

The Lord's Supper

Doctrinal Construal	Context of Use
*Christ Really Present in the Communion elements	Explicating the logic of faith
*Sacrament a "sign" (like John Calvin, Anglicanism, Methodism)	Defending faith from rational critiques
	Defending the practice of Christian living
*Christ's Body in the Sacrament only a "mystical Word"	Apologetics
*A Sacrifice, in the sense of the Church offering a sacrifice	Concern with the nature of Christian life
*A Sacrifice only in the sense that Christ is Present in the Sacrament	Exhorting faith

CHAPTER NINE

Eschatology

Doctrinal Construal	Context of Use
*Future eschatology	
—Those with faith are saved. Even keeps open the possibility that others are saved	Explicating the logic of faith Polemics with Pelagianism
—The dead judged (rewarded) by works done with grace	Exhortation to Christian living Apologetics Comforting despair
—Purgatorial fire provides opportunity for the dead to be benefited by acts of faith of the living	Exhortation to Christian living Apologetics
—Bodily resurrection	Most contexts
—Raised with a spiritual body	Responding to critics of Christianity Exhorting Christian life Comforting despair
—Millennial speculations	Exhorting Christian living; polemics with Manichees
—Rapture	Apologetics and critiquing speculation
—Millennium refers only to the history of the Church	Depicting the logic of faith
*Realized eschatology	Responding to speculations about the End Expositing the logic of faith

CHAPTER TEN

Social Ethics: The Two Cities

Doctrinal Construal	Context of Use
*Church and state in paradoxical tension	Articulating a Christian vision of world history
—Natural law the criterion for political judgments	Explicating the logic of faith
	Critiquing Pelagianism and Manicheism
*Christian principles govern the state	Responding to charges that Christianity is detrimental to society
	Addressing ecclesiastical disruptions
	Apologetics
	Exhorting Christian living

Notes

The publisher has requested that English translation citations of Augustine's works be provided. Sufficient information on the book, chapter, and section of each work cited is provided to enable scholars to identify the original Latin text. The Latin is provided in the notes for important quotations I have offered.

Introduction

1. It should be noted that this book is a conceptual study, and so is not to be regarded in the strictest sense as an historical analysis of Augustine's thought. Before proceeding further, I must offer a definition of what I mean by the "context" of Augustine's thought. The concern for the context does not obligate me to portray the full chronological development of his thought or to acknowledge every one of his intellectual debts. Of course, these historical factors must be considered to some extent, in order to avoid anachronistic interpretation. Nevertheless, my concern is not so much with Augustine's intellectual (or even his emotional) psyche as it is with a purely conceptual study of the theological concerns he had in view in deploying the various images that pertain to his theological convictions. To this end I will ask Augustine to be his own interpreter, allowing him to identify for us the concerns that he had in view. Or when failing to receive explicit clarification, I will try to surmise, on the basis of what he did say, his instructions for determining the purpose for which a given Christian image may be used.

    No exhaustive study of historical antecedents will be necessary. For "context" here refers to "literary context," an interpretive decision that should distort neither Augustine's thought nor his true intentions behind any veil of "formalism." The occasional nature of Augustine's treatises should entail that the literary context adequately reveals the historical and psychological context as well. The texts are the only legitimate access anyone has to Augustine and his world of concerns.

2. Martin Luther, *Lectures on Romans* (1515–1516), in *D. Martin Luthers Werke*, Kritische Gesamtausgabe (Weimarer Ausgabe) (56 vols.; Weimar: Hermann Bohlaus Nachfolger, 1883ff.), Vol. 56, pp. 171f. [English translation: *Luther's Works: American Edition*, ed. Jaroslav Pelikan and Helmut Lehmann (54 vols.; St.

Louis and Philadelphia: Concordia Publishing House and Fortress Press, 1955ff.), Vol. 25, p. 153]; Martin Luther, *De servo arbitrio* (1526), in *D. Martin Luthers Werke*, Vol. 18, pp. 640, 630 [*Luther's Works*, Vol. 33, pp. 72, 58]; Martin Luther, *Sermons on the Gospel of St. John* (1540), in *D. Martin Luthers Werke*, Vol. 47, pp. 216–17 [*Luther's Works*, Vol. 22, p. 512]; John Calvin, *The Necessity of Reforming the Church* (1543), in *Corpus Reformatorum* (Brunsvigae: C. A. Schwetschke et Filium, 1867), Vol. 34, p. 483.

3. Reinhold Niebuhr, *Christian Realism and Political Problems* (New York: Charles Scribner Sons, 1953), pp. 119–46; Garry Wills, *Saint Augustine* (New York: Viking, 1999), pp. 119–21.

4. Council of Trent, *Decree Concerning Justification* (1547), XI.

5. *Catechism of the Catholic Church* (1994), 1372, 1396.

6. Martin Luther, *Lectures on Romans* (1515–1516), in *D. Martin Luthers Werke*, Vol. 56, p. 356 [*Luther's Works*, Vol. 25, p. 345].

7. Martin Luther, *Temporal Authority: To What Extent It Should Be Obeyed* (1523), in *D. Martin Luthers Werke*, Vol. 11, pp. 263–264, 280 [*Luther's Works*, Vol. 45, pp. 107–08, 129].

8. Martin Luther, *That These Words of Christ, "This Is My Body," Etc., Still Stand Firm against the Fanatics* (1527), in *D. Martin Luthers Werke*, Vol. 23, pp. 209–12, 242–43 [*Luther's Works*, Vol. 37, pp. 104–06, 123–24].

9. John Calvin, *Institutes of the Christian Religion* (1559), IV.XVII.32, 33; III.XXIV.13.

10. Heinrich Bullinger, *Second Helvetic Confession* (1566), X (5.058), XII (5.085).

11. John Wesley, *The Doctrine of Salvation, Faith and Good Works, Extracted from the Homilies of the Church of England* (1738), in *John Wesley*, ed. Albert Outler (New York: Oxford University Press, 1964), p. 131.

12. Paul Tillich, *Systematic Theology*, Vol. 1 (3 vols. in 1; Chicago: University of Chicago Press, 1967), p. 62.

13. Thomas Aquinas, *Summa Contra Gentiles* (1259–1264), 1.7.6.

14. Karl Barth, *Church Dogmatics*, Vol. I/1, trans. G. T. Thomson (Edinburgh: T. & T. Clark, 1936), pp. 89, 282.

15. Paul Ricoeur, *The Conflict of Interpretations,* ed. Don Ihde (Evanston, IL: Northwestern University Press, 1974), pp. 4, 60.

Chapter 1: The African Augustine and His Context

1. Although today the Berbers closely resemble Arabs in custom, language, and appearance in most of the African regions in which they dwell, Berbers residing in Algeria to this day are Black. See Wilton Marion Krogman, "Berber," *World Book Encyclopedia,* vol. 2 (Chicago: Field Enterprises Educational Corporation, 1961), p. 200. For an example of an alternative construal of Berber ethnicity (and thereby rendering Augustine less African, more of a Moor), see Jacques Chabannes, *St. Augustine,* trans. Julie Kernan (Garden City, NY: Doubleday & Co., 1962), pp. 14–15, who claims that Berbers had intermarried with the Phoenicians prior to Augustine's lifetime. But this claim seems unsubstantiated.

2. *Conf.* II.III.5/*NPNF* 1:56.

3. For example, see Augustine, *Ep.* LXXXIV (405).2/*NPNF* 1:364.

4. This characterization of the African attitudes of the Maghrib is based on analyses of ancient tombstone inscriptions of the era in G. Charles Picard, *La civilisation de l'Afrique romaine* (Paris: Plon, 1959), especially pp. 249–54.

5. *Conf.* IX.IX.19/*NPNF* 1:136.

6. Ibid., V.VIII.14; I.IX.15/84, 49.

7. See Kim Power, "Family, Relatives," in *Augustine through the Ages: An Encyclopedia,* ed. Allan D. Fitzgerald (Grand Rapids: Eerdmans, 1999), p. 352.

8. *Ep.* XVI (390)/*NPNF* 1:233.

9. *Ep.* XVI (390).2/234: "Neque enim usque adeo teipsum oblivisci potuisses, ut homo Afer scribens Afris, cum simus utrique in Africa constituti, Punica nomina exagitanda existimares."

10. Ibid.: "Quae lingua si improbatur abs te, nega Punicis libris, ut a viris doctissimus prodifur, multa sapienter esse mandata memoriae Poenitea te certe ibi natum, ubi hujus linguae cunabula recalent."

    See *S. Dom. mon.* II.XIV–47/*NPNF* 6:49.

11. H. Basset, "Les Influences puniques chez les Berberes," *Revue Africaine,* lxii (1921): 340–75, a conclusion based on the fact that while there are a few Latin loanwords in modern Berber, there are no Punic loanwords in modern Berber. The dearth of loanwords in a language suggests that it (in this case ancient Berber) was not displaced by Punic. Similarly, W. H. C. Frend, "A Note on the Berber Background in the Life of Augustine," *Journal of Theological Studies* 43 (1942): 188–94, noted that archaeological excavations of graves in the region where Augustine resided indicates that Libyan (an ancestor of the modern Berber tongue) was used more widely than Latin or even Punic.

    Indirectly Augustine seems to confirm this observation in *Civ.* XVI.6/*NPNF* 2:314, as he notes how many diverse people in his region spoke but one language (presumably the ancestor of Berber), for he refers to these Africans as "barbaras gentes." The key question is whether this phrase should be translated as "barbarous nations," as has been the norm, or as "Berber people," which seems equally valid. In that case we can conclude that most of the "Punics" about whom Augustine spoke were Berbers.

12. W. H. C. Frend, *The Donatist Church: A Movement of Protest in Roman North Africa* (Oxford: Clarendon Press, 1952), esp. pp. 211–12, 335; Peter Brown, *Augustine of Hippo: A Biography* (Berkeley and Los Angeles: University of California Press, 1969), p. 220; Elizabeth Isichei, *A History of Christianity in Africa* (Grand Rapids: Eerdmans; Lawrenceville, NJ: Africa World Press, 1995), pp. 36–37.

13. *Ep. Joh.* II.3/*NPNF* 7:470: "Isti autem qui multum amant Christum, sic honorant Christum, ut dicant illum remanisse ed duas linguas, latinam, et punicam, it est afram."

14. For these insights see Garry Wills, *Saint Augustine* (New York: Viking, 1999), p. 2; Brown, *Augustine of Hippo,* pp. 32–33. T. Kermit Scott, *Augustine: His Thought in Context* (Mahwah, NJ: Paulist Press, 1995), p. 64, adds that the significance of "Adeodatus" is found in its Latin form "Iatanbaal," since Berbers sought names for their children that included the name of the god Baal.

15. Several scholars have concluded that Monica may have had both a Berber and a Donatist background. See Wills, *Saint Augustine,* p. 2; Frend, *Donatist Church,* pp. 186, 230. Some scholars, like Warren Thomas Smith, *Augustine: His Life and Thought* (Atlanta: John Knox Press, 1980), p. 9, and Chabannes, *St. Augustine,* p. 9, have contended that Patricius was Berber or Moor (of mixed Arab-Berber background). But the evidence does not substantiate this claim.

    Augustine himself notes the predominance of Donatism in his hometown of Thagaste. See *Ep.* XCIII (408).V.17/*NPNF* 1:388.

16. *Jul. op. imp.* VI.XVIII: "Noli istum Poenum monentem vel admonentem terra inflatus propagine spernere. Non enim quia te Apulai genuit, ideo Poenos vincendos extimes gente."

17. *Conf.* VI.IV.6–V.7; VIII.II.3/*NPNF* 1:92–93, 117.

Chapter 2: Bible and Theological Method

1. Perhaps the most influential identification of this version of the Augustinian synthesis was offered by Etienne Gilson, *Reason and Revelation in the Middle Ages* (New York: Charles Scribner's Sons, 1938), pp. 16–18. For Augustine's insistence on the relation of reason and faith, see *Doctr. Christ.* 2.12.17/*NPNF* 2:540; *Vera relig.* xxiv.45/*LCC* 247; *Praed. sanct.* 2.5/*NPNF* 5:499–500. Also see *Ep.* (c. 410) 120.3/*FC* 18:303ff. In *Conf.* III.IV-IV.V/*NPNF* 1:61–71, he describes his pilgrimage.

2. Thomas Aquinas, *Summa Theologica* (1265–1272), 1a, q.1, a.10. Aquinas's agenda in this classic work as a whole, to train beginners (foreword) and to build up and shape the advanced as well as those beginning (ibid.), is a concern with sanctification, which is one of the purposes for which Augustine employed this hermeneutic. In the section of the *Summa Theologica* in which he expressly embraces the allegorical approach with authorization from Augustine, the Scholastic Doctor was engaged in dialogue with faith's validity in face of reason (1a, q.1, a.1), an apologetic agenda similar to the purposes of the African Father. Also see Thomas Aquinas, *Summa Contra Gentiles* (1259–1264), I.7.

3. The paradigm for this approach has been Friedrich Schleiermacher, *Der christliche Glaube* (1830), 4, 15–16. Also see Paul Tillich, *Systematic Theology*, vol. 1 (3 vols. in one; Chicago: University of Chicago Press, 1951–1963), pp. 3–8, 59–66, and much Feminist Theology, for example, Mary Daly, *Beyond God the Father: Toward a Philosophy of Women's Liberation* (Boston: Beacon, 1973), pp. 28, 81.

4. Karl Barth, "The Strange New World Within the Bible," in *The Word of God and the Word of Man*, trans. Douglas Horton (repr., New York: Harper & Row, 1957), pp. 28ff.; and Hans Frei, *The Eclipse of Biblical Narrative* (New Haven, CT: Yale University Press, 1974), pp. 1–3.

5. *Conf.* III.IV.9/*NPNF* 1:62.

6. Ibid., VII.XX.26/113–14.

7. Ibid., VI.V.8/93.

8. *Trin.* I.1.2/*NPNF* 3:18.

9. *Conf.* VI.IV.6; V.XIV.24/*NPNF* 1:92, 88.

10. Ibid., IV.XII.19; VII.XVIII.24/74, 112.

11. For evidence that the letter-spirit did not always employ allegorical interpretation of Scripture for Ambrose, see his *De Abraham libri duo* (n.d.) 1. Also he broke with most allegorists in prioritizing faith over reason (ibid., 1.3.2).

12. *Vera relig.* ii.2–iii.3/*LCC* 225–27.

13. *Retrac.* I.xii.3/*FC* 60:52.

14. *Util. cred.* vii.14/*NPNF* 3:354; ibid., i.2/348; *Solilq.* I.12–14/*NPNF* 7:541–42.

15. *Vera relig.* xlii.79, iv.6; ii.2–iii.4; iv.6–iv.7/*LCC* 226–29, 266; *Nat. bon.* 24/*NPNF* 4:356; *Ep.* CXXXVII (412).18/*NPNF* 1:480.

16. *Civ.* VII.29; VIII.9/*NPNF* 2:139, 150; *Solilq.* I.9/*NPNF* 7:540; *Trin.* XV.2.2/*NPNF* 3:199.

17. *Ep.* CXXXVII (412).V.17/*NPNF* 1:480.

18. *Trin.* XV.4.6/*NPNF* 3:202; cf. *Conf.* X.VI.8/*NPNF* 1:144.

19. *De lib. arbit.* III.xxiii.70/*LCC* 212–13.

20. *Conf.* X.XXV.36–X.XXVI.37/*NPNF* 1:152; see ibid., X.VII.11; X.XVII.26.8/145, 149, for the context.

21. *Vera relig.* xxx, 56–xxxi, 578/*LCC* 253–54; cf. *Trin.* VIII.3.4–5/*NPNF* 3:117–18.

22. *Faust.* XXII.93–95/*NPNF* 4:310–11.

23. *Vera relig.* xvii.33/*LCC* 240–41; cf. l.99/275–76.

24. *Retrac.* I, xiii.13/*FC* 60:58.
25. *Util. cred.* iii.5/*NPNF* 3:349: "Omnis igitur Scriptura, quae Testamentum Vetus vocatur, diligenter eam nosse cupientibus quadrifaria traditur; secundum historiam; secundum aetiologiam; secundum analogiam; secundum allegoriam. . . . Secundum historiam ergo traditur, cum docetur quid scriptum aut quid gestum sit; quid non gestum, sed tantummodo scriptum quasi gestum sit. Secundum aetologiam, cum ostenditur quid qua de causa vel factum vel dictum sit. Secundum analogiam, cum demonstratur non sibi adverari duo Testamenta, Vetus et Novum. Secundum allegoriam, cum docetur non ad literam esse accipienda quaedam quae scripta sunt, sed figurate intelligenda." Cf. *Gen. litt. imp.* 2.5; 1.1/*WSA* I/13:116, 114.
26. *Util. cred.* vii.17/*NPNF* 3:355.
27. *Conf.* XIII.XXIV.37/*NPNF* 1:202–3. See ibid., XIII.XXII.32/201, for the context.
28. *Doctr. Christ.* III.12.18; III.22.32/*NPNF* 2:561–62, 565. See ibid., III.10.14/560–61; *Ep.* LV (400).XI.20–XII.22/*NPNF* 1:309–10.
29. *Serm.* XCIX [XLIX] (411–412)/*NPNF* 6:415–20.
30. *Doctr. Christ.* III.16.24/*NPNF* 2:563.
31. *Serm.* LXXXIX [XXXIX] (397).4–7/*NPNF* 6:390–92.
32. *Civ.* I.28; XIII.18–20; XIV.11/*NPNF* 2:18–19, 254–56, 271.
33. Ibid., XIII.21/256.
34. Ibid., XVII.3/338–39.
35. *Ep.* XCIII (408).VIII.24/*NPNF* 1:391.
36. Primary modern proponents of this hermeneutic include David Tracy, *Blessed Rage for Order* (New York: Seabury, 1978); and Karl Rahner, *Theological Investigations*, vol. 9 (New York: Crossroad, 1972), pp. 28–33.
37. *Trin.* VIII.4.6; VIII.7.101; VII.6.12/*NPNF* 3:118, 114; cf. *Ev. Joh.* XXVII.9; XXIX.6/*NPNF* 7:176–77, 184–85; *Ep. Joh.* II.8/*NPNF* 7:472. This is an affirmation Augustine made in a more apologetic context in *Conf.* XII.XV.19/*NPNF* 1:180.
38. *Trin.* X.1.1, 3/*NPNF* 3:134.
39. Ibid., X.3.5/136–37.
40. Ibid., VIII.4.7/118–19.
41. Ibid., VIII.5.8; VIII.7.10–VIII.9.13/119–20, 122–24.
42. *Ep.* XXXIV (396).6/*NPNF* 1:263.
43. *Faust.* XXXIII.6/*NPNF* 4:343; *Civ.* XV.23/*NPNF* 2:305. For references to divine inspiration, see *Trin.* XV.17.27–XV.19.33/*NPNF* 3:215–17; *De lib. arbit.* III.xxi.62/*LCC* 208; *Util. cred.* vi.13/*NPNF* 3:252; *Conf.* XII.XXX.41; XII.IX.9/*NPNF* 1:188, 178; *Nat. et grat.* XX.22/*NPNF* 5:128; *Gr. et lib. arb.* XX.41/*NPNF* 5:461; *Civ.* XVI.2; XVIII.38; XX.1/*NPNF* 2:310, 383, 421; *Cons. ev.* I.XXXV.54/*NPNF* 6:101; *Gen. ad litt.* V.8.23/*WSA* I/13:287.
44. *Enchir.* 4/*NPNF* 3:238.
45. *Civ.* XI.6/*NPNF* 2:208: "Porro si litterae sacrae maximeque ueraces ita dicunt, in principio fecisse Deum caelum et terram, ut nihil antea fecisse diceretur." Cf. ibid., XI.1/205; *Ep.* XXVIII (c. 394).III.3/*NPNF* 1:252; ibid. XL (397).III-3/273).
46. *Fid. et symb.* X.24/*NPNF* 3:332. The context for this text is the exposition of faith. Addressing those who believe there is no damnation, Augustine claims that Scripture deceives no one, in *Civ.* XXI.23/*NPNF* 2:469 (see ibid., XXI.19–20/467, for the context).
47. *Ep.* (405), LXXXII.I.3, III.24/*NPNF* 1:350, 358.
48. *Virg.* 17, 20/*NPNF* 3:422, 423; *Faust.* XI.5/*NPNF* 4:180; *Pecc. merit.* I.XXIII.33/*NPNF* 5:28.

49. *Civ.* XII.10/*NPNF* 2:252–53.
50. *Conf.* VI.V.7, 8/*NPNF* 1:92–93; cf. *Retrac.* I.3 (2)/*FC* 60:14. A similar argument is made while refuting Manichee critiques of Biblical authority in *Faust.* XXXIII.19/*NPNF* 4:339.
51. *Conf.* XII.I.1/*NPNF* 1:176; *Civ.* XI.4/*NPNF* 2:206; *Ps.* LX[LIX].1/*NPNF* 8:244.
52. This point has been made by Peter Brown, *Augustine of Hippo* (Berkeley and Los Angeles: University of California Press, 1969), p. 263. For a good example of this sort of use of the Biblical narrative in *City of God*, see I.13–14/*NPNF* 2:10.
53. *Serm.* XCIX [XLIX] (411–412).1/*NPNF* 6:415–16: "Evangelium enim cum legeretur, alttentissime audistis, et res gesta narrate atque versata est ante occulos cordis vestri."
54. *Util. cred.* ix.22/*NPNF* 3:357: "Sed quaeris fortasse vel de hoc ipso aliquam accipere rationem, qua tibi persuadeatur, non prius ratione quam fide te esse docendum. Quod facile potest, si modo aequum te praebeas."
    The quotation emerges from a context in a polemicizing against heretics who begin with reason. Cf. ibid. ix.21/*NPNF* 3:356–57.
    Also see *Fid. et symb.* I.1/*NPNF* 3:321. Its context is the exposition of The Creed. When expositing faith Augustine contends that we must believe in order to understand (*Trin.* XV.2/*NPNF* 3:200; *De lib. arb.* I.II.4; II.2.16/*LCC* 115, 137; *Symb. cat.* 4/*NPNF* 3:370).
    He also claims in *Trin.* VIII.5.8; XV.27.50/*NPNF* 3:119, 227, and in *Ev. Joh.* XXVII.9; XXIX.6/*NPNF* 7:176, 184, that before we can understand, we must believe. In *Trin.* I.2.4; XV.24.44/*NPNF* 3:19, 223, he also asserts that we cannot know the Trinity apart from faith, because it purifies the heart. Cf. *Serm.* 43 (c. 400).7, 9./*WSA* III/2:241, 242–43.
55. *Util. cred.* xii.26/*NPNF* 3:360; *Fid. et symb.* ix.20/*NPNF* 3:330, 331; *Trin.* XV.27.49; XV.28.51/*NPNF* 3:226, 227–28.
56. *De lib. arb.* I.i.1–I.iv.10; II.v.11; II.vi.14; I.xv.39/*LCC* 113–17, 141–42, 144, 159–60.
57. *Nat. bon.* xxiv/*NPNF* 4:356: "Haec quae nostra fides habet, et utcumque ratio vestigavit, divinarum Scripturarum testimoniis munienda sunt: ut qui ea minore intellectu assequi non possunt, divinae auctoritati credant, et ob hoc intelligere mereantur." Cf. *Ep.* CXXXVII (412).V.18/*NPNF* 1:480.
58. *Praed. sanct.* II.5/*NPNF* 5:499–500.
59. *Enchir.* 2/*NPNF* 3:237; cf. *Doctr. Christ.* II.39.58/*NPNF* 2:553.
60. *Enchir.* 4–5/*NPNF* 3:238.
61. *Util. cred.* xi.25; ix.22; xiii.28–29; xiv.30–31; xv.33/*NPNF* 3:358–60, 357, 361–62, 363. Augustine also makes this point in x.24/358, on behalf of the prioritizing of faith over reason that only a few can know God by reason, and that it would be wrong to deny a person who desires real truth though is not rationally equipped. See vii.20–ix.22/356–57, for the context of these passages. For another discussion of how we learn from the eternal wisdom of God who dwells in us, see *Mag.* x.35; xi.36, 38; xiv.46/*LCC* 94, 95, 100–101.
62. *Vera relig.* xxiv.45/*LCC* 247. See i.1; xiff.; xxiv.45/225, 235ff., 247, for the various contexts.
63. *Nat. bon.* xxiv/*NPNF* 4:356.
64. *Civ.* VII.29; VIII.9ff.; XXII.22, 26–28/*NPNF* 2:139, 150ff., 505–7.
65. Ibid., XI.2; VIII.10/205–6, 150–51.
66. *Doctr. Christ.* II.40.60/*NPNF* 2:554.
67. *Spir. et litt.* XII.19/*NPNF* 5:91; cf. *Serm.* CXLI [XCI] (n.d.).1–2/*NPNF* 6:531.

68. *Civ.* VIII.11/*NPNF* 2:151–52. For earlier affirmations of Plato's direct dependence on the Bible, see *Doctr. Christ.* II.28.43/*NPNF* 2:549.
69. *Civ.* XVIII.37, 39–40/*NPNF* 2:382–84.
70. Ibid., XXII.5/481–82.
71. *Serm.* LI [I] (c. 400).5/*NPNF* 6:247. A similar claim seems to be made in *Util. cred.* vi.13/*NPNF* 3:353–54; when writing against the Manichees Augustine claims that we cannot derive satisfaction from any book, including the Bible, unless we love it.
72. *Doctr. Christ.* II.41.62/*NPNF* 2:555. For Luther's Theology of the Cross, see *Dispututio Heidelbergae habita* (1518), *D. Martin Luthers Werke,* Kritische Gesamtausgabe (Weimarer Ausgabe) (56 vols.; Weimar: Hermann Bohlaus Nachfolger, 1883ff), vol. 1, pp. 353–74.
73. *Serm.* LI [I] (c. 400).35/*NPNF* 6:259; *Agon.* 13(14)/*FC* 2:332.
74. *Doctr. Christ.* II.39.58/*NPNF* 2:553.
75. Ibid., II.42.63/555; cf. Frei, *Eclipse of Biblical Narrative,* p. 3; Barth, *The Word of God and the Word of Man,* pp. 28ff.; Martin Luther, *Predigtam Tage vor Weihnachten* (1528), *D. Martin Luthers Werke,* vol. 27, p. 474ff.
76. *Util. cred.* vi.13/*NPNF* 3:353.
77. *Civ.* XVIII.10–21/*NPNF* 2:365–72.
78. Ibid., XVIII.40/384.
79. For examples of this approach, see Karl Barth, *Church Dogmatics,* Vol. I/1, trans. G. T. Thomson (Edinburgh: T. & T. Clark, 1936), pp. 373–78; ibid., Vol. IV/1, ed. G. W. Bromiley and T. F. Torrence, trans. G. W. Bromiley (1956), pp. 333–37; J. C. K. von Hofmann, *Interpreting the Bible,* trans. Otto Piper (Minneapolis: Augsburg, 1972), pp. 28, 72, 205.
80. *Ep. fund.* 5.6/*NPNF* 4:131: "Ego vero Evangelio non crederem, nisi me catholicae Ecclesiae commomveret auctoritas."
       Cf. *Util. cred.* vi, 13/*NPNF* 3:353.
81. *Mag.* xi.37/*LCC* 95.
82. *Util. cred.* xv.33; xv.34/*NPNF* 3:363–64. See ibid., vii.20; xiii.29; xiv.31/356, 361, 362, for the context for these remarks.
83. *Civ.* XXII.8/*NPNF* 2:484–85, 490.
84. Ibid., XXII.5; XXII.8/481–82, 484.
85. Ibid., XXII.9/491.
86. Ibid., XXII.8/484; *Vera relig.* xxv.47/*LCC* 248.
87. *Pecc. merit.* II.XXXVI.59/*NPNF* 5:68.
88. *Faust.* XXXIII.7–8/*NPNF* 4:343–44.
89. *Cons. ev.* III.XIII.41/*NPNF* 6:198–99; cf. III.XXIV.65/210–11; *Serm.* LI [I] (c. 400).32/*NPNF* 6:257–58.
90. *Gen. ad litt.* II.9.20/*WSA* I/13:201–2.
91. *Doctr. Christ.* III.18.26–27/*NPNF* 2:564.
92. Ibid., 2.25.40–2.3.47/548–50.
93. *Ep.* CII (409).31/*NPNF* 1:423; *Civ.* XIII.21/*NPNF* 2:256; cf. *Gen. ad litt.* VIII.6.12; 7.13/*WSA* I/13:354, 355.
94. *Doctr. Christ.* II.8.12–13/*NPNF* 2:538–39; *Faust.* XXVIII.2/*NPNF* 4:325; *Civ.* XVIII.36/*NPNF* 2:382. Augustine also makes a similar appeal to Tradition to establish the viability of the Baptism of heretics in *Ep.* XCIII (408).37/*NPNF* 1:395, the date of Easter in ibid., LIV (400).XIV.27/312; and of the Trinity in *Trin.* I.4.7/*NPNF* 3:20.
95. *Doctr. Christ.* III.2.2/*NPNF* 2:556–57; *Ep.* XXXVI (396).I.2; XIV.32/*NPNF* 1:265, 270; ibid., LIV (400).I.3–4; V.6/300–302; ibid., LV (400).XIV.27/312.
96. *Ep. Fund.* V.5.6/*NPNF* 4:131; *Util. cred.* xiv.31/*NPNF* 3:362. For his remarks

about the role of consensus in establishing the Church's teaching authority, see *Ep. fund.* V.4.5/*NPNF* 3:130; *Faust.* XI.2/*NPNF* 4:178; *C. ep. Parm.* 3.4.24.

97. *Fid. et symb.* i.1/*NPNF* 3:321; *Trin.* XIII.2.5/*NPNF* 3:169; *Enchir.* 7, 119/*NPNF* 3:238–39, 273–74.

98. *Bapt.* II.3–4/*NPNF* 4:427; *Nat. et. grat.* XXXVII.44/*NPNF* 5:136; *Ep.* XCIII (408).X./*NPNF* 1:395; cf. *Doctr. Christ.* II.42.60/*NPNF* 2:555.

99. *Spir. et litt.* XV.27/*NPNF* 5:95; see other references below to this concept's use to authorize allegory.

100. Ibid., V.8/86.

101. *Doctr. Christ.* II.7.10–11/*NPNF* 2:537–38; *Ex. Gal.* 58/*CG* 227; *C. ep. Pel.* IV.V.11/*NPNF* 5:421.

102. *Doctr. Christ.* III.11.17/*NPNF* 2:561.

103. *Spir. et litt.* XV.27/*NPNF* 5:95.

104. *Ep.* CII (409).17/*NPNF* 1:419.

105. *Faust.* VI.9/*NPNF* 4:172–73; *Conf.* V.XIV.24/*NPNF* 1:88.

106. *Util. cred.* i.2–iii.5/*NPNF* 3:348–49.

107. *Trin.* XV.9.15/*NPNF* 3:207.

108. *Doctr. Christ.* III.5.9/*NPNF* 2:559.

109. *Mend.* 26/*NPNF* 3:470.

110. *c. Adim.* 12.1–5; *Civ.* XVII.1–3/*NPNF* 2:337–39. He also affirms a correlation of the two Testaments when possible contradictions in the Bible are noted, in *Serm.* LXXXII [XXXII] (408–409).8/*NPNF* 6:359.

111. Insofar as this point appears in comments in David Dawson, "Figure, Allegory," in *Augustine through the Ages: An Encyclopedia,* ed. Allan D. Fitzgerald (Grand Rapids: Eerdmans, 1991), p. 367, it is a perspective that seems widely accepted among the guild of Augustine scholars.

112. *Ep. Joh.* I; II; X/*NPNF* 7:460–75, 520–29.

113. *Serm.* XCI [XLI] (n.d.); XCVIII [XLVIII] (c. 418); CXXXVI [LXXXVI] (418–420)/*NPNF* 6:397–400, 413–15, 514–17. The second of these sermons is the one in which he dialogues with Donatism. For his figural approach, also see *Serm.* 2 (c. 391).2–6/*WSA* III/1:176–79; ibid., 245 (c. 410–412).(3)–(4)/*FC* 38:289–91; *Ev. Joh.* XV.10–22/*NPNF* 7:101–5; ibid., CXXII/439–43. For occasions when a concern with Christian living overrides the narrative sense of the Biblical text, see *Serm.* 232 (c. 412–413)/*FC* 38:209–217; ibid., 248 (c. 410–412)/*FC* 38:300–304. For more retelling of the Biblical story, see *Ev. Joh.* CXX/*NPNF* 7:434–36; ibid., CXXI/436–39.

114. Bertrand de Margerie, *An Introduction to the History of Exegesis,* vol. 3: *Saint Augustine,* trans. Pierre de Fontnouvelle (Petersham, MA: Saint Bede's Publications, 1991), pp. 60–61; G. H. Allard, "L'articulation de sens et du signe dans le *De Doctrina Christiana* des Augustin," *Texte und Unterschungen zur Geschichte der altchristlichen Literatur* 117 (Berlin: Akademie Verlag, 1976), p. 386; Curtis W. Freeman, "Figure and History: A Contemporary Reassessment of Augustine's Hermeneutic," in *Collectanea Augustiniana,* ed. J. T. Lienhard, E. C. Muler, and R. J. Teske, vol. 2 (New York: Peter Lang, 1993), pp. 319–29; S. M. Zarb, "Unité ou multiplicité des sens littéraux dans la Bible?" *Revue Thomiste* 37 (1932): 251–300, distinguishes various literal senses of a Biblical text.

115. *Mag.* xiii.43/*LCC* 98–99; also see *Doctr. Christ.* III.25/*NPNF* 2:566. For the context for the first citation, see *Mag.* xiv.46/*LCC* 100–101.

116. *Conf.* XII.XXXI.42/*NPNF* 1:188; ibid., XII.XXIV.33/185. Also see *Doctr. Christ.* III.27.38/*NPNF* 2:567. This text challenges the argument of F. Talon, "S. Augustin a-t-il enseigné réellement la pluralité des sens littéraux dans l'Écriture?"

Recherches de Science Religieuse, vol. 11 (1921): 1–28, who posited a unity of Augustine's view of the literal sense in the Biblical author's intention.

117. *Trin.* XI.2.3/*NPNF* 3:145–46; *Lib. arb.* II.VII, 15–II.X, 28/*LC* 144–52.

118. *Gen. ad litt.* I.21.41/*WSA* I/13:188: "Et cum divinos Libros legimus in tanta multitudine verorum intellectum, qui de paucis verbis eruunt, et sanitate catholicae fidei muniuntur, id potissimum deligamus quod certum adparuerit eum sensisse quem legimus."

119. *Mag.* i.2; vii.19/*LCC* 70–71, 82–83. For the preoccupation with memory, see *Conf.* X.VIII.12–15/*NPNF* 1:145–46.

120. *Mag.* vi.17; vi.18/*LCC* 81–82; ibid., vii.19–vii.20; x.30–x.31/83–84, 91.

121. Ibid., viii.22/85–86; *Doctr. Christ.* I.2.2; II.1.1/*NPNF* 2:523, 535.

122. *Mag.,* ix.25; ix.27; x.31/*LCC* 87–88, 89.

123. Ibid., x.33–34; xiv.46/93–94, 100–101.

124. Ibid., xi.38/95. Also see ibid., xiv.46/100–101.

125. Ibid., xii.39/96. See Immanuel Kant, *Kritiker reinen Vernunft* (Leipzig, 1877), pp. 17–18, 156–57, 231ff.

126. *Mag.* xii.39/*LCC* 96.

127. Ibid., xiii.42–43; xiv.46/98–99, 100–101.

128. *Gen. ad Man.* II.4.5–II.5.6/*WSA* I/13:73–75; *Ev. Joh.* XXXV.9/*NPNF* 7:207.

129. *Doctr. Christ.* I.13.12/*NPNF* 2:526.

130. Ibid., I.4.4/523.

131. Ibid., I.1.1/522–23.

132. *Serm.* LXXIV [XXIV] (n.d.).1/*NPNF* 6:335. Cf. the *analogia fidei* of Karl Barth, *Church Dogmatics,* III/2, ed. G. W. Bromiley and T. F. Torrance (Edinburgh: T. & T. Clark, 1960), p. 6; ibid., vol. I/1, trans. G. T. Thomson (1936), pp. 3ff.; Frei, *Eclipse of Biblical Narrative,* p. 3.

133. *Vera relig.* l.99–li.100/*LCC* 275–76.

134. *Doctr. Christ.* III.10.14–15/*NPNF* 2:560–61.

135. *Ps.* CXLVI [CXLVII].10.12/*NPNF* 8:667–68; *Doctr. Christ.* II.6.7/*NPNF* 2:537. Also see *Spir. et litt.* IV.6/*NPNF* 5:85, for Augustine's appreciation that not all parts of Scripture should be read literally.

136. *Ps.* XCIII [XCIV].1/*NPNF* 8:459.

137. *Civ.* XI.19/*NPNF* 2:215.

138. *Doctr. Christ.* II.9.14; III.26.37/*NPNF* 2:539, 566; *Serm.* LXXI [XXI] (c. 417).11/ *NPNF* 6:321–22.

139. *Conf.* XII.XVIII.27; XII.XXXI.42; XIII.XXV.38./*NPNF* 1:183, 188, 203.

140. *Doctr. Christ.* III.28.39/*NPNF* 2:567.

141. *Ep.* LXXXII (405).V.34/*NPNF* 1:361; cf. *Gen. ad litt.* V.9.24/*WSA* I/13:287. In *Ep.* CII (409).37/*NPNF* 1:425, he urges that the diversity be in harmony with the Rule of Faith.

142. *Serm.* LXXXIX [XXXIX] (397).4–5/*NPNF* 6:390–91; *Doctr. Christ.* III.5.9/*NPNF* 2:559.

143. *Doctr. Christ.* III.10.14/*NPNF* 2:560.

144. *Conf.* XII.XXV.34/*NPNF* 1:185. See XII.XV.18–19/180, for the context.

145. *Doctr. Christ.* III.9.14/*NPNF* 2:539.

146. Ibid., I.35.39–I.36.41/532–33; *Ps.* XCVIII [XCIX].1; XLV [XLVI].1; XVI [XVII].51/*NPNF* 8:483, 155, 54; *Enchir.* 5/*NPNF* 3:238.

147. *Ep. Joh.* VII.4/*NPNF* 7:503.

148. *Doctr. Christ.* III.10.15; III.15.23/*NPNF* 2:561, 563.

149. Ibid., III.10.14/560–61.

150. *Faust.* XIII.18/*NPNF* 4:206–7; *Trin.* VIII.4.6/*NPNF* 3:118.

151. *Doctr. Christ.* I.2.2/*NPNF* 2:556–57.

152. *Nat. et grat.* LXVII.81/*NPNF* 5:149–50. Even in the texts in which he is self-critical of his previous writings Augustine points out how he had taught the priority of grace. See *Retrac.* I.22(2)/*FC* 60:98–99; *Praed. sanct.* III.7/*NPNF* 5:500–501.

153. *Persev.* XX.53/*NPNF* 5:547.

154. Ibid., XXI.55/548.

155. Ibid., XX.53/547.

156. Ibid., XVI.40; XXII.57–59/541–42, 549.

157. Ibid., XXII.61/549–50.

158. *Spir. et litt.* XXX.52/*NPNF* 5:106.

159. *Doctr. Christ.* III.14.22/*NPNF* 2:562–63.

160. *Retrac.* I.8(2)/*FC* 60:32–33: "De gratia uero [*sic* "vero"] Dei, qua suos electos sic praedestinavit, ut eorum qui jam in eis utuntur libero arbitrio, ipse etiam praeparet uoluntates [*sic* "voluntates"], nihil in his libris disputatum est propter hoc proposita quaestione. Ubi autem incidit locus, ut hujus gratiae fieret commemoratio, transeunter commemorate est, non, quasi inde ageretur, operosa ratiocinatione defensa. Aliud est enim quaerere, unde sit malum, et aliud quaerere, unde redeatur ad pristinum vel ad maius perueniatur bonum."
      Cf. ibid., (6)/38–39.

161. For such a characterization of Western theology since the Enlightenment as especially preoccupied with apologetics, see Frei, *The Eclipse of Biblical Narrative*, esp. pp. 128–29; Jaroslav Pelikan, *Christian Doctrine and Modern Culture (since 1700)* (Chicago and London: University of Chicago Press, 1989), esp. 184–86.

162. Barth, *Church Dogmatics,* I/1:ix–x, 119, 141–49; Hans Frei, *The Identity of Jesus Christ* (Philadelphia: Fortress Press, 1975), xii–xvi, 7–8.

163. Tracy, *Blessed Rage for Order,* pp. 9–10, 32ff.; Paul Ricoeur, *Essays on Biblical Interpretation,* ed. Lewis S. Mudge (Philadelphia: Fortress Press, 1980), pp. 64–73, 98, 108, 143.

164. Aquinas, *Summa Contra Gentiles* I.4; John Calvin, *Institutes of the Christian Religion* (1559), Pref.; I.III.2; I.XIV–I.XVI.

165. *Util. cred.* 9, 23, 26–27/*NPNF* 3:351, 357–58, 360; *Civ.* XVIII.XLII.41/*NPNF* 2:384–85; *Serm.* CXVII (418).3, 5/*NPNF* 459–60.

166. Luther sees him as an ally in teaching that God commands the impossible (*Lectures on Romans* [1515–1516], in *D. Martin Luthers Werke,* vol. 56, p. 356 [*Luther's Works,* vol. 25:345]) and the letter-spirit (Law-Gospel) dialectic (*Dispututio Heidelbergae habita* [1518], in *D. Martin Luthers Werke,* vol. 1, pp. 355–56, 369 [*Luther's Works,* vol. 31:42–43, 62–63]). He attributed to Augustine the position that what the Law demands is given by the Gospel, without the Law (p. 364). He cites Augustine as wishing to be unfettered by other writings unless they agree with Scripture, in *Preface to the Wittenberg Edition of Luther's Writings* (1539), in *D. Martin Luthers Werke,* vol. 50, p. 657 [*Luther's Works,* vol. 34:285].

167. *Ex. Gal.* Pref. (2); 57 (4)/*CG* 125, 227; *Ep. Joh.* VII.8/*NPNF* 7:504; *Gr. et lib. arb.* 32, 37/*NPNF* 5:457, 459; *Spir. et litt.* XVII.29/*NPNF* 5:95; *Ep.* CXLV (c. 412).3/*NPNF* 1:496. For other affirmations of the Law-Gospel distinction when dialoguing with Pelagius, see Augustine, *Doctr. Christ.* III.33.46/*NPNF* 2:569.

168. See note 146, above.

Chapter 3: God/Trinity/Christology

1. *Civ.* VIII.11/*NPNF* 2:151; *Solilq.* I.9/*NPNF* 7:540.

2. *Conf.* VIII.I.1; VII.II.4; XII.VII.7; XII.XI.11/*NPNF* 1:102, 103–4, 177, 178; *Nat. bon.* 24/*NPNF* 4:356; *Ep. fund.* 21/*NPNF* 4:138; *Vera relig.* xii.25/*LCC* 237; *Retrac.* II.35/*FC* 60:137; *Nat. bon.* 1, 19, 24/*NPNF* 4:351, 355, 356; *Doctr.*

Christ. I.6.6ff./*NPNF* 2:524–25; *Gen. ad litt.* VIII.20.39; 21.40; 23.44/*WSA* I/13: 368, 369; *Ep.* CXVIII (410).III.154/*NPNF* 1:444; *Ep.* CXXX (412).XV–28/*NPNF* 1:468; *Ep.* XVIII (390).2/*NPNF* 1:236.

3. *Conf.* V.X.20/*NPNF* 1:86–87, 91; *Ep. fund.* 21/*NPNF* 4:138.

4. *Fid. et symb.* 2.2/*NPNF* 3:322; *Gen. ad litt.* IV.16.27/*WSA* I/13:257.

5. *Conf.* VI.X.16; VII.XX.26/*NPNF* 1:109, 114; *Ep.* CXXVI (412).II.4/*NPNF* 1:474; *Ibid.*, CXVIII (410).IV.23/*NPNF* 1:446.

6. *Conf.* VII.XIV.22/*NPNF* 1:111; ibid., VII.V.7/104–5; *Mor.* VIII.13/*NPNF* 4:44–45; *Nat. bon.* 1/*NPNF* 4:351.

7. *Civ.* VIII.6/*NPNF* 2:148; *Conf.* IV.XVI.28–30/*NPNF* 1:77.

8. *Doctr. Christ.* I.6.6/*NPNF* 2:524.

9. *Conf.* II.I.1; II.VI.13/*NPNF* 1:55, 58.

10. Ibid., X.I.1; XI.II.3/141, 163–64.

11. Ibid., IV.V.10/71.

12. Ibid., I.III.3; IV.XII.19/46, 76; *Gen. ad litt.* V.16.34/*WSA* I/13:293.

13. *Conf.* III.VI.11; VI.III.3/*NPNF* 1:63, 91; *Ep.* CXXXVII (412).II.4/*NPNF* 1:474; *Ep.* CXVIII (410).IV.23/*NPNF* 1:446.

14. *Conf.* VII.I.2/*NPNF* 1:102; ibid., VII.V.7/104. Note similarities to the concept of Panentheism in some forms of Process Theology. See John B. Cobb Jr. and David R. Griffin, *Process Theology: An Introductory Exposition* (Philadelphia: Westminster Press, 1976), esp. p. 62.

15. *Solilq.* I.15/*NPNF* 7:542; cf. *Ep.* CXXXII (412).I.2/*NPNF* 1:474.

16. *Conf.* I.VI.10/*NPNF* 1:48; *Ps.* CI [CII].27–28/*NPNF* 8:501–2.

17. *Conf.* XI.XIII.16/*NPNF* 1:168; *Ev. Joh.* XXI.5/*NPNF* 7:190; *Civ.* XI.21/*NPNF* 2:216.

18. *Vera relig.* xlix.97/*LCC* 275. Also see *Conf.* XII.XI.13/*NPNF* 1:179.

19. *Conf.* VII.X.12/*NPNF* 1:109.

20. Ibid., X.VII.11–VIII.12, 15; X.XVIII.26/*NPNF* 1:145, 146, 149.

21. Ibid., X.XX.29; X.XXIII.33/150, 151.

22. Ibid., X.X.17–XI.18; X.XV.23/146–47, 148.

23. Ibid., X.XXV.36–XXVI.37/152; cf. *Ep.* CXVIII (410).IV–23/*NPNF* 1:446.

24. *Conf.* X.XL.65/*NPNF* 1:161.

25. *Mag.* XI.38/*LCC* 95; cf. *Solilq.* I.15/*NPNF* 7:542; *Faust.* XX.7/*NPNF* 4:254–55. For a helpful discussion of the various schools of interpretation regarding God's role in relation to human cognition, see Ronald H. Nash, "Illumination, Divine," in *Augustine through the Ages: An Encyclopedia*, ed. Allan D. Fitzgerald (Grand Rapids: Eerdmans, 1999), pp. 438–40.

26. *Mag.*, XII.40; XIV.45, 46/*LCC* 96–97, 100, 101.

27. *Ps.* XLI [XLII].6–8/*NPNF* 8:133–34; *Serm.* CXXXVII [LXXXVII] (c. 408).9/*NPNF* 6:520; *Conf.* VII.X.16; VII.XVII.23; IX.X.23–26/*NPNF* 1:109, 111, 137–38; cf. Plotinus, *Enneads* VI.9.

28. *De lib. arbit.* II.xiii.35/*LCC* 157; *Gen. ad litt.* V.16.34/*WSA* I/13:293; *Conf.* V.IV.7/*NPNF* 1:81.

29. *Ep.* CXVIII (400).II.15/*NPNF* 1:443–44.

30. Ibid., CXXX (430).7.11/463.

31. *De lib. arbit.* II.v.12/*LCC* 142; cf. I.i.1–II.i.5/113–37, for the context.

32. Ibid., II.vi.14/144.

33. Ibid., II.xii.33–34; II.xv.39/156, 159–60.

34. See p. 17, above.

35. *Retrac.* I.1.4/*FC* 60:10.

36. *Trin.* VIII.2.3; VI.4.6; I.1.3/*NPNF* 3:116, 99–100, 18; *Civ.* VIII.6; XI.2, 6/*NPNF* 2:148, 205–6, 208 (to depict how God is simple and different from the world);

Pat. 1/*NPNF* 3:527 (when exhorting Christian life); *Ev. Joh.* XIX.11/*NPNF* 7:126 (when exhorting faith); *Civ.* XI.22/*NPNF* 2:217 (against the Manichees); *Civ.* XXII.6/*NPNF* 2:480 (engaging in apologetics). For the rejection of attributing femininity to God, see *Trin.* XII.5.5/*NPNF* 3:156–57. God is identified as changeless Good in *Spir. et. litt.* iii.5/*NPNF* 5:84 (against Pelagianism, much as Luther portrayed God in his *Bondage of the Will,* in *Luther's Works,* vol. 33, ed. Philip Watson [Philadelphia: Fortress Press, 1972]).

37. *Trin.* I.1.1–2/*NPNF* 3:17–18; *Civ.* XXII.2/*NPNF* 2:480; cf. ibid., XVII.7/347, as Augustine deals with apologetic questions.

38. *Trin.* XV.6.9; I.2.4–5/*NPNF* 3:203, 117–18; *Ep. Joh.* I.5/*NPNF* 7:462–63; *Conf.* VII.X.16/*NPNF* 1:109.

39. *Civ.* XI.2/*NPNF* 2:205–6; ibid., XI.10/211; see the reference above in note 7; cf. *Conf.* VII.X.16/*NPNF* 1:109; *Ep.* CXLVII (413).31/*FC* 20:199.

40. *Civ.* XIV.11/*NPNF* 2:272.

41. Ibid., XXII.29, 30/508, 511; *Serm.* LXIX [XIX] (413).3/*NPNF* 6:316; *Trin.* VIII.II.3/*NPNF* 3:116.

42. *Civ.* XI.21/*NPNF* 2:216.

43. *Ep. Joh.* XXXI.5, 4/*NPNF* 7:190; cf. Albert Einstein, "Zur Elektrodynamik bewegter Korper," *Analen dir Physik* (1905): 891–921.

44. *Trin.* XV.7.13/*NPNF* 3:206.

45. *Conf.* XIII.III.4/*NPNF* 1:191.

46. *Trin.* III.5.2/*NPNF* 3:57–58; ibid., III.2.7/57ff.; Plotinus, *Enneads,* VI.9; cf. Lewis Ayres and Michael R. Barnes, "God," in Allan D. Fitzgerald, ed., *Augustine through the* Ages, p. 387.

47. Plotinus, VI.

48. *Civ.* XII.18/*NPNF* 2:238; *Trin.* V.16.17/*NPNF* 3:95–96.

49. *Pat.* 19/*NPNF* 3:534; *S. Dom. mon.* II.VIII.28/*NPNF* 6:42–43; *Nat. bon.* 31/*NPNF* 4:357–58. See *Pecc. merit.* II.XVIII–XIX.32/*NPNF* 5:57.

50. *Enchir.* 27, 3/*NPNF* 3:246, 238; *Serm.* LXXVII [XXVII] (n.d.).3, 1/*NPNF* 6:343, 342. Also see *Civ.* I.8–9/*NPNF* 2:5–6; ibid., I.34/21; ibid., XIII.4/246–47; *Cat. rud.* VI.9/*NPNF* 3:288.

51. *Enchir.* 33, 31/*NPNF* 3:249, 247–48.

52. *Trin.* XV.19.37/*NPNF* 3:219–20. Here and in the next citation from *On the Trinity* Augustine moves from responding to critics merely to expositing faith. See ibid., VIII.Preface/115. Also see *Symb. cat.* 13/*NPNF* 3:374; *Ev. Joh.* CX.6/*NPNF* 7:411; *Ep. Joh.* VII.6, 4/*NPNF* 7:503, 502. *Pat.* 15/*NPNF* 3:532.

53. *Ep. Joh.* IX.9/*NPNF* 7:513–14; *Serm.* 299 D (c. 412).6/*WSA* III/8.260.

54. *Trin.* VIII.8.12/*NPNF* 3:123.

55. Ibid., XV.25.44/223.

56. Ibid., XIV.12.15/191; *Spir. et litt.* 18.31/*NPNF* 5:96; *Gr. et lib. arb.* XII.24/*NPNF* 5:453; *Ev. Joh.* XXVI.1/*NPNF* 7:168; cf. Martin Luther, *Preface to the Complete Edition of Luther's Latin Writings* (1545), *Luther's Works,* vol. 34, ed. Lewis Spitz (Philadelphia: Muhlenberg Press, 1960), p. 337.

57. *Conf.* IV.V.10/*NPNF* 1:71; *Serm.* CXXIV [LXXIV] (c. 410).4–5/*NPNF* 6:478; *Ps.* CXVII [CVIII]:1; II.2/*NPNF* 8:557, 2–3; cf. *Trin.* IV.I.2/*NPNF* 3:70.

58. *Conf.* XII.XV.18; XIV.XXXVII.52–XXXII.53/*NPNF* 1:180, 207; cf. *Gen. ad litt.* IV.16.27/*WSA* I/13:257.

59. *Ps.* CV [CVI].31, 6/*NPNF* 8:531, 527; *Civ.* XIV.11/*NPNF* 2:271.

60. *De lib. arbit.* III.iv.11/*LCC* 177. See *Ep. fund.* 41.47, 37.42–43/*NPNF* 4:150, 148.

61. *Pat.* 1–2/*NPNF* 3:527–28.

62. *Fid. et symb.* 9.20/*NPNF* 3:330–31.

63. *Trin.* XV.VII.11/*NPNF* 3:204–5.

64. *Conf.* XIII.V.5/*NPNF* 1:191.
65. Ibid., XIII.XI.12/193–94.
66. *Civ.* XI.24–26/*NPNF* 2:218–20.
67. *Trin.* X.12.19/*NPNF* 3:143; ibid., XIV.12.15/191–192; *Serm.* LII [II] (c. 410–412).19–23/*NPNF* 6:264–66; cf. *Civ.* XI.26/*NPNF* 2:220; *Conf.* XII.XI.12/*NPNF* 1:193.
68. *Trin.* XIV.6.9/*NPNF* 3:187–88; ibid., IX.5.8/128–29; ibid., IX.12.18/133.
69. Ibid., X.10.13/140–41; ibid., IV.7.10/188; ibid., XIV.6.8/187; *Serm.* LII [II] (c. 410).19–23/*NPNF* 6:264–66; cf. *Ev. Joh.* XXIII.10–11/*NPNF* 7:155.
70. *Trin.* VIII.8.12/*NPNF* 3:123; ibid., VIII.10.14/124; ibid., IX.2.2/126–27.
71. *Civ.* XI.25/*NPNF* 2:219.
72. *Trin.* V.3.4; VI.4.6; VII.1.2–2.3/*NPNF* 3:88, 99–100, 105–7.
73. Ibid., VI.5.7/100; *Civ.* XI.10/*NPNF* 2:210–11.
74. *Fid. et symb.* IX.17/*NPNF* 3:328.
75. *Trin.* XV.26.47/*NPNF* 3:224; *Ep.* 238 (n.d.).2.24/*FC* 32:206.
76. *Trin.* XV.14.23ff./*NPNF* 3:213–14.
77. Ibid., XV.14.23–24/213.
78. Ibid., XV.11.20; XV.14.23/209–10, 213.
79. *Fid. et symb.* IX.19/*NPNF* 3:329–30; *Doctr. Christ.* I.5.5/*NPNF* 2:524.
80. *Trin.* IV.20.29, XV.17.29; XV.26.45–27.48/*NPNF* 3:84, 216, 223–25; *Ev. Joh.* XCIX.6, 7/*NPNF* 7:383–84.
81. *Ev. Joh.* XCIX.7/*NPNF* 7:383–84.
82. *Trin.* VI.5.7/*NPNF* 3:100: "Spiritus ergo sanctus commune aliquid est patris et filii, quid-quid illud est, aut ipsa communio consubstantialis et coaeterna; quae si amieitia convenienter dici potest, dicatur, sed apitus dicitur caritas . . ." Ibid., VIII.10.14/124; ibid., XV.17.27/215; ibid., XV.19.37/219; ibid., V.11.12/93; *Ev. Joh.* IX.7; XIV.9/*NPNF* 7:65, 97; *Fid. et symb.* IX.19/*NPNF* 3:329–30.
83. *Trin.* V.11.12; XV.19.37/*NPNF* 3:93, 219–20.
84. Ibid., XV.4.6–5.7; V.8.9/*NPNF* 3:202, 91; *Praed. sanct.* VIII.13/*NPNF* 5:504–5.
85. *Enchir.* 38/*NPNF* 3:250.
86. *Ep.* XI (389).2, 3/*NPNF* 1:229; *Serm.* LXXI [XXI] (c. 471).27–28/*NPNF* 6:328. Cf. *Ep.* CLXIX (415).6/*NPNF* 1:546; *Serm.* LII [II] (410–412).23/*NPNF* 6:265.
87. *Enchir.* 5/*NPNF* 3:238: "Certum uero propriumque fidei catholicae fundomentum Christus est . . ."
88. Adolf von Harnack, *Monasticism and the "Confessions" of Saint Augustine: Two Lectures,* trans. E. E. Kellett and F. A. Marseille (London: Williams & Norgate, 1913), pp. 140–41, 166–67; Adolf von Harnack, *History of Dogma,* vol. 5, trans. J. Millar (London: Williams & Norgate, 1898), pp. 128, 129; cf. William Mallard, "Jesus Christ," in *Augustine through the Ages,* 466–67.
89. *Vera relig.* xvi.30, 32; xxxviii.71/*LCC* 239, 240, 261.
90. *Fid. et symb.* 4.6,8/*NPNF* 3:324, 325. A similar view of Christ's atoning work appeared in another early treatise when dealing with Christian life in response to skeptics, in *Agon.* 2(2)/*FC* 2:316–17.
91. *Fid. et symb.* 4.5/*NPNF* 3:324–25, *Agon.* 14(16), 16(18)/*FC* 2:332, 333.
92. *Fid. et symb.* 4.8/*NPNF* 3:325; *Enchir.* 108/*NPNF* 3:272; cf. *Conf.* X.XLII.67/*NPNF* 1:161. For an early insistence on Christ's full humanity, see *Agon.* 18(20)/*FC* 2:335.
93. *Ep.* CXXXV (412).11/*NPNF* 1:477.
94. *Ep.* 187 (417).34/*FC* 30:249; *Ev. Joh.* XXXVII.1/*NPNF* 7:213; cf. *Conf.* X.III.4/*NPNF* 1:143; *Doctr. Christ.* I.14/*NPNF* 2:526; *Ps.* LVIII [LIX].14/*NPNF* 8:240.

95. *Ps.* XCVII [XCVIII].1/*NPNF* 8:483; *Conf.* XI.II.4/*NPNF* 1:164; *Enchir.* 36, 37, 40/*NPNF* 3:249, 250, 251; *Trin.* XIII.10.3/*NPNF* 3:174; ibid., IV.1.2/70.
96. *Trin.* I.11.22; I.7.14; I.1.1/*NPNF* 3:29, 24, 17.
97. *Ep.* 187 (417).3–10/*FC* 30:223–29; *Nat. bon.* XXXI/*LCC* 336; *Serm.* LXXVII [CXXVII] (c. 410–420).8/*NPNF* 6:489.
98. *Fid. et symb.* 4.8–9/*NPNF* 3:225; cf. *Ev. Joh.* VIII.9/*NPNF* 7:61.
99. *Trin.* VIII.5.7/*NPNF* 3:119.
100. Ibid., I.13.28/33; *C. serm. Ar.* VIII.6/*WSA* I/18:146; *Faust.* XXVI.6, 7/*NPNF* 4:3, 23; cf. *Agon.* 23(25)/*FC* 2:340–41.
101. *Trin.* XII.18.23/*NPNF* 3:180; *Enchir.* 41/*NPNF* 3:251; *Serm.* LI [I] (c. 400).26/*NPNF* 6:244.
102. *Serm.* 186 (411–412).1/*WSA* III/6.24; *Haer.* 56, 82/*WSA* I/18:48, 53; *Fid. et symb.* 5.11/*NPNF* 3:326.
103. *Nat. et grat.* 36.42/*NPNF* 5:135.
104. *Ep. fund.* 6.7–10.11/*NPNF* 4:131–34.
105. *Simpl.* II.21/*LCC* 405.
106. *Vera relig.* xii.24/*LCC* 236–37; *Fid. et symb.* 9.19/*NPNF* 3:329.
107. *Spir et litt.* XXI.36; XXVII.47/*NPNF* 5:98, 103; *Ep Joh.* III.12/*NPNF* 7:480–81; *Correct.* XI.50/*NPNF* 4:651; *Trin.* XV.20.39/*NPNF* 3:221; *Serm.* 267 (412).4/*WSA* III/7:276; cf. *Pat.* 20/*NPNF* 3:534.
108. *Nat. et grat.* LXX.84/*NPNF* 5:151.
109. *Spir. et litt.* XIV.26/*NPNF* 5:95; *Cat. rud.* 20.35/*NPNF* 3:305; *Ps.* XC(XCI).16/*NPNF* 8:451.
110. *Spir. et litt.* III.5/*NPNF* 5:84–85; *Ep.* XI (389).4/*NPNF* 1:230; *Ps.* CI [CII].20/*NPNF* 8:500.
111. *Ev. Joh.* XXV.4–8/*NPNF* 7:169–70; *Pecc. mer.* II.XIX.32/*NPNF* 5:57; *c. ep. Pel.* I.XII.27/*NPNF* 5:385–86; *Enchir.* 31, 118/*NPNF* 3:247–48, 275; *Jul op. imp.* 1.107; 2.217; 2.226; /*WSA* I/25: 128, 263, 271.
112. *Anim.* IV.IX.13/*NPNF* 5:359–60.
113. *Trin.* XV.17.31–XV.18.32; XV.17.27/*NPNF* 3:216–17, 215; *Ev. Joh.* XXXIX.5; CX.4–5/*NPNF* 7:223, 410–11; cf. *Ep. Joh.* VII.7/*NPNF* 7:303.
114. *Pat.* 14/*NPNF* 3:532; *Trin.* XV.19.37/*NPNF* 3:219; cf. *Serm.* LXXI [XXI] (c. 417).19/*NPNF* 6:324; *Conf.* XIII.XI.10/*NPNF* 1:193; *Ev. Joh.* XXVII.9/*NPNF* 7:175.
115. *Ev. Joh.* XXVI.3/*NPNF* 7:168–69; *Spir. et litt.* 17.29/*NPNF* 5:95.
116. *Mor.* 13.22/*NPNF* 4:48.
117. *Conf.* XIII.VII.8–VIII.9/*NPNF* 1:192; cf. ibid., XII.XXX.41/188.
118. *Civ.* XI.24/*NPNF* 2:218–19.
119. *Trin.* XV.6.10; XV.17.27–28; XV.21.40–22.42/*NPNF* 3:204, 215, 221–22.

Chapter 4: Creation and Providence

1. *Solilq.* I.2/*NPNF* 7:537; *Nat. bon.* 26/*NPNF* 4:356; *Ep. fund.* 25.27/*NPNF* 4:140–41; *Fid. et symb.* 2.2/*NPNF* 3:322; *Conf.* XI.IX.6/*NPNF* 1:164.
2. *Retrac.* 1.3/*FC* 60:14.
3. *C. Acad.* 3.17(37); 3.19(42)/*FC* 5:213, 214, 219; *Div. qu.* 46/*FC* 70:79–81; *Ord.* II.11(30); *FC* 5:308; *Imm. an.* 15(24)/*FC* 4:43–44.
4. *Retrac.* I.3; I.10.4/*FC* 60:14, 47–48.
5. *Civ.* XI.22, XII.5; XIX.13/*NPNF* 2:217, 228–29, 409; *Enchir.* 10, 12/*NPNF* 3:240; *Gen. ad litt.* III.24.37/*WSA* I/13:239–40.
6. *Civ.* XXII.24/*NPNF* 2:502; f. *Ord.* I.1(2)/*FC* 5:241; *Serm.* XCVI [XLVI] (416–17). 4–6/*NPNF* 6:410.

7. *Ps.* CXLVIII.1ff./*NPNF* 8:673ff.
8. *Enchir.* 10/*NPNF* 3:240. Also see *Gen. ad litt.* III.16.25/*WSA* I/13:231, where a similar point is made while explicating the faith with an apologetic concern in view (ibid., I.19.39/186–87). For a reference to the Stoic belief in cosmic harmony, see Marcus Aurelius, *Meditations,* II.3; III.1; VII.9.
9. *B. vid.* 9/*NPNF* 3:444.
10. *De lib. arbit.* III.ix.25/*LCC* 186.
11. *Vera relig.* XI.46/*LCC* 264.
12. *Civ.* XXII.24/*NPNF* 2:504, 503; *Soliloq.* I.2/*NPNF* 7:538.
13. *Ep. Joh.* II.11/*NPNF* 7:473.
14. *Civ.* XI.16, 22; XII.2, 5; XIV.10/*NPNF* 2:214, 217, 227, 228–29, 271; *Ord.* II.8(25)/*FC* 5:301; *C. Acad.* 1.4(11)/*FC* 5:119. For the Stoic commitment to controlling emotion, see Aurelius, I.15; II.1; VII.8; VIII.4. For Augustine's rejection of the possibility that since the Fall humans can avoid passions and emotions, see *Ev. Joh.* LX.3/*NPNF* 7:309–10; *Civ.* XIV. 8–9/*NPNF* 2:267–71.
15. *Civ.* XI.16/*NPNF* 2:214; cf. *Trin.* III.4.9/*NPNF* 3:58–59.
16. *Civ.* XII.4/*NPNF* 2:228.
17. Ibid., XI.24, 26/219, 220.
18. *Spir. et litt.* XXI.36; XXVI.43/*NPNF* 5:98, 101; *Faust.* XXII.27/*NPNF* 4:283; *S. Dom. mon.* II.IX.32/*NPNF* 6:44.
19. *De lib. arbit.* II.xvii.46; II.xviii.49; II.xv.39; III.xiii.36/*LCC* 164, 166, 159–60, 193.
20. *Civ.* XI.26/*NPNF* 2:220.
21. *Conf.* XII.III.3; XII.XII.15; XII.XV.19; XII.XXIX.40/*NPNF* 1:176, 179, 180, 188. In ibid., XIII.XXXIV.49/206, he indicates his awareness of an apologetic agenda.
22. *Civ.* XI.5–6/*NPNF* 2:207–8; cf. ibid., XII.15/235–36; *Gen. ad litt.* V.5.12.
23. *Civ.* VII.30; XI.9/*NPNF* 2:140, 209–10.
24. Ibid., XI.29/222; *Gen. ad litt.* V.20.41; VIII.24.25/*WSA* I/13:297, 372.
25. *Civ.* XI.11, 13–15, 17–19, 28, 32–33; XII.1/*NPNF* 2:211–12, 213–15, 222, 223–24, 227; *Ev. Joh.* III.7/*NPNF* 7:21.
26. *Conf.* XII.XII.15/*NPNF* 1:179; cf. *Civ.* XII.15/*NPNF* 2:236.
27. *Conf.* XIII.XXXVII.52/*NPNF* 1:207; cf. *Gen. ad litt.* IV.12.22–23; 35–36; V.4.10/*WSA* I/13:253–54, 275, 281.
28. *Conf.* IV.X.15; IV.XII.18/*NPNF* 1:172–74.
29. Ibid., XI.IV.6; XIII.XX.28/165, 199.
30. Ibid., XII.IX.9/178.
31. Ibid., XI.X.12; XI.XII.14; XI.XIII.16/167, 168; cf. *Ev. Joh.* XXI.5/*NPNF* 7:190.
32. *Conf.* X.XIII.15–16; XI.XXX.40/*NPNF* 1:167–68, 174.
33. Ibid., XI.XV.18; XI.XVII.22; XI.XX.26–XXI.27/168–69, 170.
34. Ibid., XI.XX.26–XXI.27/170; ibid., XI.XVII.36/173.
35. Ibid., XI.XI.14/179.
36. Ibid., XI.XVIII.37–38/173–74.
37. Ibid., XI.XXX.40–XXXI.41/174–75.
38. *Civ.* XXII.24/*NPNF* 2:502; *Gen. ad litt.* I.17.32–35; IV.27.44ff. (esp. 30.47); V.23.44–45/*WSA* I/13:183–84, 267ff., 299–300. See *Conf.* XII.2.2ff.; XII.12.15/*NPNF* 1:176ff., 179, for the point about how Augustine envisages God establishing patterns of created realities, like the forms. Also see *Trin.* III.9.16/*NPNF* 3:62.
39. *Ep.* CXVIII (410).IV.31/*NPNF* 1:449.
40. *Conf.* XII.XII.15/*NPNF* 1:179; ibid., XI.XXX.40/174; *Civ.* XI.6/*NPNF* 2:208; *De lib. arbit.* III.xvi.42/*LCC* 196–97; *Gen. litt. imp.* 3.8./*WSA* I/13:117–18; *Gen. ad Man* I.2.3/*WSA* I/13:40–41; *Gen. ad litt.* V.5.13/*WSA* I/13:282; cf. Albert Einstein, "Letter to W. De Sitter," March 25, 1917.

41. *Conf.* XI.XI.13/*NPNF* 1:167; cf. Albert Einstein, "Zur Elektrodynamik bewegter Korper," *Analen der Physik* (1905): 891–921.
42. *Conf.* XIII.37.52/*NPNF* 1:207; cf. *Trin.* XII.7.10/*NPNF* 3:159.
43. *Conf.* VII.V.7; IV.XI.18/*NPNF* 1:104–5, 74.
44. *Ev. Joh.* II.10/*NPNF* 7:16–17.
45. *Civ.* I.28; XII.4/*NPNF* 2:18, 228.
46. *Enchir.* 106/*NPNF* 3:271.
47. Ibid., 11/240; *Civ.* XI.9/*NPNF* 2:210.
48. *Civ.* XI.34/*NPNF* 2:225.
49. *Vera relig.* XXV.47/*LCC* 248.
50. *Retrac.* I.12(7)/*FC* 60:55; *Util. cred.* 34/*NPNF* 3:364. Also see *Serm.* LXXVII [XXVII] (n.d.).9/*NPNF* 6:376; *Ep.* CXXXVII (412).16/*NPNF* 1:479; and *Retrac.* I.12(8)/*FC* 60:55, for Augustine's construal of the Pentecost experience.
51. *Doctr. Christ.* I.31–32/*NPNF* 2:531; *Civ.* XXII.24/*NPNF* 2:502.
52. *De lib. arbit.* III.iii.6, 8; III.iv.11/*LCC* 174, 175, 177; *Civ.* V.10/*NPNF* 2:93.
53. *De lib. arbit.* III.ix.9.26; III.xxiii.70; III.xxiii.68/*LCC* 186, 212, 211.
54. *Nat. bon.* 16/*NPNF* 4:354; *Ep. fund.* 41.47–42.48/*NPNF* 4:150; *Solilq.* I.2/*NPNF* 7:537; cf. *Ord.* II.4(12)/*FC* 5:287–88.
55. *Serm.* 286 (c. 425–430).6, 5/*WSA* III/8:103–3; *Serm.* LXXVII [XXVII] (410–412).3/*NPNF* 6:343.
56. *Vera. relig.* vi.11; xiv.27/*LCC* 231, 238; *Ev. Joh.* LIII.6, 7/*NPNF* 7:293.
57. *Ep.* LXXVIII (404).7/*NPNF* 1:348; *S. Dom. mon.* III.IX.30–34/*NPNF* 6:43–45; *Ep.* CIV (409).5/*NPNF* 1:435; *Agon.* 7(8)–8(9)/*FC* 2:323–35; *Serm.* LVII [VII] (c. 412–416).9/*NPNF* 6:282–83; *Civ.* XX.1/*NPNF* 2:421.
58. *Vera. relig.* xvii.34/*LCC* 241: "Ut enim ars medicinae, cum eaden maneat, neque ullo pacto ipsa mutetur, mutat tamen praecepta languentibus, quia mutabilis est nostra valetudo: ita divina providentia, cum sit ipsa omnino incommutabilis, mutabili tamen creaturae varie subvenit, et pro diversitate morborum alias alia jubet out vetat . . ."
59. Ibid., xxv,46/247.
60. *Pecc. merit.* II.32/*NPNF* 5:57; *Ps.* CXLVIII.8ff./*NPNF* 8:675ff.; *Civ.* XIII.4/*NPNF* 2:228; cf. ibid., V.11/93.
61. *Gr. et lib. arb.* XXII.43/*NPNF* 5:463; *Corrept.* VIII.18/*NPNF* 5:479.
62. *Gr. et lib. arb.* XXIII.45/*NPNF* 5:464; *Praed. sanct.* XIV.26/*NPNF* 5:511; cf. *Gen. ad litt.* XI.10.13/*WSA* I/13:435.
63. *Civ.* I.1, Pref./*NPNF* 2:2, 1; ibid., I.8–9/5–6; ibid., II.23/38.
64. Ibid., XIII.4/246–47.
65. *Gr. et lib. arb.* XX.41; XXI.42–43/*NPNF* 5:461, 463.
66. Ibid., XXI.42/462. Also see ibid., XVI.32/457.
67. *Nat. et grat.* 27.32/*NPNF* 5:132; ibid., 23.25/129; ibid., 24.27/130. He was comforting despair when making this point in *Ep.* CXXXI (411/412)/*NPNF* 1:469. See the exhortation to faith agenda in *Nat. et grat.* 68.82/*NPNF* 5:50. Also see *Corrept.* X.27/*NPNF* 5:482; *Enchir.* 11/*NPNF* 3:240; 100/269; *Gen. ad litt.* XI.6.8; 11.14–15/*WSA* I/13:433, 436–37; *Ev. Joh.* XVII.10/*NPNF* 7:177.
68. Martin Luther, *Disputatio Heidelbergae habita* (1518), in *D. Martin Luthers Werke*, Kritische Gesamtausgabe (Weimarer Ausgabe) (56 vols., Weimar; Hermann Bohlaus Nachfolger, 1883ff.), vol. 1, pp. 353–74 [*Luther's Works*, vol. 31, ed. Harold J. Grimm (Philadelphia: Fortress Press, 1957), pp. 39–70].
69. *Civ.* XIV.27, 26/*NPNF* 2:282.
70. *Enchir.* 11, 96, 100, 101/*NPNF* 3:240, 267, 269–70; cf. ibid., 3–5/238, for the context.

71. *Vera relig.* xl.74/263–64; *Gen. ad litt.* V.20.40–41; VI.15.26; 17.28; 18.29; VIII.19.38–20.39; 23.44–24.45/*WSA* I/13:240–47, 315, 316, 317, 368–69; 371–72, 436–38; *Gen. litt. imp.* 5.25/*WSA* I/13:127–28; cf. *Doctr. Christ.* I.16.15/*NPNF* 2:526.
72. *Conf.* IX.IV.11–12; IX.VI.14/*NPNF* 1:133–34.
73. Ibid., VII.III.5; VII.XVI.22/104, 111.
74. Ibid., VII.XVI.22/111.
75. *Civ.* V.9.10/*NPNF* 2:92.
76. Ibid., V.10/92–93.
77. Ibid.
78. Ibid., XX.2/480.
79. Ibid., XII.5/229.
80. Ibid., XII.7–8/230–31.
81. Ibid., V.1, 21/84, 102–3.
82. Ibid., V.9/90; cf. VII.30; XIX.12/140, 409.
83. Ibid., X.14/189.
84. Ibid., V.20/102.
85. Ibid., XXII.2/480.
86. *Serm.* CXXIV [LXXIV] (c. 410).4–5/*NPNF* 6:478.
87. *Civ.* XIV.11/*NPNF* 2:271.
88. Ibid., XI.18/214–15.
89. Ibid., V.10/93.
90. Ibid., XXII.22; XXII.24/500, 502, 503.
91. Ibid., XX.1/421.
92. Ibid., XXII.22/500.
93. *Enchir.* 100/*NPNF* 3:269; see ibid., 3, 98/238, 268, for the context.
94. *Nat. et grat.* XLVI.54–XLVII.55/*NPNF* 5:139–40.
95. *De lib. arbit.* xviii.48/*LCC* 165; *Solilq.* II.3–5/*NPNF* 7:548–49; *Mor.* 1.22.40/*NPNF* 4:53. For another affirmation of this dualism when doing apologetics, see *Gen. litt. imp.* 5.24; 1:1/*WSA* I/13:126–27, 114. Such a view is implied when doing apologetics in *Civ.* XIX.3/*NPNF* 2:400.
96. *Ep. Joh.* XIX.12/*NPNF* 7:127; *Ps.* CXLV [CXLVI].2,1/*NPNF* 8:661–62.
97. *Ps.* CI [CII].31, 27/*NPNF* 8:502, 501.
98. *Conf.* X.VI.8; IX.XI.28/*NPNF* 1:144, 138; cf. *Civ.* X.6/*NPNF* 2:184 (see ibid., and ibid. X.1/180, for context).
99. *Anim.* IV.XXII.36–XXIII.37/*NPNF* 5:369–70; IV.XIIff./361ff; cf. *Fid.et symb.* 10.23/*NPNF* 3:331, articulated in the context of polemics with heretics.
100. *Conf.* XXXV.36/*NPNF* 1:152; *Trin.* XV.1.1/*NPNF* 3:199; *Mor.* 5.7, 8; 4.6/*NPNF* 4:43.
101. *Imm. an.* 15(24)/*FC* 4:43; *Mus.* VI.5(10)/*FC* 4:336; *Ps.* CXLV [CXLVI].2/*NPNF* 8:661–62.
102. *Fid. et symb.* 10.23/*NPNF* 3:331.
103. *Civ.* XXII.24/*NPNF* 2:503–4.
104. *De lib. arbit.* 2.3.8/*LCC* 138–39; *Mor.* 4.6; 5.7.8/*NPNF* 4:43.
105. *Conf.* III.VII.14/*NPNF* 1:65; *Ev. Joh.* XIX.12/*NPNF* 7:127; *Faust.* XII.1ff./*NPNF* 4:183–85; *Gen. ad litt.* VII.18.24/*WSA* I/13:335.
106. *Serm.* 155 (417).15/*WSA* III/5:93; *Conf.* VI.IV.6/*NPNF* 1:92.
107. *Trin.* XIV.4.6; XII.7.10, 12/*NPNF* 3:185–86, 159; *Civ.* XXII.24/*NPNF* 2:502; *Ps.* XLII [XLIII].6/*NPNF* 8:140.
108. *Trin.* VII.6.12; XIV.8.11/*NPNF* 3:113, 189. The latter text, though emerging in an apologetic context, still locates this intuitive tendency to God in the mind. Also see *Civ.* XIV.28/*NPNF* 2:220; *Conf.* XIII.XI.12/*NPNF* 1:193.

109. *Gen. ad litt.* VI.24.35; VI.27.38/*WSA* I/13:321, 322.
110. *Civ.* XXII.24/*NPNF* 2:502.
111. *Spir. et litt.* XVIII.48/*NPNF* 5:103; cf. *Trin.* XIV.8.11/*NPNF* 3:189; *Retrac.* II.50/*FC* 60:169.
112. *Conf.* X.V.7; X.XVII.26; X.XXXIII.50; X.VI.10/*NPNF* 1:144, 149, 156, 145.
113. *C. Acad.* I. 2(5)/*FC* 5:111; *De lib. arbit.* III.xxiv.71–72/*LCC* 213–14.
114. Ibid., I.viii.18; I.xiii.29/123, 129.
115. Ibid., I.xiv.30/130; *B. vita.* 2(10)/*FC* 5:55; *Retrac.* I.13(4)/*FC* 60:61; *Civ.* XIX.12/*NPNF* 2:407.
116. *Civ.* XI.26; XII.1/*NPNF* 2:220, 226; *De lib. arbit.* III.vi.18/*LCC* 181; *Conf.* IV.X.15/*NPNF* 1:72–73; cf. *Ep.* 155 (c. 414)/*FC* 20:35; *B. vita.* 2(11)/*FC* 5:58–59.
117. *De lib. arbit.* I.xv.31/*LCC* 131.
118. Ibid., II.x.28/152–53; cf. *Praed. sanct.* V.10/*NPNF* 5:503.
119. *Civ.* XXII.24/*NPNF* 2:503.
120. *Gr. et pecc. or.* I.XVIII.19–XXI.22/*NPNF* 5:224–25; cf. *Faust.* V.11/*NPNF* 4:167; *Ep. Joh.* V.7/*NPNF* 7:490; *Enchir.* 117/*NPNF* 3:274. Also see *Doctr. Christ.* I.23.22–I.24.24/*NPNF* 2:528, on self-love. See ibid., I.22.20/527, for the context.
121. *Civ.* XIX.1/*NPNF* 2:397.
122. *Trin.* XIV.14/18/*NPNF* 3:192–93; *Ep.* CXXX (412).VII.14/*NPNF* 1:463. For this critique of Augustine's view of love, see Anders Nygren, *Agape and Eros,* trans. Philip Watson (London: S. P. C. K., 1953); Karl Rahner, *Theological Investigations,* vol. 6, trans. K. H. Kruger and B. Kruger (Baltimore: Darton, Longan & Todd, 1969), pp. 231–49.
123. *Trin.* IX.6.9/*NPNF* 3:129.
124. Ibid., IX.7.12–IX.8.13/130–31.
125. Ibid., IX.9.14–11.16/131.
126. Ibid., XIV.1.1/183.
127. Ibid., VIII.10.14/124; see pp. 47–48, for other references to this and the next two points.
128. *Trin.* IX.5.8; IX.12.18; XIV.16.8/*NPNF* 3:128–29, 133, 187.
129. Ibid., X.10.13; XIV.6.8–7.10; XIV.8.11; XV.6.10/140–41, 187–88, 189, 204.
130. Ibid., XIV.10.13–12.15/190–91.
131. *De lib. arbit.* III.xxi.62/*LCC* 208; *Civ.* XI.23/*NPNF* 2:217–218. Also see *Ep.* CXLIII (c. 412).11/*NPNF* 1:492–94; *Ep.* CLXIV (414/415).VII.20/521; *Ep.* CLXVI (415).10ff/526ff.; Origen, *On First Principles,* I.VII.5.
132. *Ev. Joh.* XIX.6/*NPNF* 7:126; *Trin.* X.10.13–14/*NPNF* 3:140–41; cf. Plato, *Phaedo* 78–79.
133. *Civ.* XXII.24/*NPNF* 2:503.
134. *Ep. Joh.* III.1/*NPNF* 7:476.
135. *Civ.* XII.15/*NPNF* 2:236.
136. *B. conjug.* 1/*NPNF* 3:399; *Civ.* XIX.5/*NPNF* 2:403–4; ibid., XIV.1/262; ibid., XII.27/243–44.
137. *Civ.* XIV.1; XII.27, 27/*NPNF* 2:262, 243–44, 241.
138. *Ep.* CXXX (430).6.13/*NPNF* 1:463.
139. *Civ.* XIV.26/*NPNF* 2:281–282. See ibid., XIV.25/281, for a reference to the treatise's context.
140. *Enchir.* 106/*NPNF* 3:271. See n. 93 for a reference to the treatise's context.
141. *Gr. et lib. arb.* XIII.25/*NPNF* 5:454; cf. *Nat. et grat.* XLII.49/*NPNF* 5:138.
142. *Corrept.* 31/*NPNF* 5:484.

Chapter 5: Sin, Free Will, and Atonement

1. *Conf.* VII.III.4–5; VII.XVI.22/*NPNF* 1:103–4, 111 (in dialogue with the Manichees); *De lib. arbit.* I.xvi.35; II.xx.54; III.xii.35; III.xxiv.71/*LCC* 133–34, 168, 192, 213; *Nat. bon.* xxviii/*LCC* 335.
2. *De lib. arbit.* II.x.29/*LCC* 189.
3. *Vera relig.* xiv.27/*LCC* 238; *Gr. et lib. arb.* II.3–6/*NPNF* 5:444–45.
4. *Retrac.* I.8.2–3, 4/*FC* 60:32–33, 36: "Qwa propler novi haeretici Pelaglani, qui liberum sic asserunt voluntatis arbitrium, ut gratiae. Dei non relinquant locum, quandoquidem eam secumdum merita nostra dari asserunt, non se extollani, quasi eorum egerim causam; quia multa in his libris dixi pro libero arbitrio, quae illius disputationis causa pascelat."
5. Ibid., I.12.5/53–54; cf. *Gr. et lib. arb.* III.5/*NPNF* 5:446.
6. *De lib. arbit.* III.xviii.52/*LCC* 201–2.
7. Ibid., III.xviii.52; III.xix.53/202, 203.
8. Ibid., II.xx.54/168–69; *Vera relig.* xi.21/*LCC* 235.
9. *De lib. arbit.* III.xvii.48/*LCC* 199–200.
10. *Vera relig.* x.18; xxxvii.68; xiv.84/*LCC* 234, 259–60, 269; *Trin.* XII.11.16; XII.9.14/*NPNF* 3:161, 160.
11. A. Sage, "Le péché originel dans la pensée de saint Augustin, de 412 à 430," *Revue des études augustiniennes* 15 (1969): 75–112; J. Patout Burns, *The Development of Augustine's Doctrine of Operative Grace* (Paris: Etudes Augustiniennes, 1980).
12. *Simpl.* I.II.20; I.I.10/*LCC* 403–4, 380; *Gen. ad litt.* VI.24.35/*WSA* I/13:321.
13. *Bapt.* 1.15.23/*NPNF* 4:421; *Correct.* 9.40/*NPNF* 4:647. The latter document, it must be conceded, was written after the beginning of the Pelagian controversy, and so is not as important as the rest in making the case for continuity in Augustine's thought.
14. *Conf.* I.VII.12/*NPNF* 1:48–49.
15. Among those who have advocated for the compatibility of Augustine's mature doctrine of sin and that of his pre-Pelagian days, see W. S. Babcock, "Augustine's Interpretation of Romans (A.D. 394–396)," *Augustinian Studies* 10 (1979): 55–74; Paul Rigby, *Original Sin in Augustine's Confessions* (Ottowa: Ottowa University Press, 1987); T. G. Ring, *Ad Simplicianu, zwei Bucher über verschiedene Fragen* (Würzberg: Augustinus Verlag, 1991).
16. *Conf.* I.VII.11/*NPNF* 1:48; *Grat. Christ.* II.XIX.21/*NPNF* 5:244.
17. *Conf.* I.IX.15/*NPNF* 1:49.
18. Ibid., II.IV.9/57.
19. Ibid., II.V.10/57.
20. *Trin.* XIV.14.18/*NPNF* 2:192–93; *Conf.* II.VI.12/*NPNF* 1:58; *Nat. bon.* 34/*NPNF* 4:358; *Simpl.* II.18/*LCC* 400; *Civ.* XII.6/*NPNF* 2:229; ibid., XIV.28/282–83.
21. *Conf.* II.VIII.16; V.X.18/*NPNF* 1:59, 86.
22. Ibid., VI.VI.9; X.XX.29; X.XXI.30/93–94, 151–52.
23. Ibid., X.II.2, 3/142.
24. Ibid., X.XXVII.39/153.
25. Ibid., XIII.XX.28/109.
26. *Trin.* IX.4.4/*NPNF* 3:127; cf. *Civ.* XIII.13/*NPNF* 2:251.
27. *Trin.* X.5.7–7.9; VIII.34/*NPNF* 3:138–39, 117.
28. *Nat. et grat.* XX.22/*NPNF* 5:128; *Grat. Christ.* I.XIX.20/*NPNF* 5:225; *Nupt. et concup.* II.XXIV.39/*NPNF* 5:298–99; cf. *Civ.* XXII.1/*NPNF* 2:479; *Enchir.* 11/*NPNF* 3:240.
29. *Spir. et litt.* XII.19/*NPNF* 5:91; cf. *Civ.* XIV.13/*NPNF* 2:273.

30. *Serm.* LXXVI [XXVI] (410–412).14/*NPNF* 6:346; *Civ.* XXI.14; XXII.22–23/*NPNF* 2:464, 499–501.
31. *Civ.* XIV.13/*NPNF* 2:273: cf. *Nat. bon.* 10/*NPNF* 4:353.
32. *Civ.* XIV.3, 5/*NPNF* 2:263, 265; ibid., XIV.15/274; cf. ibid., XV.22/303.
33. Serm. LX [X] (397).1–2/*NPNF* 6:290.
34. *Civ.* XIV.28/*NPNF* 2:282–83. Also see p. 184 n. 120.
35. Ibid., XIX.10; I.9/406, 7; *Ev. Joh.* X.6/*NPNF* 7:71.
36. *Enchir.* 23/*NPNF* 3:245.
37. Ibid., 80/263.
38. Ibid., 83/264; *Ep.* 185 (417).49–50/*FC* 188–89; *S. Dom. mon.* I.XXII.75/*NPNF* 6:31.
39. *C. Fort.* 22/*NPNF* 4:21; *De lib. arbit.* I.xiv.30/*LCC* 6:130.
40. *Simpl.* I.I.10/*LCC* 380.
41. Ibid., I.I.11–12; I.II.21/381, 404–5; *Corrept.* I.2/*NPNF* 5:472; *Gr. et lib. arb.* VI.7/*NPNF* 5:447; *Nat. et grat.* LV.65/*NPNF* 5:144; *C. ep. Pel.* I.II.5/*NPNF* 5:378.
42. *Civ.* XXI.6/*NPNF* 2:229.
43. *Spir. et litt.* III.5; II.3–4/*NPNF* 5:84–85; *Enchir.* 30/*NPNF* 3:247.
44. *Spir. et litt.* III.5–IV.6/*NPNF* 5:85; cf. Martin Luther, *Lectures on Romans* (1515–1516), in *D. Martin Luthers Werke*, Kritische Gestamtausgabe (Weimer Ausgabe) (56 vols.; Weimar: Hermann Bohlaus Nachfolger, 1883ff.), vol. 56: 356f. [*Luther's Works,* vol. 25, ed. Hilton C. Oswald (St. Louis: Concordia, 1972), p. 345].
45. *Corrept.* XI.29/*NPNF* 5:483.
46. *Gr. et lib. arb.* XI.23; XV.31/*NPNF* 5:453, 456; *Nat. et grat.* LIII.61–62/*NPNF* 5:142.
47. *Nat. et grat.* V.5/*NPNF* 5:123; *Grat. Christ.* I.XLIX.54/*NPNF* 5:235; *Persev.* II.4; VIII.20/*NPNF* 5:527, 532.
48. *Conf.* X.XXIX.40/*NPNF* 1:15; *Spir. et litt.* XXIX.51/*NPNF* 5:105; cf. *Ep.* 157 (416)/*FC* 20:344.
49. *Gr. et lib. arb.* XVI.32/*NPNF* 5:547; *Perf. just.* VI.6/*NPNF* 5:161; Martin Luther, *Against Latomus* (1521), in *D. Martin Luthers Werke*, vol. 8, p. 93 [*Luther's Works,* vol. 32, ed. George Forrell (Philadelphia: Fortress Press, 1958), pp. 151–57, 209–10].
50. *Fid. et symb.* 4.6/*NPNF* 3:324; *Civ.* XII.6; XIV.14, 13/*NPNF* 2:229, 273, 274; ibid., XII.3/273; *Ev. Joh.* XXV.15.16/*NPNF* 7:165, 166.
51. *Nat. et grat.* XXIX.33; XXXI.35/*NPNF* 5:132, 133.
52. *Ep.* CVIII (410).III.22/*NPNF* 1:445–46.
53. *Civ.* XIX.25/*NPNF* 2:418–19; *c. Jul.* IV.3.16–17/*FC* 35:179–82.
54. *Civ.,* XIV.13/*NPNF* 2:273.
55. *Conf.* VIII.V.10/*NPNF* 1:120.
56. Ibid., VIII.V.12; VIII.IX.21; VIII.XI.26/121, 125, 126.
57. *Nat. et grat.* XXII.24/*NPNF* 5:129; *Gr. et pecc. or.* I.XXI.22/*NPNF* 5:225.
58. *Simpl.* II.20/*LCC* 404.
59. *Civ.* I.9/*NPNF* 2:6; *Perf. just.* XI(28)/*NPNF* 5:168.
60. *C. ep. Pel.* I.II.5/*NPNF* 5:378.
61. *Nat. et grat.* XXXI.25/*NPNF* 5:129.
62. Ibid., XLVI.54–XLVII.55/139–40; *C. ep. Pel.* I.5/*NPNF* 5:378.
63. *Civ.* XIV.15–16, 13.3/*NPNF* 2:275–76, 246; *Perf. just.* XIII.31/*NPNF* 5:170. See *Pecc. merit.* II.IV.4/*NPNF* 5:45, where concupiscence is identified as "the law sin."

64. *Nupt. et concup.* I.XXIV.27/*NPNF* 5:274–75; *Corrept.* XIII.42/*NPNF* 5:489; *Gr. et pecc. or.* II.XXIII.38/*NPNF* 5:250–51; *Enchir.* 26/*NPNF* 3:246. For the affirmation of the inherited character of original sin without reference to concupiscence, see *Pecc. merit.* I.IX.9/*NPNF* 5:18.

65. See *Conf.* II.I.1ff/*NPNF* 1:55ff.

66. Ibid., III.I.1; VI.XII.22; VI.XVI.26/60, 99, 100–101.

67. Ibid., XIII.VII.8/192.

68. *Gr. et lib. arb.* 8/*NPNF* 5:447.

69. Ibid., XVI.32/457.

70. *Civ.* XIV.3; XIII.13/*NPNF* 2:263–64, 251.

71. *Enchir.* 24/*NPNF* 3:245–46.

72. *Spir. et litt.* XXVI.48/*NPNF* 5:104; *Perf. just.* IX(20)/*NPNF* 5:165–66; *Nupt. et concup.* I.XXIV.27/*NPNF* 5:274–75; *Cat. rud.* 15/*NPNF* 3:374; *Enchir.* 78/*NPNF* 3:262–63; *Ep. Joh.* I.6/*NPNF* 7:464; *Ep.* CLXVII (c. 414/415).VI–17/*NPNF* 1:537; cf. *Catechism of the Catholic Church* (1994), pp. 1854–55.

73. *Enchir.* 18/*NPNF* 3:243. These remarks suggest an openness on Augustine's part to a situational ethic. Perhaps the fact that he was not just exhorting Christian life, a context in which the standard for Christian behavior is the Law of God, but also included a concern with apologetics accounts for his affirmation of such an ethic. On grading sins see *S. Dom. mon.* I.IX.24/*NPNF* 6:11.

74. *C. ep. Pel.* 1.13.27/*NPNF* 5:385–86; *Pecc. merit.* XXI.44/*NPNF* 5:176; *Nupt. et concup.* I.XXIV.27/*NPNF* 5:275.

75. *Nupt. et concup.* I.XXIII.25; I.XXV.28/*NPNF* 5:274, 275; cf. *C. Jul.* VI.15.47/*WSA* I/24:507. See *Apology of the Augsburg Confession (1531),* II/*The Book of Concord,* ed. Robert Kolb and Timothy J. Wengert (Minneapolis: Fortress, 2000), p. 117.35–118.38; *Catechism of the Catholic Church,* 1264.

76. *Conf.* IV.XII.19; V.IX.16/*NPNF* 1:74, 84–85; *Corrept.* X.27; XI.30/*NPNF* 5:482–84; *Trin.* XII.13.7; XIII.15.19; XIII.17.22; XV.19.34/*NPNF* 3:176, 178, 180, 128; ibid., XII.13.17/176; ibid., IV.13.17/78; *Serm.* CXXX [LXXX] (n.d.).2/*NPNF* 6:499; *Serm.* CXXXIV [LXXXIV] (c. 420/413).6/*NPNF* 6:511; *Ex. Gal.* 22(8)/*CG* 163; *Enchir.* 108/*NPNF* 3:272; *Ep. Joh.* II.14/*NPNF* 7:474–75; *Ev. Joh.* III.3; XLI.5; L.2; LXXIX.2/*NPNF* 7:19–20, 231, 279, 283, 343.

77. *Enchir.* 27, 33, 41, 62/*NPNF* 3:246, 248–49, 251, 257. The treatise's preoccupation with Christian life is evident in ibid., 7/239; *Ep. Joh.* VII.9/*NPNF* 7:504, when dealing with love (Christian life); *Trin.* IV.14.19/*NPNF* 3:79; *Civ.* X.6, X.19–20/*NPNF* 2:184, 192–93, also in a context of addressing how to live one's life as a sacrifice to God. *Trin.* IV.XIV.19; IV.XIII.18/*NPNF* 3:79, when critiquing pride. Likewise, see *Simpl.* I.2.16/*LCC* 398, 386; *Pecc. merit* II.I.1/*NPNF* 5:44. Themes suggestive of both the classic view, the Satisfaction Theory, and the Moral Influence Theory appear side-by-side in *Conf.* X.XLII.68–69/*NPNF* 1:162, as he considered both the logic of Christ's atoning work and how to live the Christian life. Also see Anselm, *Cur Deo Hom.* (n.d.) bk. 2, ch. 6, for a later proponent of the Satisfaction Theory, who articulates this vision while considering the nature of the Christian life with apologetic concerns in view (ibid., bk. 2, ch. 1; Pref.).

78. *Conf.* XIII.I.1/*NPNF* 1:190.

79. *Fid. et symb.* IV.6/*LCC* 357; *c. Acad.* III.19(42)/*FC* 5:219; *Vera relig.* xvi.32/*LCC* 240; *Mus.* 6.4.7/*FC* 4:322; *Cat. rud.* 48/*NPNF* 3:287; *Ex. Gal.* 24(10), 25(3)/*CG* 167, 169. Also see *Enchir.* 108/*NPNF* 3:472, for a reliance on both the classic view and the Moral Influence Theory. Again both the logic of Christ's Work and how to live the Christian life are considered.

Chapter 6: Salvation, the Christian Life, and Predestination

1. *Spir. et litt.* XXVI.45; X.16/*NPNF* 5:102, 89.
2. *Enchir.* 30/*NPNF* 3:247; *Spir. et litt.* IX.15; XIII.22; XXIX.51; XXXII.56/*NPNF* 5:89, 92, 105, 108; *Pecc. merit.* I [XIII].18/*NPNF* 5:21; *Gr. et pecc. or.* I.XIII.14/*NPNF* 5:223; *Praed. sanct.* VIII.12/*NPNF* 5:504; *Civ.* XXII.22/*NPNF* 2:501; *Ex. Gal.* 15(14ff.); 19/*CG* 147, 153, *Serm.* CX [LX] (c. 410).2/*NPNF* 6:444.
3. *Ps.* CX [CXI].3/*NPNF* 8:545; *Gest. Pelag.* I.II.6; II.V.10/*NPNF* 5:379, 395; *Persev.* XIII.32–33/*NPNF* 5:538; *Spir. et litt.* X.16/*NPNF* 5:89; *Enchir.* 30/*NPNF* 3:247; *Ex. Gal.* Pref. 2/*CG* 125; *Ep.* CXLV (c. 412–413)/*NPNF* 1:496; *Ev. Joh.* III.8,9/*NPNF* 7:21–22.
4. *Gr. et lib. arb.* 13.25/*NPNF* 5:454. Some recent critics like Alister E. McGrath, *Iustitia Dei: A History of the Christian Doctrine of Justification* (2nd ed.; Cambridge: University Press, 1998), esp. pp. 35–36, 204–7, have sought to argue for a dichotomy between the Protestant Reformers and Augustine, even when the African Father addressed Pelagianism. But this interpretation overlooks the external character of righteousness that Augustine affirms when depicting justification forensically, and in this text how it contradicts human conceptions and is rooted in Christ's Cross.
5. *Spir. et litt.* XIX.34; XVIII.31; X.16; VII.11/*NPNF* 5:97, 96, 89, 87; *Trin.* I.10.21/*NPNF* 3:29; *Ex. Gal.* Pref. (4); 15(17)/*CG* 125. 147.
6. *Conf.* X.II.2/*NPNF* 1:142. For a similar definition of confession as aiming to glorify God in tandem with an awareness of our sin, see *Serm.* LXVII [XVII] (n.d.).2/*NPNF* 6:311.
7. *Conf.* XI.I.1–II.2/*NPNF* 1:163.
8. Ibid., XI.II.4; XIII.I.1/164, 190; *Gr. et lib. arb.* XVIII.38/*NPNF* 5:460.
9. *Spir. et litt.* IX.15; XXXII.56/*NPNF* 5:88–89, 108; *Ev. Joh.* XXVI.1/*NPNF* 7:168.
10. *Gr. et pecc. or.* I.XIII.14/*NPNF* 5:223; *Enchir.* 41/*NPNF* 3:251; cf. Martin Luther, *Preface to the Complete Edition of Luther's Latin Writings* (1545), in *D. Martin Luthers Werke*, Kritische Gesamtausgabe (Weimarer Ausgabe) (56 vols., Weimar: Hermann Bohlaus Nachfolger, 1883ff.), vol. 56, p. 186 [*Luther's Works*, vol. 34, ed. Lewis L. Spitz (Philadelphia: Muhlenberg, 1960), p. 337].
11. *Civ.* XIV.13; XXII.22/*NPNF* 2:273, 501; cf. Martin Luther, *Disputatio Heidelbergae habita* in *D. Martin Luthers Werke*, vol. 1, pp. 353ff. [*Luther's Works*, vol. 31, ed. Lewis L. Spitz (Philadelphia: Muhlenberg, 1957), pp. 39ff.].
12. *Gr. et lib. arb.* 16.32/*NPNF* 5:457.
13. *Spir. et litt.* 36.64/*NPNF* 5:112; cf. *Pecc. merit.* II.VIII.10/*NPNF* 5:48.
14. *Ep. Joh.* IX.4/*NPNF* 7:515–16; *Ep.* LV (400).XIV.25–26/*NPNF* 1:311; cf. *Civ.* XIV.27/*NPNF* 2:419.
15. *Nat. et grat.* LIII.61/*NPNF* 5:142; *Gr. et pecc. or.* 2.39.44/*NPNF* 5:253; *Nupt. et concup.* I.XXX.33; I.XXII.30–XXVIII.31/*NPNF* 5:277, 276; *Persev.* XII.35/*NPNF* 5:486; *Pecc. merit.* II.VII.9/*NPNF* 5:48; *Praed. sanct.* IV.8/*NPNF* 5:502; *Spir. et litt.* 14.25/*NPNF* 5:94; *Ep. Joh.* I.6; VII.8/*NPNF* 7:463–64, 504; *Civ.* XIX.4, 27/*NPNF* 2:402, 419; *Retrac.* I.23; II.27/*FC* 60:103, 119; *Correct.* 9–40/*NPNF* 4:647; *Serm.* 9 (n.d.).73/*WSA* III/1: 270–71; *Serm.* LVII [VII] (c. 409).9/*NPNF* 6:283, *Serm.* XC [XL] (c. 411–416).3/*NPNF* 6:392–93; *Conf.* VIII.V.10; VIII.IX.21/*NPNF* 1:120–21, 125.
16. *De lib. arbit.* III.xix.53/*LCC* 202; *Nat. bon.* 31/*NPNF* 4:358; cf. *Ps.* IX.14/*NPNF* 8:36.
17. *Praed. sanct.* III.7/*NPNF* 5:500; *Persev.* XVI.41; XX.52/*NPNF* 5:542, 547.
18. *Conf.* I.I.1; VIII.IV.9/*NPNF* 1:45, 119–120; cf. *Ev. Joh.* XXVI.4/*NPNF* 7:169.

19. *Conf.* IX.I.1; VIII.X.22/*NPNF* 2:129, 125; *Ps.* LXX [LXXI].19 XXXIV [XXXIII]/*NPNF* 8:322, 73.
20. *Spir. et litt.* XXX.52/*NPNF* 5:106; ibid., XXXI.53/106; cf. *Praed. sanct.* V.10/ *NPNF* 5:503.
21. *Simpl.* II.11–13/*LCC* 393–95; ibid., II.2/386.
22. *Spir. et litt.* III.5/*NPNF* 5:85; *Gr. et lib. arb.* XIV.28–29/*NPNF* 5:455.
23. *Spir. et litt.* XXXII.56/*NPNF* 5:108.
24. *Praed. sanct.* II.3; IV.8; VII.12; VIII.16/*NPNF* 5:499, 504, 506; *C. ep. Pel.* II.20/*NPNF* 5:400–401.
25. *Gr. et lib. arb.* XIV.28/*NPNF* 5:455; *C. litt. Pet.* I.7–8/*NPNF* 4:522; *Spir. et litt.* XXIX.50/*NPNF* 5:105; *Serm.* CV [LV] (410–411).5/*NPNF* 6:431; *Enchir.* 30/*NPNF* 3:247; *Ep.* 194 (418)/*FC* 30:304, 309, 311, 318. This point is implied in *Ex. Gal.* 19(1); 37(4); 46(1)/*CG* 153, 173, 209, as he speaks of "the grace of faith."
26. *C. ep. Pelag.* I.XIX.37/*NPNF* 5:388–89; *Gr. et lib. arb.* XIV.29/*NPNF* 5:455; *Praed. sanct.* II.3; XIX.39/*NPNF* 5:499, 517; *Ep.* 215 (c. 426/427)/*FC* 32:65; *Corrept.* XI.31/*NPNF* 5:485.
27. *Ev. Joh.* 26.3/*NPNF* 7:168–69; cf. *Spir. et litt.* XXXI.54/*NPNF* 5:107.
28. *Spir. et litt.* XXXIII.57; XXXIV.60/*NPNF* 5:109, 110.
29. *Persev.* XXI.54, 55; XIII.33/*NPNF* 5:547–48, 538.
30. *Gr. et lib. arb.* XVI.32/*NPNF* 5:457; *Civ.* XXII.30/*NPNF* 2:510; cf. *Persev.* XII.35/*NPNF* 5:486; *Perf. just.* IV.9/*NPNF* 5:161–62. Similar affirmations are made in controversies with the Manichees in *C. fort.* 22/*NPNF* 4:122–22.
31. *Praed. sanct.* VII.12; VIII.16/*NPNF* 5:504, 506: "Ex fide autem ideo dicit justificari hominem, non ex operibus, quia ipsa prima datur, ex qua impetrentur caetera, quae proprie opera nun cuptantur, in quibus juste vivitur."
    "Fides igitur, et inchoate, et perfecta, donum Dei est: et hoc donum quibusdam dari, quibusdam non dari, omnio non dubiety, qui non vult manifestissimis sacris Literis repugnare."
    Cf. *Persev.* 25/*NPNF* 5:534–35.
32. *Spir. et litt.* XXXIV.60/*NPNF* 5:110.
33. Ibid., 110–11.
34. Ibid., XXX.52/106; *Ep.* 157 (414).2.10/*FC* 20:325; cf. *Retrac.* II.92/*FC* 60:268.
35. Council of Trent, *Decree Concerning Justification* (1547), V–VII; *The [Lutheran] Augsburg Confession,* IV, in *The Book of Concord,* ed. Robert Kolb and Timothy J. Wengert (Minneapolis: Fortress, 2000), 38–40.1; *The [Reformed] Westminster Confession* (1646), XIII, 6.608.
36. *Praed. sanct.* III.7/*NPNF* 5:501.
37. *Trin.* XIV.8.11/*NPNF* 3:189–90.
38. *Ep.* 147 (413).7/*FC* 20:175–76; *Trin.* XIV.2.4/*NPNF* 3:184.
39. *Praed. sanct.* II.5/*NPNF* 5:499–500; *Enchir.* 20/*NPNF* 3:244; *Symb. cat.* 1/*NPNF* 3:369.
40. Philo, *Enneads,* VI.9.7.
41. *Conf.* I.V.6; V.VII.13; X.I.1/*NPNF* 1:46, 83, 142; *Enchir.* 31/*NPNF* 3:247–48; *Serm.* 155 (417).15/*WSA* III/5:93; *Ep.* CXXXI (412–413) *NPNF* 1:469.
42. *Serm.* CXXVIII [LXXVIII] (412–416).4/*NPNF* 6:492; *Serm.* LXXX [XXX] (c. 410).5/*NPNF* 6:351; *Ep.* CLXXXVIII (416).II.5–6/*NPNF* 1:550; cf. *Ex. Gal.* 17(7–9)/*CG* 149–51, 173.
43. *Mor.* 13.22/*NPNF* 4:48; *Enchir.* 31/*NPNF* 3:248.
44. *Gr. et lib. arb.* XIV.30/*NPNF* 5:456; *Praed. sanct.* VIII.13/*NPNF* 5:505; *Ps.* IV.2/*NPNF* 8:8.
45. *Ep.* XCII (408).3/*NPNF* 1:380; *Conf.* XI.IX.11/*NPNF* 1:166–67. In *Conf.* X.XXVII.39/*NPNF* 1:153, such a vision emerges when comforting despair.

46. *Nupt. et concup.* I.XXV.28/*NPNF* 5:275: "Si autem quaeritur, quomodo ista concupiscentia carnis maneat in regenerato, in quo universorum facta est remissio peccatorum . . . ad haec responditur, dimitti concupiscentiam carnis in Baptismo, non ut non sit, sed ut in peccatum non imputetur."
    Conf. XI.11/*NPNF* 1:164; *Pecc. merit.* I.XIII.18; I.XXVII.43/*NPNF* 5:21–22; 31–32; *Trin.* XIV.18.24; *Enchir.* 41/*NPNF* 3:251; also see *Perf. just.* XI.27/*NPNF* 5:168. For an affirmation of this view or similar contexts, see Martin Luther, *The Holy and Blessed Sacrament of Baptism* (1519), in *D. Martin Luthers Werke,* vol. 2, 731 [*Luther's Works,* vol. 35, ed. E. Theodore Bachman (Philadelphia: Fortress Press, 1960), pp. 34–35]; *[Methodist] Articles of Religion* (1783–1784), 9.
47. *Ep.* XCII (408).5/*NPNF* 1:381.
48. Author trans.; *Trin.* XIV.XIX.25; XIV.XIV.20/*NPNF* 3:197, 194: "Propter cuius perfectionem dictum intelligendum est: Similes ei erimus quoniam uidebimus eum sicuti est. . . . Qui autem adhaeret domino unus spiritus est, accedente quidem ista ad participationem naturae, ueritatis et beatitudinis illius, non tamen crescente illo in natura, ueritate et beatitudine sua. In illa itaque natura cum feliciter adhaeserit immutabile uidebit onme quod uiderit."
49. *Ev. Joh.* XXI.8/*NPNF* 7:140: "Ergo gratulemur et agamus gratias, non solum nos christianos factos esse, sed Christum . . . si enim caput ille, nos membra; totus homo, ille et nos."
    Cf. *Ep. Joh.* II.14/*NPNF* 7:475; *Trin.* IV.24/*NPNF* 3:71; *Ep.* XCII (408).4/*NPNF* 1:381; *Ps.* XLIX [L].2/*NPNF* 8:178.
50. *Quant.* 33(76), 35(79)/*FC* 4:143, 146–47, *Conf.* VII.X.16/NPNF 1:109; ibid., IV.XII.19; XII.XVII.23; IX.X.23–26; XIII.VII.8; XIII.IX.10/74, 111–12, 137–38, 192; cf. *S. Dom. mon.* I.IV.11/*NPNF* 6:6; *Ep. Joh.* II.14/*NPNF* 7:475.
51. For Augustine's unambiguous affirmation of free will against the Manichees, see his *De lib. arbit.* III.xx.55; xxii.65/*LCC* 203, 209–10. Also see *Simpl.* I.14/*LCC* 382, for such an affirmation when addressing the importance of works.
52. *Civ.* XXII.29/*NPNF* 2:507; *Ep.* XIX(390)/*NPNF* 1:236; cf. *Ep.* 157 (414)/*FC* 20:323–24; *Ep. Joh.* IV.7/*NPNF* 7:485.
53. *De lib. arbit.* III.xx.55/*LCC* 203; *Nat. bon.* 31/*NPNF* 4:357.
54. *S. Dom. mon.* II.VIII.29; I.VIII.20; I.I.1/*NPNF* 6:43, 70, 3; *Civ.* XXI.27/*NPNF* 2:475, 476, 477; *De lib arbit.* III.x.29, 30/*LCC* 189, 190; *Ps.* XXXII [XXXIV].3–4, 22; XXXVIII [XXXIX].18; LXXVIII [XXXIX].10/*NPNF* 8:73, 77, 117, 371; *Ep.* CXVIII (410).III.22–IV.23/*NPNF* 1:445–46. *Gr. et lib. arb.* XVI.32/*NPNF* 5:457 (see *Gr. et lib. arb.* II.4/*NPNF* 5:444–45, for this passage's context).
55. *Vera relig.* xlii.79; xxix.73ff.; i.1/*LCC* 266, 262ff., 225; *Ord.* I.9(27)/*FC* 5:264; cf. Gabriel Biel, *Commentary on the Sentences,* II.27, 28.
56. *Vera relig.* vii.13; lv.113/*LCC* 232, 282; cf. *De lib. arbit.* III.xxii.64/*LCC* 209.
57. *Vera relig.* xii.24/*LCC* 236–37; *Retrac.* I.13.4/*FC* 60:52–53.
58. *Vera relig.* xlii.79/*LCC* 266; *B. vita* 3(21)/*FC* 5:69; *De lib. arbit.* II.xx.54/*LCC* 169; *Util. cred.* 24/*NPNF* 3:358.
59. *Gr. et lib. arb.* XVII.33/*NPNF* 5:458: "Ut ergo velimus, sine nobia operatur; cum autem, volumus, et sic volumus ut facismus, nobiscum cooperatur: tamen sine ilio vel operante ut velimus, vel cooperante cum volumnus, ad bona pietatis opera nihil valemus."
    See *Nat. et grat.* LXVI.79/*NPNF* 5:149, where he refers to the assistance of grace and only of a tendency to sin. Cf. *Ep.* XCV (408).6/*NPNF* 1:403; *Corrept.* I.2/*NPNF* 5:472; *Pecc. merit.* II.V.5; VI.7/*NPNF* 5:43–44; *Ep. Joh.* IV.7/*NPNF* 7:485; *Ps.* CXLIII [CXLII].12/*NPNF* 8:654; *Ex. Gal.* 24(10), 25(3), 32(3)/*CG* 167, 169, 183. See n. 35 above for the Catholic view.

60. *Gr. et lib. arb.* VI.15/*NPNF* 5:450; *Ps.* CII.6/*NPNF* 8:505; *Serm.* 298 (c. 416).4–5. See *Grat. Christ.* I.XXVI.27/*NPNF* 5:227–28, where he also claims that merits do not precede grace.

61. *Simpl.* I.7; II.2/*LCC* 379, 386; *Gr. et pecc. or.* I.XIII.14/*NPNF* 5:222; *Ev. Joh.* XXIX.6/*NPNF* 7:185; *Ep. Joh.* X.2/*NPNF* 7:521; *Serm.* 169 (416).3, 18/*WSA* III/5:225–26, 234–35; *Ex. Gal.* 32(3)/*CG* 183; cf. Thomas Aquinas, *Summa Theologica* (1266–1273), I2ae, q.113, a.2; II2ae, q.4, a.7.

62. *Pecc. merit.* II.VIII.10/*NPNF* 5:48; cf. Council of Trent, *Decree Concerning Justification* (154.7), x.
    C. ep. Pel. II.IX.21; IV.VI.15/*NPNF* 5:400–401, 427; *Gr. et lib. arb.* I.1; II.2; IV.6; VI.15; XV.31; XVII.33/*NPNF* 5:444, 446, 450, 456, 458; *Nat. et grat.* XXIII.25; LXVI.79/*NPNF* 5:130, 149; *Ep.* CCXIV (426/427).1, 4, 7/*NPNF* 1:437, 438; ibid., CCXV.7–8/*NPNF* 5:440.

63. *Gr. et lib. arb.* VII.18/*NPNF* 5:451; *Enchir.* 67/*NPNF* 3:259.

64. Methodist-Roman Catholic Dialogue, *Denver Report* (1971), 7. See p. 170 n. 2, for primary-source documentation for this contemporary observation. Also see John Wesley, *Minutes of the First Annual Conference* (1741), in *John Wesley,* ed. Albert Outler (New York: Oxford University Press, 1964), p. 137.

65. *Vera relig.* vi.11; xii.24; xiii.28/*LCC* 231–32, 236–37, 238. Also see *Spir. et litt.* II.4/*NPNF* 5:84; *Gest. Pelag.* XIV.32/*NPNF* 5:197.

66. *Enchir.* 32/*NPNF* 3:248; cf. Aquinas, *Summa Theologica,* I2ae, q.109, a.6.

67. *Enchir.,* 82/*NPNF* 2:264.

68. *Spir et. litt.* XXXII.56/*NPNF* 5:108.

69. *Enchir.* 46, 65/*NPNF* 3:252–53, 258.

70. Ibid., 67/259.

71. Ibid., 72, 73, 110/260–61, 272–73; cf. *Civ.* XXI.27/*NPNF* 2:477, 475; *Cura mort.* 22/*NPNF* 3:550.

72. *Enchir.* 75/*NPNF* 3:261–62; cf. *Catechism of the Catholic Church* (1974), 1032, 1434.

73. *Enchir.* 69/*NPNF* 3:260; *Civ.* XXI.26/*NPNF* 2:474–75.

74. *Civ.* XXII.9/*NPNF* 2:491: *Ev. Joh.* LXXXIV.1/*NPNF* 7:350.

75. *Fid. et symb.* I.1/*NPNF* 3:321.

76. *Simpl.* I.II.8–9, 21/*LCC* 392, 405.

77. *Conf.* X.VI.81/*NPNF* 1:144.

78. Ibid., X.XXIX.40; X.XXXVII.60/153, 159.

79. *Praed. sanct.* X.21/*NPNF* 5:508.

80. *Persev.* XIV.36–37/*NPNF* 5:539–40.

81. *Persev.* XXII.61/*NPNF* 5:549–50.

82. For instances when he posits a relationship between predestination and divine foreknowledge, see *De lib. arbit.* III.iii.8; III.iv.11/*LCC* 175–76, 177. In his *Ep. Rom.* 60–61/*FC* 60:98–99, 97 he also teaches predestination based on foreknowledge. As previously noted, he renounced this in his *Retrac.* I.22 (2)/*FC* 60:98–99, with his dialogue with Pelagianism in mind. Also see *Praed. sanct.* III.7, 18, 37, 39/*NPNF* 5:501, 507, 515–16, 517; *Simpl.* II.5–6, 2, 22/*LCC* 389–91, 386, 405; *Corrept.* XII.36/*NPNF* 5:486.

83. *Gr. et lib. arb.* XVIII.38/*NPNF* 5:460; *Praed. sanct.* XVII.34; XVIII.35, 37; XIX.38/*NPNF* 5:514–15, 516, 517; *Ep.* 194 (418)/*FC* 30:327; cf. *Ev. Joh.* LXXXVI.1–2/*NPNF* 7:353.

84. *Civ.* V.9; XXII.2/*NPNF* 2:90–91, 480; *Corrept.* XII.38/*NPNF* 5:487.

85. *Persev.* XVII.41; XVIII.47/*NPNF* 5:542, 544.

86. *Trin.* XV.7.13/*NPNF* 3:206.

87. *Praed. sanct.* III.7; VI.11; VIII.14.16; XIX.38–XX.40/*NPNF* 5:501, 503–4, 505,

506, 517; *Anim.* IV.11.16/*NPNF* 5:361; *Gr. et lib. arb.* XXIII.45/*NPNF* 5:464; *Ep.* 194/*FC* 30:303–4, 305, 308–10, 321, 327.

88. *Ev. Joh.* XLVIII.3–4; LIII.6/*NPNF* 7:266–67, 293; *Enchir.* 95, 96, 100, 102/*NPNF* 3:267, 268, 269, 270. In *Enchir.* 98/*NPNF* 2:268, he asserts unequivocally that predestination is not based on foreknowledge.

89. *Civ.* XXII.24; XV.1/*NPNF* 2:504, 284–85; cf. ibid., XVII.5/344–45; *Imm. an.* IV [XI].16/*NPNF* 5:361.

90. *Simpl.* I.II.13, 15–18/*LCC* 395, 397, 398–401; see ibid., II.2, 6/386–87, 391, for the context.

91. Ibid., II.18/400.

92. Ibid., II.19/401–2. With regard to his views of Judaism, and Jewish-Christian relations, Augustine regards the Jews as incorrect interpreters of their own Scriptures (*Ps.* LVIII [LIX].2.1/*NPNF* 8:241–42) and as Christ-killers (LXV [LXVI].4/275). However, he hastens to add, the Jews were not God-killers, for they would never have killed Jesus had they known Who He was. Although those who reject Christ will be crushed when He comes again (*Serm.* 91 [n.d.].1/*WSA* III/3:458–59), the African Father praises the Jews over other nations (*Ps.* LXXXIV [LXXXV].8/*NPNF* 8:408). He also insists that Judaism will continue to be preserved as a witness to the Church of divine Prophecy before Jesus (*Civ.* XVIII.46/*NPNF* 2:389; cf. *Faust.* XII.12/*NPNF* 4:187–88) and that as such the Jews should be treated with humility and love (*Adv. Jud.*).

93. *Persev.* IX.21; XI.25/*NPNF* 5:532, 534–35.

94. Ibid., VIII.16–17; XII.28/531, 536.

95. *Corrept.* XIV.44/*NPNF* 5:489; *Praed. sanct.* VIII.14/*NPNF* 5:505.

96. *Ev. Joh.* LXXXVII.3/*NPNF* 7:355.

97. *Civ.* XIV.27/*NPNF* 2:282. Also see ibid., XI.13/212–13, for a similar affirmation in the same context.

98. *Ev. Joh.* XIX.19/*NPNF* 7:131; cf. *Pecc. merit.* II.XVIII.31/*NPNF* 5:56–57.

99. *Enchir.* 62/*NPNF* 3:257; *Trin.* XV.25.44/*NPNF* 3:223; *Ps.* CXLVI [CXLVII].24/ *NPNF* 8:671.

100. *Conf.* XIII.XXXIV.49/*NPNF* 1:206.

101. *Persev.* XXIV.67/*NPNF* 5:552; *Ev. Joh.* CV.7/*NPNF* 7:398; cf. *Praed. sanct.* XV.30–XVI.31/*NPNF* 5:512–13. The last text includes more direct attention to a polemical concern, which may account for why there is at least a hint of double predestination along with the teaching of election in Christ.

102. *Ev. Joh.* LIII.5–6/*NPNF* 7:292–93.

103. *Spir. et litt.* XXXIV.60/*NPNF* 5:110.

104. *Civ.* XI.13/*NPNF* 2:213.

105. Ibid., XXI.23/468–69; cf. XXI.19–20/467, for the context.

106. *Enchir.* 97, 103/*NPNF* 3:267–68, 270.

107. *Ep.* CII (409)/*NPNF* 1:417–19.

108. *Ep.* CLXIV (414). II.3ff./*NPNF* 1:515–20; *Corrept.* XV.47, 49; XVI.49/*NPNF* 5:491.

109. *De lib. arbit.* I.ii.6/*LCC* 115. Also see p. 185 nn. 1–3 for other references.

110. *Retrac.* I.8(2)/*FC* 60:32–33.

111. *Persev.* XV.38; XVI.40; XXII.57–60/*NPNF* 5:541–42, 549.

112. Ibid., XXII.61/550.

113. *Spir. et litt.* XXX.52/*NPNF* 5:106.

114. See n. 15 above for references.

115. *Civ.* XIX.25/*NPNF* 2:418–19.

116. *Enchir.* 22, 21/*NPNF* 3:245; *Ep. Joh.* VII.8/*NPNF* 7:504; *Ex. Gal.* 57(4)/*CG* 227.

117. *Simpl.* I.I.17/*LCC* 384; *Spir. et litt.* X.16/*NPNF* 5:89.
118. *Nupt. et concup.* I.XXX.33/*NPNF* 5:277; *Enchir.* 31/*NPNF* 3:248; *Spir. et litt.* XXIX.5/*NPNF* 5:105–6.
119. *Cat. rud.* IV.7/*NPNF* 3:286–87; *Ev. Joh.* LII.2/*NPNF* 7:287; *Pat.* 15, 20, 24/*NPNF* 3:532, 534, 535; *Serm.* 2 (c. 391).9/*WSA* III/1:181. That good works are works of grace is also affirmed against Pelagianism in *Ep.* 215 (c. 426–427)/*FC* 32:65–67; *Gr. et lib. arb.* VIII.19; IX.21/*NPNF* 5:451, 452; *Agon.* 10(11)/*FC* 2:326. Also in response to Pelagianism, see *Spir. et litt.* IV.6/*NPNF* 5:84. Cf. *Ps.* XXXV [XXXVI].12/*NPNF* 8:89, where a reference is also made to the soul becoming divine. This may relate to the fact that the Psalms' overall context is an exhortation to Christian living.
120. *Ep.* 186 (417)/*FC* 30:194; *Simpl.* II.2/*LCC* 386; *Pecc. merit.* II.XVIII.28/*NPNF* 5:56; *Grat. Christ.* I.XXI.22/*NPNF* 5:225; *Civ.* XIV.11/*NPNF* 2:271.
121. *Ev. Joh.* 51.10/*NPNF* 7:285; *Civ.* X.6/*NPNF* 2:184; cf. *Agon.* 7(7), (8)/*FC* 2:322–23.
122. *Ep.* CXVIII (410).I.15/*NPNF* 1:443; ibid., CXXX (412).V.11–VII.15/*NPNF* 1:462–64; *Mag.* xiv.46/*LCC* 6:100; *Conf.* V.IV.7; X.XXIII.33.34/*NPNF* 1:81, 151–52; *Trin.* XI.14.18/*NPNF* 3:192–93; *Civ.* X.3/*NPNF* 2:182. For a reference to self-love, see *Ep.* CXXX (412).VI.14/*NPNF* 1:463. For reference to enjoyment of oneself, see *Doctr. Christ.* III.10.16/*NPNF* 2:561.
123. *Trin.* VIII.6.9/*NPNF* 3:122.
124. *Conf.* XII.XXXV.50; X.XXXVIII.63; XI.I.1/*NPNF* 1:207, 160, 163; *Pecc. merit.* II.XXXIV.56/*NPNF* 5:66–67.
125. *Civ.* XIX.10/*NPNF* 2:406.
126. *Ev. Joh.* XL.10/*NPNF* 7:228–29.
127. *Doctr. Christ.* I.22.20–21; I.33.36–37/*NPNF* 2:527–28, 532.
128. *Trin.* X.7–8.13/*NPNF* 3:130–31; *Conf.* IV.XII.18/*NPNF* 1:73–74.
129. See *Vera relig.* i.1–ii.2/*LCC* 225, for the context of this treatise.
130. Ibid., vi.11/231; cf. *Serm.* 4 (c. 410–419).37/*WSA* III/1:206.
131. *Vera relig.* xxxv.65/*LCC* 258.
132. Ibid., xlv.84–xlvi.86, 88–89, 92–xlvii.93/269, 270–71, 273.
133. *Conf.* XIII.XXI.30/*NPNF* 1:200; *De lib. arbit.* III.x.30; III.xxv.76/*LCC* 190, 216–17; *Ex. Gal.* 38(5), (7–8)/*CG* 193; *Ev. Joh.* CV.4/*NPNF* 7:396–97; ibid., LII/282; *Serm.* 325 (408).1/*WSA* III/9:167.
134. *Enchir.* 53/*NPNF* 3:254–55. Augustine also relies on the concept imitation of Christ in order to condemn sin, in *Trin.* XIII.17.22/*NPNF* 3:179–80.
135. *Conf.* X.VIII.12; X.XVII.26/*NPNF* 1:145, 149; cf. *Quant.* 33(70)–35(79)/*FC* 4:136–47; Plotinus *Enneads* VI.9.4.
136. *Conf.* X.XXXVI.58/*NPNF* 1:158–59; cf. ibid., X.XXXIf.43ff./151ff.
137. *Nat. et grat.* LXVIII.82/*NPNF* 5:150; *Perf. just.* VIII.19; XIII.31/*NPNF* 5:165, 170; *Ev. Joh.* LIII.8/*NPNF* 7:293; *Trin.* XIV.17.23; XIV19.25/*NPNF* 3:196, 197; *Ep.* CXII (408).3/*NPNF* 1:380; cf. *Ev. Joh.* CVIII.2/*NPNF* 7:404–5.
138. *Ep.* LV (400).III–5/*NPNF* 1:304; *Perf. just.* XVIII.39/*NPNF* 5:173–74; *Serm.* 158 (c. 417).4/*WSA* III/5:116.
139. *Conf.* X.XXX.41–42; X.XXXVII.61; X.XXXIX.63–64/*NPNF* 1:153–54, 159–60.
140. *Vera relig.* xxvii.50/*LCC* 250; *Fid. et symb.* 10.22/*NPNF* 3:331.
141. *Serm.* 158 (n.d.).5.
142. *Spir. et litt.* III.5/*NPNF* 5:84–85.
143. *Ep. Joh.* II.8; X.1/*NPNF* 7:472, 520. Also see n. 61 above.
144. Aquinas, *Summa Theologica* II-2ae, q.4, a. 3.
145. See p. 170 n. 2.

146. *Ep. Joh.* X.2/*NPNF* 7:521; Martin Luther, *Treatise on Good Works* (1520), in *D. Martin Luthers Werke,* vol. 6, p. 216 [*Luther's Works,* vol. 44, ed. James Atkinson (Philadelphia: Fortress Press, 1966), pp. 38–39].
147. *Enchir.* 118–19/*NPNF* 3:275; *Vera relig.* xxvi.48–49/*LCC* 248–49.
148. *Ep.* LV (400).III.5/*NPNF* 1:304–5. Against the Manichees, in *Faust.* XII.8ff/*NPNF* 4:185ff., Augustine identifies six periods of world history.
149. *Civ.* XI.12, 11/*NPNF* 2:212; *Gr. et lib. arb.* XXIII.45/*NPNF* 5:464; *Corrept.* VI.10; VII.15–VIII.18; IX.20–23/*NPNF* 5:475, 477–78, 479–81; *Ev. Joh.* XLV.12–13/*NPNF* 7:254. Also see *Corrept.* XIII.40/*NPNF* 5:488, where Augustine affirms perseverance of the elect while comforting from despair along with the Pelagian critique. Cf. *Persev.* XXI.56/*NPNF* 5:549, where he is again critiquing Pelagianism and affirming continuity with his past writings.
150. *Persev.* II.4; V.9; XIII.13/*NPNF* 5:528, 529, 538.
151. *Corrept.* XIII.40; VII.15/*NPNF* 5:488, 477.
152. See pp. 85, 79, above for references.
153. *Civ.* XIX.14/*NPNF* 2:410.
154. *Simpl.* I.I.2/*LCC* 377; *Spir. et litt.* XXI.36/*NPNF* 5:98.
155. *Simpl.* I.I.2–3, 6/*LCC* 377, 378; *Ex. Gal.* 25(9)/*CG* 171.
156. *Conf.* II.VI.14/*NPNF* 1:58–59; *Civ.* XIII.5/*NPNF* 2:247; *Simpl.* I.I.5/*LCC* 378.
157. *Serm.* CXXV[LXXV] (416–417).2/*NPNF* 6:476; *Civ.* XIII.5/*NPNF* 2:247; *Enchir.* 118/*NPNF* 3:275.
158. *Conf.* X.XXXVIII.63; XI.I.1/*NPNF* 1:160, 162.
159. *Gr. et lib. arb.* X.22/*NPNF* 5:452; *Gr. et pecc. or.* VIII.9/*NPNF* 5:221; *Spir. et litt.* VI.6/*NPNF* 5:85; *Corrept.* I.2/*NPNF* 5:472; *Gest. Pelag.* VI.20–IX.21/*NPNF* 5:191–92; *Ep.* CXLV (c. 413/414).3/*NPNF* 1:496.
160. *Gr. et lib. arb.* XVIII.37/*NPNF* 5:459; *Corrept.* I.2/*NPNF* 5:472.
161. *Nat. et grat.* XII.13/*NPNF* 5:125; *Spir. et litt.* XVII.29–30/*NPNF* 5:95–96.
162. *Spir. et litt.* IX.15/*NPNF* 5:88–89; cf. *Grat. Christ.* I.VIII.9/*NPNF* 5:220–21.
163. *Ep.* 157 (414)/*FC* 20:321.
164. *Gr. et lib. arb.* XI.23; XVII.39–XIX.40/*NPNF* 5:453, 460.
165. *Corrept.* V.7/*NPNF* 5:473–74; cf. *Ep.* CXLV (412–413).3/*NPNF* 1:496.
166. *Enchir.* 117–118/*NPNF* 3:274–75; cf. *Ep.* 177 (c. 416)/*FC* 30:97.
167. *Simpl.* I.I.17/*LCC* 385; *Spir. et litt.* V.8/*NPNF* 5:86. Also see p. 28 nn. 100–101.
168. *Spir. et litt.* XII.19; XIII.22/*NPNF* 5:91, 92–93.
169. *Simpl.* I.I.17/*LCC* 384.
170. *Corrept.* esp. 1.3.5/*NPNF* 5:473; *Serm.* LXXXII [XXXII] (408–409).1–3/*NPNF* 6:357–58; *C. ep. Parm.* 3.2.16.
171. *Ep.* XXII (392).3/*NPNF* 1:239–40; also *Ep.* XXIX (395).3ff./*NPNF* 1:253ff.; *Conf.* XII.XXIII.34/*NPNF* 1:202.
172. *Fid. et symb.* 10.21/*NPNF* 3:331; cf. *Retrac.* II.27/*FC* 60:119–20.
173. *Simpl.* I.I.6/*LCC* 378; *Nat. et grat.* XLIII.50/*NPNF* 5:138.
174. *Civ.* XIX.14, 13/*NPNF* 2:410, 408. These references may refer not to specifically Christian behavior, but to the behavior expected of all citizens in government. In any case, the point is still valid, in noting that when Augustine expressly addresses the topic of Christian behavior he uses the Law as a guide. See Chapter 10 for more details on the civil righteousness expected of all citizens of a state.
175. *Fid. et symb.* 4.6/*NPNF* 3:324; cf. *Ep.* CLXXXIX (418).2/*NPNF* 1:553.
176. *Civ.* IV.27/*NPNF* 2:595–96.
177. Ibid., XX.30/2:451.
178. *Ep. Joh.* I.9/*NPNF* 7:465.
179. *Div. qu.* 76.2/*FC* 70:196, 194.

180. See p. 85, above.
181. *Ev. Joh.* XLI.12/*NPNF* 7:234; *Pecc. merit.* II.VI.7/*NPNF* 5:46–47; *Spir. et litt.* XXXV.62/*NPNF* 5:111; *Nat. et grat.* LXVIII.82/*NPNF* 5:150; *Perf. just.* VIII.17–18; XX.43/*NPNF* 5:164, 175–76; *Grat. Christ.* XLVIII.53/*NPNF* 5:235; *S. Dom. mon.* XXIII.80/*NPNF* 6:33. Cf. Clement of Alexandria, *The Stromata, or Miscellanies* (c. 194), IV.XIX,XXV; VI.XII/*Ante-Nicene Fathers,* ed. Alexander Roberts and James Donaldson (2nd print., Peabody, MA: Hendrickson, 1995), vol. 2, pp. 431, 438, 502; Athanasius, *Life of St. Anthony* (c. 356), 19/*NPNF* 2nd series 4:200; Pseudo-Macarius, *The Fifty Spiritual Homilies* 17, 19; John Wesley, *A Plain Account of Christian Perfection* (1725–1777); John Wesley, *Brief Thoughts on Christian Perfection* (1767).175. See *Civ.* IV.27/*NPNF* 2:595–96.
182. *Mor.* 13.22–23/*NPNF* 4:48; *Conf.* X.XXXVIII.63/*NPNF* 1:160.
183. *Nat. et grat.* LXIV.77/*NPNF* 5:148.
184. *Perf. just.* III.7/*NPNF* 5:161.
185. Martin Luther, *Ninety-Five Theses* (1517), 1, in *D. Martin Luthers Werke,* vol. 1, 233 [*Luther's Works,* vol. 31, ed. Harold J. Grimm (Philadelphia: Muhlenberg, 1957), p. 25].
186. *Perf. just.* XI.28–29; XIII.31–XIV.32/*NPNF* 5:168–69, 170–71; cf. ibid., VIII.19/165.
187. *Ep.* LV (400).XIV.26/*NPNF* 1:311–12.
188. *Nupt. et concup.* I.XXIX.32–XXX.33/*NPNF* 5:276, 277.
189. Ibid., I.XXV.28; I.XXIII.25/275, 274.
190. *Perf. just.* III.5ff. (XIII.31)/*NPNF* 5:160ff.(170); *Nat. et grat.* VII.8/*NPNF* 5:123; *Spir. et litt.* XXXVI.66/*NPNF* 5:113–14.
191. *Nat. et grat.* XLII.49/*NPNF* 5:138. This commitment also surfaces in his *Ep.* 157 (414)/*FC* 20:320–21, where he both affirms and denies the possibility of perfection.
192. *Ep.* CXXX (412).II.3/*NPNF* 1:460.
193. *Ep. Joh.* X.7/*NPNF* 7:524; ibid., VIII.10/510.
194. See above, pp. 84, 100.
195. *Ep. Joh.* X.4, 3, 2/*NPNF* 7:522, 521.
196. *Nat. et grat.* LXIX.83/*NPNF* 5:150–51; *Gr. et lib. arb.* XVIII.38/*NPNF* 5:459.
197. See p. 193 n. 116, above for references.
198. *Conf.* III.IX.17/*NPNF* 1:66.
199. Ibid., IX.I.1/129.
200. *Ep. Joh.* VIII.10/*NPNF* 7:510. This hiddenness of the Christian life is asserted in a slightly different way in this context in *Trin.* XIV.18.24/*NPNF* 3:197.
201. *Trin.* VIII.8.12; VIII.10.14; IX.2.2–3.3; XIV.14.18/*NPNF* 3:123, 124, 126–27, 193; *Grat. Christ.* I.XXVI.27/*NPNF* 5:227.
202. *Gr. et lib. arb.* XIV.30/*NPNF* 5:456.
203. *Nat. et grat.* XXVI.29/*NPNF* 5:131.
204. Ibid., LXVII.80; XXXII.36/149, 133.
205. *Trin.* XV.17.31/*NPNF* 3:217; cf. *Ex. Gal.* 46(6ff.)/*CG* 211.
206. *Conf.* X.II.2; XIII.XXXVIII.53/*NPNF* 1:142, 207; *C. ep. Pel.* IX.21/*NPNF* 5:400–401; *Civ.* XIII.15/*NPNF* 2:251.
207. *Gr. et lib. arb.* XIII.26–XIV.27/*NPNF* 5:454, 455; cf. *Grat. Christ.* I.II.2/*NPNF* 5:218.
208. *Praed. sanct.* X.22/*NPNF* 5:509; *Corrept.* XII.35/*NPNF* 5:486.
209. *Gr. et pecc. or.* I.XIII.14/*NPNF* 5:223.
210. *Retrac.* I.8.4/*FC* 60:35–36.

Chapter 7: Church and Ministry

1. *Virg.* 2/*NPNF* 3:417; *Bapt.* I.16–25/*NPNF* 4:422; *Nat. et grat.* XXI.23/*NPNF* 5:128; *Serm.* (c. 410) LVII [VII].2/*NPNF* 6:281; *Symb. cat.* 1/*NPNF* 3:369; *Ep.* XXIII (392).4/*NPNF* 1:243; *Ep.* XLVIII (398).2/*NPNF* 1:294; *Ep.* LXIX (402).1/*NPNF* 1:325; *Ep.* LXXXIV (405).1/*NPNF* 1:363; *Ep.* XCVIII (408).3/*NPNF* 1:407–8; *Ep.* 104 (409)/*FC* 18:205–6; *Quant.* 33(76)/*FC* 4:143; *Ep.* 185 (417)/*FC* 30:190; *Ps.* CXXVII [CXVIII].4–6/*NPNF* 8:60–61.
2. *Fid. et symb.* IX.21/*NPNF* 3:331: ". . . si auten ista fides congregationem societatemque hominum non teneat, qua fraterna charitas operetur, minus fruc tuosa est."
3. *Serm.* 341 (n.d.).11, 12/*WSA* III/10.26. 27; *Ev. Joh.* XXI.8/*NPNF* 7:140: "Ergo gratulemur et agamus gratias, non solum nos christianos factos esse, sed Christum."
   Cf. *Doctr. Christ.* I.16.15/*NPNF* 2:526; *Ps.* LXII [LXI].2/*NPNF* 8:251.
4. *Ep.* XCIII (408).IX.28/*NPNF* 1:392.
5. *Ps.* CI [CII].21/*NPNF* 8:500; *Bapt.* III.18.23/*NPNF* 4:443–44.
6. *Ep. fund.* 5.6/*NPNF* 4:131; *Bapt.* IV.1.1; IV.17.25/*NPNF* 4:447, 458; *Pecc. merit.* III.XXII.21/*NPNF* 5:78.
7. *Civ.* XIX.17, 19/*NPNF* 2:412–13; *Ep.* LV (400).XVIII.34/*NPNF* 1:314; cf. *Conf.* III.VII.13/*NPNF* 1:64.
8. *Ep. Joh.* X.8, 10/*NPNF* 7:524, 525–26.
9. Ibid., II.3/470.
10. Ibid., I.12, 13/468, 470. See *Ev. Joh.* XXVII.6/*NPNF* 7:176, for another affirmation that one cannot be in Christ outside the Church.
11. *Ep. Joh.* III.5/*NPNF* 7:477.
12. Ibid., III.7/478.
13. *Bapt.* I.1–2/*NPNF* 4:411–12.
14. *Ep. Joh.* III.4/*NPNF* 7:477.
15. *Faust.* 13.5/*NPNF* 4:201.
16. *Ep.* LIII (400).2–3/*NPNF* 1:298.
17. *Serm.* LXXXVIII [XXXVIII] (c. 400).18/*NPNF* 6:385; *Ps.* XCIX [C].5/*NPNF* 8:488; *Doctr. Christ.* 3.32.45/*NPNF* 2:569; *Ep.* XCIII (408) IX.33–34/*NPNF* 1:394; *Bapt.* VI.2.4–4.6/*NPNF* 4:480–81; *Agon.* 12(13)/*FC* 2:331.
18. *Bapt.* V.27.38; IV.9.13/*NPNF* 4:476–77, 452–53.
19. *C. litt. Pet.* II.48.111–12; II.81.178; II.109.246/*NPNF* 4:559–60, 571, 595; *Retrac.* II.44/*FC* 60:156.
20. *Gest. Pelag.* XII.27/*NPNF* 5:195; *Ep.* 185 (417).38/*FC* 30:171; *Fid. et op.* I.1. See *Bapt.* VI.I.1/*NPNF* 4:479, and *Correct.* 9–38/*NPNF* 6:647, where he takes this position against the Donatists.
21. *Civ.* I.35/*NPNF* 2:21; *Cat. rud.* XIX.31–32/*NPNF* 3:303; *Ps.* VIII.1, 13/*NPNF* 8:28, 31; cf. *Ep.* 157 (416)/*FC* 20:353, 340.
22. *Ep. Joh.* X.1/*NPNF* 7:520; *Ps.* CXXI [XCCII].4, 5, 1/*NPNF* 8:594, 593. For denominations with a parallel construal of the Church, a view that emerges in relation to their preoccupation with living the Christian life, see *[Baptist] Second London Confession* (1677/1688), XVI, Preface; Southern Baptist Convention, *Baptist Faith and Message* (1968), VI; Church of God in Christ, *Official Manual* (1973), pp. 61, 83–84. Protestant traditions not as single-mindedly preoccupied with issues related to sanctification but in contrast define the Church, as Augustine did in such contexts, in more objective terms that construe it as God's act, include *The [Lutheran] Augsburg Confession* (1530), VII; *The [Anglican] Thirty-Nine Articles* (1549), XIX; *The [Reformed] Heidelberg Catechism* (1563), Q.54.
23. *Ep. Joh.* X.3/*NPNF* 7:521.

24. *Ep.* XXXV (396).1–4/*NPNF* 1:264–65; ibid., LXV (404).2/322–23; ibid., XCIII (404).V.16–17/388; *Ep.* 153 (413/414)/*FC* 20:284, 298. *C. litt. Pet.* III.37–43/*NPNF* 4:614.
25. *Civ.* XXI.20–21/*NPNF* 2:467–68.
26. *Enchir.* 56, 61/*NPNF* 3:255, 257; *Civ.* XX.9/*NPNF* 2:430.
27. *Ep.* XII (391).1/*NPNF* 1:237.
28. *C. ep. Parm.* II.13.28; *B. conjug.* 32/*NPNF* 3:412; *Ep.* LIII (400).3, 2/*NPNF* 1:298. For the affirmation of Apostolic Succession, see *Ep.* XLIV (398).III.5/*NPNF* 1:287; *Faust.* XXXIII.9/*NPNF* 4:345; *Ep. fund.* 4.5/*NPNF* 4:130.
29. *Util. cred.* 35/*NPNF* 3:364–65.
30. *Ep.* CXXXIII (412).2/*NPNF* 1:471; *Ps.* CXXVI [CXXVII].2/*NPNF* 8:606–7.
31. *Ep. fund.* 4.5/*NPNF* 4:130; *Ep.* XLIII (397).III.7/*NPNF* 1:278; cf. *Serm.* CXLVII [XCVII] (409).2/*NPNF* 6:544.
32. *Ps.* LXXVII [LXXVIII].35/*NPNF* 8:379; *Civ.* XVII.5/*NPNF* 2:345; *Ev. Joh.* LI.13/*NPNF* 7:286–87; cf. *Ep.* 134 (412)/*FC* 20:9.
33. *Conf.* IV.XII.19/*NPNF* 1:74; *Ps.* VIII.7/*NPNF* 8:29.
34. *Conf.* XI.II.2/*NPNF* 1:163; *Ep.* XXI (391).3/*NPNF* 1:238; cf. *C. litt. Pet.* III.55–67/*NPNF* 4:625, as he makes this point against the Donatists.
35. See below, n. 4, for references.
36. *Perf. just.* XVII (38)/*NPNF* 5:173; *Ep.* LXV (402).1–2/*NPNF* 1:322–23.
37. *Doctr. Christ.* IV.27.59/*NPNF* 2:595–96.
38. Ibid., IV.16.33/585.
39. *Cat. rud.* 10.15/*NPNF* 3:293–94.
40. *Ep.* LIV (400).II.2/*NPNF* 1:300; ibid., LV (400).XVIII.34/*NPNF* 1:314; ibid., XXXVI (396).I.2ff./*NPNF* 1:265–70.
41. Ibid., XXII (392) II.8/*NPNF* 1:241; *Ep. Joh.* V.15; LVII.3/*NPNF* 7:37, 304.
42. *Enchir.* 3/*NPNF* 3:238; *Trin.* XII.14.22/*NPNF* 3:165.
43. *Conf.* IX.VII.15–16/*NPNF* 1:134.
44. Ibid., X.XXXIII.50/256.
45. *Ep.* LV (400).XVIII.34/*NPNF* 1:314–15.
46. *Ep.* CCXIII (42).1ff./*NPNF* 1:569–70; *Ev. Joh.* III.21; XLV.13/*NPNF* 7:25, 254; cf. *Ep. Joh.* V.7/*NPNF* 7:490; *Cat. rud.* IX.13/*NPNF* 3:292.
47. *Ev. Joh.* XXXVI.15/*NPNF* 7:173.
48. *Persev.* XXIII.63/*NPNF* 5:551; *Ep.* CXXX (412).X.20/*NPNF* 1:465.

Chapter 8: Sacraments

1. *Ep.* LIV (400).I-1/*NPNF* 1:300: ". . . unde Sacramentis numero paucissimis, observatione facillimis, significatione praestantissimis, societatem novi populi coligavit, sicuti est Baptismus Trinitatis nomine consecratus, communicatio corporis et sanguinis ipsius, et si quid aliud in Scripturis canonicis commendatur. . . ."
2. *Simpl.* II.2/*LCC* 386; *Ev. Joh.* LXXX.3/*NPNF* 7:344.
3. *Faust.* XIX.16/*NPNF* 4:244; *Ev. Joh.* LXXX.3/*NPNF* 7:344. This theme was employed by seventeenth-century Protestant Orthodoxy (see John Gerhard, *Loci communes theologici* [1610–1622], XVIII.11) and by modern heirs like Robert W. Jenson, *Visible Words: The Interpretation and Practice of Christian Sacraments* (Philadelphia: Fortress Press, 1978), pp. 3ff.
4. *Bapt.* III.10.15; IV.10.17; VI.2.4/*NPNF* 4:439–40, 454, 480; *Ev. Joh.* V.15/*NPNF* 7:37; *C. litt. Pet.* II.47–110, 48–112, 30–69/*NPNF* 4:559–60, 547; *Ep.* XCVIII (408).5/*NPNF* 1:408; *Bapt.* III.15–20/*NPNF* 7:294.
5. *C. litt. Pet.* II.105.39/*NPNF* 4:592.

6. *B. conjug.* 21, 32/*NPNF* 3:408, 412; *C. Jul.* V.12(46)/*FC* 35:288; *Adul. conjug.* I.1(1); I.9(9); I.11(12); I.25(31); II.4(3)–(4); II.19(20)/*FC* 27:62, 71–72, 75–76, 97–98, 104–105, 128–29; cf. *Nupt. et concup.* I.XXI.23/*NPNF* 5:273.

7. *Sym. cat.* 15/*NPNF* 3:374–75; *Serm.* LXXXII [XXXII] (408–9).7/*NPNF* 6:359; *Ep.* 153 (413/414)/*FC* 20:284; *Ep.* 265 (c. 396)/*FC* 32:280–81; *Enchir.* 46, 65, 71/*NPNF* 3:252, 258, 260.

8. *Pecc. merit.* I.xxiv.63/*NPNF* 5:40; *Nupt. et concup.* X.XXIX.50/*NPNF* 5:303.

9. *Trin.* XIV.17.23/*NPNF* 3:196; *Ep.* XCVIII (408).1–2/*NPNF* 1:406–7; *Bapt.* I.14.22–15.23/*NPNF* 4:421; *Pecc. merit.* I.XXIII.33; III.II.2/*NPNF* 5:28, 70.

10. *Enchir.* 42, 52, 53/*NPNF* 3:252, 254–55.

11. *Trin.* XIV.17.23; XIV.19.25/*NPNF* 3:196, 197. There are significant similarities here to Martin Luther's concept of living one's Baptism (*The Small Catechism* [1528], sec. 4, in *The Book of Concord,* ed. Robert Kolb and Timothy J. Wengert [Minneapolis: Fortress Press, 2000], 360.12.)

12. *Vera relig.* 5/*LCC* 219–20.

13. *Bapt.* I.I–2/*NPNF* 4:411–12; cf. *Pelag.* III.III.5/*NPNF* 5:404; *Gr. et pecc. or.* II.XXXIX.44–45/*NPNF* 5:253.

14. See p. 187 n. 74, for references. See Council of Trent, *Decree Concerning Original Sin* (1546), 5.

15. *Nupt. et concup.* I.XXIII.25; I.XXV.28; I.XXVI.29/*NPNF* 5:274, 275; *Pecc. merit.* II.IV.4/*NPNF* 5:45.

16. *Ep.* XCIII (408).X/37/*NPNF* 1:395; *Bapt.* III.13.18–III.18.23; III.5–7/*NPNF* 4:440–44, 438.

17. *Ep.* XCVIII (408).5/*NPNF* 1:408. Also see n. 4 above.

18. *Conf.* I.XI.17/*NPNF* 1:50.

19. *Gr. et lib. arb.* XXII.44/*NPNF* 5:463; *Pecc. merit.* I [XX]28; III.II[2]/*NPNF* 5:25, 70.

20. *Enchir.* 45/*NPNF* 3:252.

21. *Jul. op. imp.* 3.149; *Pecc. merit.* I.XXVI.39/*NPNF* 5:30.

22. *Pecc. merit.* I.XXXIII.62/*NPNF* 5:40; *Ep.* XCVIII (408).9–10/*NPNF* 1:410.

23. *De lib. arbit.* III.xxiii.67; xxii.64/*LCC* 211, 209; *Pecc. merit.* I.XXXIII.62/*NPNF* 5:40.

24. *Serm.* 293 (413).10/*WSA* III/8; 155.

25. *Civ.* XIII.7/*NPNF* 2:248; *Bapt.* IV.22.30/*NPNF* 4:460–61; cf. *Ep.* CLXVI (415).III–6ff./*NPNF* 1:525–30; ibid., 157 (414)/*FC* 20; 326ff.; *Anim.* I.IX.11; IV.XI.16/*NPNF* 5:319, 361; *C. ep. Pel.* II.IV.8/NPNF 5:394; *Pecc. merit.* III.IV.7/*NPNF* 5:71; ibid., I.XCI.21/22–23 (posits that unbaptized infants received the lightest punishment). Also see *Enchir.* 93/*NPNF* 3:267.

26. *Civ.* XXII.12–14/*NPNF* 2:493–95; *Enchir.* 83–86/*NPNF* 3:264–65; *Bapt.* II.15–20/*NPNF* 4:434.

27. *Civ.* X.5, 6/*NPNF* 2:183, 184; ibid., X.6/187; *Cura mort.* XXII/*NPNF* 3:550; *Serm.* 227 (414–415)/*WSA* III/6:255. For the Eucharistic Sacrifice benefitting the dead, see *Enchir.* 110/*NPNF* 3:272–73; *Cura mort.* 22/*NPNF* 3:550. Cf. *Catechism of the Catholic Church,* 1994), 1368.

28. *Civ.* X.20/*NPNF* 2:193; *Ep.* XCVIII (408).9/*NPNF* 1:410; cf. Martin Luther, *That These Words of Christ, "This Is My Body," Etc. Still Stand Firm against the Fanatics* (1527), in *D. Martin Luthers Werke,* Kritische Gesamtausgabe (Weimarer Ausgabe) (56 vols.; Weimar: Hermann Bohlaus Nachfolger, 1883ff.), vol. 23, p. 271 [*Luther's Works,* vol. 37, ed. Robert H. Fischer (Philadelphia: Fortress Press, 1961), pp. 143–44].

29. *Enchir.* 110/*NPNF* 3:272–73; cf. *Catechism of the Catholic Church,* 1371.

30. *Ep.* LIV (400).III–4/*NPNF* 1:301.

31. *Trin.* III.X.21/*NPNF* 3:64; *Bapt.* V.8–9/*NPNF* 4:466–67; *Ep.* XCVIII (408).9/

NPNF 1:410; *Serm.* 227 (412–13)/*WSA* III/6:254; ibid., 272 (c. 405–411)/*WSA* III/7:301; cf. *Catechism of the Catholic Church*, 1375.
32. *Bapt.* V.8–9/*NPNF* 4:466–67; *Ep.* LIV (400).VI.8/*NPNF* 1:302.
33. *Ps.* III:1/*NPNF* 8:5: "ipsa Domini nostri tanta et tam miranda patientia, quod eum tamdiu pertulit tamquam bonum, cum eius tamdiu pertulit tamquam bonum, cum eius cogitationes non ignoraret, cum adhibuit ad conuiuium in quo corpis et sanguinis sui figuram discipulis commendauit et tradidit." Cf. *Ev. Joh.* XXV.12; XXVI.11, 13, 16–18/*NPNF* 7:164, 171, 172, 173; *Civ.* X.5/*NPNF* 2:183; *Doctr. Christ.* II.2.3–II.3.4/*NPNF* 2:536; John Calvin, *Institutes of the Christian Religion* (1559), 4.14, 17.
34. *Ev. Joh.* XXVII.1/*NPNF* 7:174.

Chapter 9: Eschatology

1. *Ep.* 199 (c. 419).3, 24/*FC* 30:359, 375.
2. *Civ.* XIX.4, 8/*NPNF* 2:403, 406.
3. *Ps.* CI[CII].26–27/*NPNF* 8:501–2; ibid., VI.6/17.
4. *Spir. et litt.* XXVII.48/*NPNF* 5:104; *Civ.* XXII.30/*NPNF* 2:510. See *Spir. et litt.* I.1/*NPNF* 5:83–84; *Civ.* XXII.4; XXII.23; XXII.25–28/*NPNF* 2:481, 501, 504–7, for the contexts. Also see *S. Dom. mon.* I.VIII.20/*NPNF* 6:10.
5. *Gr. et lib. arb.* VIII.19–IX.21/*NPNF* 5:451–52; *Ep.* 215 (426/427).1, 7/*NPNF* 5:439, 440; cf. *Serm.* LX [X] (n.d.).9, 1/*NPNF* 6:293, 290, where the context is comfort from despair.
6. *Civ.* XXII.29/*NPNF* 2:507.
7. Ibid., XXI.24/470. On purgatory also see *Enchir.* 69/*NPNF* 3:260; *Civ.* XXI.13/*NPNF* 2:463.
8. *Cura mort.* 1, 3, 22/*NPNF* 3:539, 540, 550. For the context for this assertion, see ibid., 1/539. Also see *Enchir.* 109/*NPNF* 3:272.
9. *Civ.* XX.9/*NPNF* 2:491; *Enchir.* 109–110/*NPNF* 3:272. Also see p. 191 n. 74.
10. *Civ.* X.25; XX.5, 6; XXII.29/*NPNF* 2:195, 425, 509; *Ps.* XCVI.15/*NPNF* 8:474–75; *Perf. just.* XV.34/*NPNF* 5:171; *Persev.* XII.31/*NPNF* 5:537.
11. *Ev. Joh.* XLIX.9/*NPNF* 7:273; cf. *Ep.* LIV (400).XIII–23/*NPNF* 1:310; *Enchir.* 109/*NPNF* 3:272.
12. *Conf.* X.XXVIII.39/*NPNF* 1:153.
13. *Civ.* XXII.30/*NPNF* 2:510. Also see n. 4 above for the context.
14. *Enchir.* 105, 111/*NPNF* 3:271, 273. See ibid., 2/237–38, for the overall context.
15. *Fid et symb.* 7.14/*NPNF* 3:326–27; cf. *Agon.* 26(28)/*FC* 2:342–43.
16. *Civ.* XXII.30, 29; XIX.14/*NPNF* 2:570, 507, 410–11; cf. *Ep.* LV (400).IX.17/ *NPNF* 1:308.
17. *Civ.* XXII.30/*NPNF* 2:509–10; *Faust.* XV.11/*NPNF* 4:219.
18. *Civ.* XXII.30/*NPNF* 2:510–11.
19. *Conf.* IX.III.6/*NPNF* 1:130–31; *Civ.* XXII.29, 30/*NPNF* 2:509, 510–11; *B. conjug.* 21/*NPNF* 3:408; *Ep.* XCII (408).2/*NPNF* 1:380; ibid., XCV (408)/404; *Serm.* 243 (c. 410) (5)/*FC* 38:216.
20. *Vera relig.* xlix.97/*LCC* 6:275; *Ev. Joh.* XXXI.4–5/*NPNF* 7:190.
21. *Trin.* XIV.9.12/*NPNF* 3:190.
22. *Civ.* XXII.25, 5; XXI.7/*NPNF* 2:504–5, 481–82, 457–58.
23. *Vera relig.* xliv.82/*LCC* 268; *Civ.* XXII.XIXff./*NPNF* 2:497ff.; *Enchir.* 91/*NPNF* 3:266. In the first text Augustine was engaged in apologetics.
24. *Civ.* XIII.18; XXII.11/*NPNF* 2:254, 492–93; *Serm.* 242 (c. 405) (8)/*FC* 38:270.
25. *Civ.* XXII.12–21, 30/*NPNF* 2:493–99, 509–10.
26. *Enchir.* 87, 90/*NPNF* 3:265, 266.

27. *Retrac.* 29/*FC* 60:124; cf. *Fid. et symb.* 10.24/*NPNF* 3:332; *Agon.* 32(34)/*FC* 2:351–52.
28. *Ep.* XCV (404).6/*NPNF* 1:403; *Enchir.* 91/*NPNF* 3:266.
29. *Serm.* 259 (c. 400).2 *WSA* III/7:178–79; *Faust.* XII.14/*NPNF* 4:276; cf. *Civ.* XX.7/*NPNF* 2:426–28. Ibid., XX.9/429–31.
    In his *The Emergence of the Catholic Tradition (100–600)* (Chicago: University of Chicago Press, 1971), p. 129, Jaroslav Pelikan claims it is just a matter of development in Augustine's thought. In *Cat. rud.* XVII.28/*NPNF* 3:301, while dealing with disciplining the Christian life, Augustine speaks of Christ resting with His saints in a seventh age, at the end of time. Addressing a similar concern in *Ps.* XCII.1/*NPNF* 8:456–57, he refers to six periods of world history.
30. *Enchir.* 29, 63/*NPNF* 3:247, 257.
31. Ibid., 92/266.
32. *Civ.* XX.30/*NPNF* 2:449ff; *Agon.* 27(29)/*FC* 2:343–44.
33. *Gen. ad litt.* XII.26.53–54/*WSA* I/13:494–95. For his context, see ibid., I.19.38–39; XII.1.1/186–87, 464.

Chapter 10: Social Ethics

1. *Civ.* XIV.28; XVIII.2; XIX.5ff., 21/*NPNF* 2:282–83, 361–62, 403ff., 414; *Ps.* LXXXIII [LXXXIV].11/*NPNF* 8:403; cf. James Madison, *The Federalist Papers* (1788), 10, 51; Martin Luther, *Temporal Authority: To What Extent It Should Be Obeyed* (1523), in *D. Martin Luthers Werke*, Kritische Gesamtausgabe (Weimarer Ausgabe) (56 vols.; Weimar: Hermann Bohlaus Nachfolger, 1883ff.), vol. 11, pp. 251–252 [*Luther's Works,* vol. 45, ed. Jaroslav Pelikan and Helmut Lehmann (54 vols.; St. Louis and Philadelphia: Concordia Publishing House and Fortress Press, 1955ff.), pp. 91–92].
2. *Civ.* XIV.1/*NPNF* 2:262.
3. Ibid., XIV.28; V.24ff.; I.Pref./282–83, 104ff., 1.
4. Ibid., II.4/74–75; *Trin.* XIV.15.21/*NPNF* 3:194; *Conf.* II.V.9/*NPNF* 1:57; *Spir. et litt.* XX.35–XXI.36/*NPNF* 5:98.
5. *Civ.* V.21/*NPNF* 2:102–3; cf. *Ep.* CXXXVIII (412).III–17/*NPNF* 1:487.
6. *Civ.* V.12ff; IV.2–3/*NPNF* 2:93ff., 65.
7. Ibid., I.1, 7; II.2/2, 5, 23–24.
8. *Spir. et litt.* XXVII.48/*NPNF* 5:103; *Nat. et grat.* LXI.72/*NPNF* 5:147; *Ex. Gal.* 21(12)/*CG* 159.
9. *Civ.* XIV.28/*NPNF* 2:283.
10. *C. ep. Pelag.* 3.20–21/*NPNF* 5:411–12.
11. *De lib. arbit.* vi.14–15/*LCC* 120–21.
12. *Conf.* III.VII.15/*NPNF* 1:65.
13. *Civ.* IV.4/*NPNF* 2:66.
14. Ibid., XVIII.2; XIX.17/361–62, 412: cf. *Ep.* CXXXVIII (412).II–14/*NPNF* 1:485.
15. *Civ.* XIX.11, 13–17/*NPNF* 2:407, 409–13.
16. Ibid., XIX.12/408.
17. See n. 1.
18. *Civ.* IX.6/*NPNF* 2:404–5.
19. Ibid.; cf. ibid., V.19/202.
20. Ibid., II.21/36.
21. Ibid., XIX.21/414–15.
22. Ibid., XIX.13/409; ibid., XIX.17, 26–27/412–13, 419.
23. *Ep. Joh.* II.3/*NPNF* 7:470.

24. *Simpl.* II.16/*LCC* 398; *Ev. Joh.* VI.25/*NPNF* 7:47.
25. *Ep.* XXXIV (396).1/*NPNF* 1:262; *Ep.* XLIV (398).IV.7–11/*NPNF* 1:287–89.
26. *Conf.* X.XXXVI.59/*NPNF* 1:159.
27. *Civ.* XIV.28/*NPNF* 2:283.
28. Ibid., V.24; IV.4/104–5, 66: *Ep.* 134 (412)/*FC* 20:10; *Ep.* CXXXVIII (412).II–13/*NPNF* 1:485.
29. *Ep.* XCI (408).4/*NPNF* 1:377; ibid., XCVII (408).3/406; ibid., CXXXVIII (412).II.9–10, 15/483–84, 486; *Civ.* II.19/*NPNF* 2:34; *Ev. Joh.* XI.14/*NPNF* 7:80; *C. litt. Pet.* II.98–224/*NPNF* 4:586; *Ep.* 155 (c. 414)/*FC* 20:310; cf. John Calvin, *Institutes of the Christian Religion* (1559), IV.XI.3–4; Thomas Aquinas, *De Regimine Principum* 1.14; Henrich Bonkamm, *Luther's Doctrine of the Two Kingdoms in the Context of His Theology,* trans. Karl H. Hertz (Philadelphia: Fortress Press, 1966), esp. p. 24; Bruno Seidel, *Die Lehre des heiligen Augustus vom Staate* (Breslau: Kirchengeschichtliche Abhandlungen, 1909).
30. *Ep.* LXXXIII (405)/*NPNF* 1:362–63; *Ep.* XXXIII (396).51/*NPNF* 1:261–62.
31. *Cons. ev.* 1.15.23; 1.26.41/*NPNF* 6:86, 93–94; *Ep.* XCIII (408).II.5–III.10/*NPNF* 1:383–85.
32. *Civ.* XIX.21, 23/*NPNF* 2:414–15, 418: cf. ibid., XIX.4/403.
33. Ibid., XIX.4; II.21/402, 36; *Ep.* 153 (414)/*FC* 20:282–83, 295–96.
34. *Civ.* XIX.1, 4, 21ff./*NPNF* 2:397, 402, 414ff; *Ep.* 153 (414)/*FC* 20:281.
35. For this discussion see E. L. Saak, "Scholasticism, Late," in *Augustine through the Ages: An Encyclopedia,* ed. Allan D. Fitzgerald (Grand Rapids: Eerdmans, 1999), p. 755.
36. *Ps.* XXXIX[XL].7/*NPNF* 8:121–22: "Quo ducit et quo perducit terrena avaritia? Fundos quaerebas, terrum possidere cupiebas, vicinos excludebas; illis exclusis, aliis vicinis inhiabas; et tamdiu tendebas avaritiam, donee ad littora pervenires; perveniens ad littora, insulas concupiscis; possessa terra, coelum forte vis prendere."
37. *Civ.* XIX.14/*NPNF* 2:410; *Ev. Joh.* VI.25–26/*NPNF* 7:47–48.
38. *Ps.* XXXVI [XXXVII].3.5/*NPNF* 8:99; ibid., CXXVIII [CXXIX].6/612; *Serm.* 239 (410).4,5; *WSA* III/7:61–62.
39. *Serm.* LXXXVI [XXXVI] (n.d.).3/*NPNF* 6:369.
40. *Serm.* 206 (n.d.).2/*WSA* III/6:107. See *Serm.* LXXXV [XXXV] (c. 426–430).5–6/ *NPNF* 6:367–68.
41. *Ep.* 113–115 (n.d.)/*FC* 18:256–60.
42. *Ep.* 153 (414)/*FC* 20:302: "Omne igitur quod male possideteur, alienum est; male autem possidet, qui male utitur. . . . Sed tamen etiam hic non intercedimus ut secundum mores legesque terrenas non restituantur aliena . . ."
       Also see Herbert A. Deane, *The Political and Social Ideas of St. Augustine* (New York and London: Columbia University Press, 1963), p. 107, for a discussion of the whole letter.
43. *Ep.* CXXII (410).2/*NPNF* 1:451: *Ep.* 155 (c. 414)/*FC* 20:314; *Serm.* LX [X] (397).8/*NPNF* 6:292–93; ibid., XCI [XLI] (n.d.).9/*NPNF* 6:400; ibid., CIV[LIV] (n.d.).4–5/*NPNF* 6:428; ibid., 25 (c. 410–412). 8/*WSA* III/2:86.
44. *Ep.* CXXXVII (412).2.14/*NPNF* 1:485.
45. *Conf.* XIV.24/*NPNF* 1:99–100.
46. *Civ.* XIX.15/*NPNF* 2:411.
47. *Ps.* C [XCL].7/*NPNF* 8:489.
48. *Civ.* XIX.16/*NPNF* 2:411; *S. Dom. mon.* 1.19.59/*NPNF* 6:26.
49. *Civ.* XIX.15/*NPNF* 2:411.
50. Ibid., XXII.22/500.
51. *Ep.* 10* (c. 422/423) (2), (7)/*FC* 81:76–77, 79–80.

52. *Civ.* XIX.5/*NPNF* 2:403–4.
53. Ibid./404: "Sed in huius moltalitatis aerumna quot et quantis abundet malis humana societas, quis enumerare ualet? quis aestimare sufficiat? . . . Duxi uxorem; quam ibi miseriam uidi! Nati filii, Alia cura. . . . Qui porro inter se amiciores solent esse uel debent, quam qui una etiam continentur domo? Et tamen quis inde securus est, cum tanta saepe mala ex eorum occultis insidiis extiterint, tanto amariora quanto pax dulcior fuit, quae uera putata est, cum astitussime fingeretur?"
54. *Solilq.* I.17/*NPNF* 7:543; cf. *Conf.* II.I.2/*NPNF* 1:55, for a similar assessment, offered while recounting his spiritual pilgrimage.
55. *B. conjug.* 9, 10/*NPNF* 3:403, 404; cf. *Mor.* 35.79/*NPNF* 4:62–63; *Nupt. et concup.* I.IV.5/*NPNF* 5:265. See *Retrac.* II.79/*FC* 60:236, for a reference to Augustine's perception that he was also addressing Pelagianism in *Nupt. et concup.*
56. *Civ.* XIX.6/*NPNF* 2:404–5.
57. Ibid., XIX.16, 14/412; 410–11; cf. *B. conjug.* 1/*NPNF* 3:399.
58. *Civ.* XIX.15/*NPNF* 2:411.
59. *B. conjug.* 11–12, 5/*NPNF* 3:404–5, 401; *Nupt. et concup.* I.XI.17/*NPNF* 5:270–71; cf. *C. Jul.* V.12(46)/*FC* 35:287–88. For the context see *B. conjug.* 1, 8/*NPNF* 3:399, 402–3; *Nupt. et concup.* I.1/*NPNF* 5:263; *C. Jul.* I.1(1)–I.3(5); V.1(1–4)/*FC* 35:3–7, 241–44.
60. *Nupt. et concup.* I.XV.17/*NPNF* 5:270–71; *B. conjug.* 5/*NPNF* 3:401.
61. *Civ.* XIV.22–24/*NPNF* 2:278–81; *Gen. ad litt.* IX.3.5–6/*WSA* I/13:378–79.
62. *B. conjug.* 1/*NPNF* 3:399.
63. *Cat. rud.* XVIII.29/*NPNF* 3:302; *Faust.* XXII.31/*NPNF* 4:284; *Serm.* 9 (n.d.).3/*WSA* III/1:262; cf. *Conf.* III.I.1; IV.II.2; VI.XV.25/*NPNF* 1:60, 68, 100.
64. *Serm.* 9 (n.d.).4, 11–12/*WSA* III/1:263, 268–70; *Vera relig.* xli.78/*LCC* 265–66.
65. *Trin.* XII.7.9–10, 12/*NPNF* 3:158–160; *Gen. ad litt.* III.22.34/*WSA* I/13:237–38; *Ord.* II.11(31), (32)/*FC* 5:269–71: *B. vita.* 2(10)/*FC* 5:55–56; cf. *Gen. ad litt.* XI.42.58/*WSA* I/13:462.
66. *Fid. et symb.* 4.9/*NPNF* 3:325; *Agon.* 22(24)/*FC* 2:339.
67. *Serm.* 354A (n.d.).4/*WSA* III/11:323–24; *B. conjug.* 5/*NPNF* 3:401; *Conf.* VI.XV.25/*NPNF* 1:100, for information about Augustine's concubine and lifestyle choices; cf. *Civ.* I.16–19, 28; II.2/*NPNF* 2:12–14, 24; *Ep.* CXI (409).9/*NPNF* 1:436.
68. *Civ.* I.20, 27/*NPNF* 2:14–15, 18; cf. ibid., I.21/15.
69. Ibid., I.21/15.
70. Ibid., XIX.7/405.
71. *Qu. Hept.* 6.10.
72. *Civ.* XIX.7/*NPNF* 2:405; ibid., XV.4/286.

Conclusion

1. Philip Schaff, "Prolegomena: St. Augustine's Life and Work" (1886), *NPNF* 1:19ff. (esp. 23, 24).
2. *Spir. et litt.* XXX.52/*NPNF* 5:106: "Ac per hoc, sicut lex non evacuatur, sed statuitur per fidem, quia fides impetrat gratium, qua lex impleatur: ita liberum arbitrium non evacuatur per gratiam, sed statuitur, quia gratia sanat voluntatem, qua justitia libera diligatur. Omnia haec quae velut catenatim connexi, habent voces suas in Scripturis sanctis."
3. *Persev.* XX.53/*NPNF* 5:547: "Haec est praedestinatio manifesta et certa sanctorum: quam postea diligentius et operosius, cum jam contra Pelagianos disputare mus, defendere necessitas compulit. Didicimus enim singulas quasque haereses

intulisse Ecclesiae proprias quaestiones contra quas diligentus defenderetur Scriptura divina, quam si nulla talis necessitas cogeret."

4. For a detailed analysis of this pattern in the theology of a number of theologians, see my *Common Sense Theology: The Bible, Faith, and American Society* (Macon, GA: Mercer University Press, 1995), pp. 216–20.

5. Additional examples of the presence of the pattern to the use of Christian concepts identified in Augustine reflected in other great contextual theologians may be found in some of my other publications and presentations. See ibid., pp. 207–29; "The Development of Luther's Thought: Context Dependency," *Dialog* 21, no. 4 (1982): 283–92; "Luthers katholische Amtsvorstelling," *Una Sancta* 39, no. 3 (September 1984): 240–53; "Wesley As Contextual Theologian: A New Paradigm for Overcoming Tensions in the Wesleyan/Holiness Heritage" (paper presented to the Wesleyan/Holiness Studies Conference; Wilmore, KY, 2003).

6. *Spir. et litt.* XXX.52/*NPNF* 5:106.

7. *Doctr. Christ.* I.35.39, I.36.40/*NPNF* 2:532–533: "Omnium igitur quae dicta sunt, ex quo de rebus tractamus, haec summa est, ut intelligatur Legis et omnium divinarum Scripturarum plenitudo et finis esse dilectio rei qua fruendum est, et rei quae nobiscum ea frui potest. . . . Quisquis igitur Scripturas divinas vel quamlibet earum partem intellexisse sibi videtur, ita ut eo intellectu non aedificet istam gemeinam charitatem Dei et proximi, nodum intellexit."

Selected Bibliography

Allard, G. H. "L'articulation de sens et du signe dans le *De Doctrina Christiana* de S. Augustin," *Texte und Unterschungen zur Geschichte der altchristlichen Literatur* 117 (Berlin, 1976): 386.

Basset, H. "Les Influences puniques chez les Berberes," *Revue Africaine,* vol. lxii (1921): 340–75.

Bonner, Gerald. *St. Augustine of Hippo: Life and Controversies.* Rev. ed. Norwich: Canterbury Press, 1986.

Brown, Peter. *Augustine of Hippo: A Biography.* Berkeley and Los Angeles: University of California Press, 1969.

———. *Religion and Society in the Age of Saint Augustine.* New York: Harper & Row, 1972.

Burnaby, J. *Amor Dei: A Study in the Religion of Saint Augustine.* London: Hodder & Stoughton, 1938.

Burns, J. Patout. *The Development of Augustine's Doctrine of Operative Grace.* Paris: Etudes Augustiniennes, 1980.

Chabannes, Jacques. *St. Augustine.* Trans. by Julie Kernan. Garden City, NY: Doubleday & Co., 1962.

Chadwick, H. *Augustine.* Oxford: Oxford University Press, 1995.

Comeron, M. "Transfiguration: Christology and the Roots of Figurative Exegesis in Augustine," *Studia Patristica* 33 (1997): 40–47.

Cooper, Stephen A. *Augustine for Armchair Theologians.* Louisville, KY: Westminster John Knox Press, 2002.

Deane, Herbert A. *The Political and Social Ideas of St. Augustine.* New York: Columbia University Press, 1963.

Duchrow, Ulrich. "'Signum' u. 'Superbia' beim jungen Augustine," *Revue des études augustiniennes* 7 (1961): 369–72.

Ellingsen, Mark. *Blessed Are the Cynical: How Original Sin Can Make America a Better Place.* Grand Rapids: Brazos, 2003.

———. *A Common Sense Theology: The Bible, Faith, and American Society.* Macon, GA: Mercer University Press, 1995.

———. "The Development of Luther's Thought: Context Dependency," *Dialog* 21, no. 4 (1982): 283–92.

———. "Luthers katholische Amtsvorstelling," *Una Sancta* 39, no. 3 (September 1984): 240–53.

———. "Wesley As Contextual Theologian: A New Paradigm for Overcoming Tensions in the Wesleyan/Holiness Heritage" (paper presented to the Wesleyan/Holiness Studies Conference; Wilmore, KY, 2003).

Fitzgerald, Allan D., ed. *Augustine through the Ages: An Encyclopedia*. Grand Rapids: Eerdmans, 1999.

Frend, W. H. C. *The Donatist Church: A Movement of Protest in Roman North Africa*. Oxford: Clarendon, 1952.

———. "A Note on the Berber Background in the Life of Augustine." *Journal of Theological Studies* 43 (1942): 188–94.

Freeman, C. W. "Figure and History: A Contemporary Reassessment of Augustine's Hermeneutic," in *Collectanea Augustiniana*, vol. 2: *Augustine: Presbyter factus sum*, ed. E. C. Muller and R. J. Teske. New York: Peter Lang, 1993, pp. 319–29.

Gilson, Etienne. *The Christian Philosophy of Saint Augustine*. Trans. L. E. M. Lynch. New York: Random House, 1960.

———. *Le métamorphoses de la Cité de Dieu*. Paris: Vrin, 1952.

Harnack, Adolf von. *Augustine: Reflexionen und Maximen*. Tübingen: Mohr, 1922.

——— *Monasticism and the "Confessions" of Saint Augustine: Two Lectures*. Trans. E. E. Kellett and F. A. Marseille. London: Williams & Norgate, 1913.

Harrison, Carol. *Augustine: Christian Truth and Fractured Humanity*. London: Oxford University Press, 2000.

de Lubac, Henri. *Augustinianism and Modern Theology*. New York: Herder & Herder, 1969.

de Margerie, Bertrand. *An Introduction to the History of Exegesis*, vol. 3: *Saint Augustine*, trans. Pierre de Fontnouvelle. Petersham, MA: Saint Bede's Publications, 1991. He argues in pp. 60–61 that there is no single literal meaning, but several related meanings. He thereby endorses the views of Allard, "L'articulation de sens et du signe dans le *De Doctrina Christiana* de S. Augustin." *Texte und Unterschungen zur Altchristlichen Literatur*.

Marrou, Henri Irénée. *Saint Augustine and His Influence through the Ages*. Trans. P. Hepburne-Scott. London: Longmans, 1957.

Nygren, Gotthard. *Das Prädestinationsproblem in der Theologie Augustins*. Studia Theologica Lundensia 12. Lund: Gleerup, 1956.

O'Connell, R. J. *Images of Conversion in St. Augustine's "Confessions."* Bronx: Fordham University Press, 1995.

———. *Saint Augustine's Platonism*. Villanova, PA: Villanova University Press, 1984.

O'Donovan, O. *The Problem of Self-Love in St. Augustine*. New Haven, CT: Yale University Press, 1980.

O'Meara, John J. *The Young Augustine*. London: Longmans, Green, 1954.

Pelikan, Jaroslav. *The Mystery of Continuity: Time and History, Memory and Eternity in the Thought of Saint Augustine*. Charlottesville: University of Virginia Press, 1986.

Pontet, Maurice. *L'Exégèse de s. Augustin prédicateur*. Paris: Aubier, 1945.

Portalie, E. *A Guide to the Thought of Saint Augustine*. Trans. R. J. Bastian. Chicago: Henry Regnery, 1960.

Ratzinger, Joseph. *Volk und Haus Gottes in Augustins Lehre der Kirche*. St. Ottilien: EOS Verlag, 1992.

Ruokanen, Miika. *Theology and Social Life in Augustine's City of God*. Göttingen: Vandenhoeck & Ruprecht, 1993.

Schaff, Philip. "Prolegomena: St. Augustine's Life and Work" (1886), in *Nicene and Post-Nicene Fathers*, First series, vol. 1. Reprint, Peabody, MA: Hendrickson, 1995, pp. 1–24.

Scott, T. Kermit. *Augustine: His Thought in Context.* New York and Mahwah, NJ: Paulist Press, 1995.

Smith, Warren Thomas. *Augustine: His Life and Thought.* Atlanta: John Knox Press, 1980.

Talon, F. "S. Augustin a-t-il enseigné réellement la pluralité des sens littéraux dans l'Écriture?" *Recherchés de Science Religieuse* 11 (1921): 1–28, sees Augustine positing a unity of the literal sense defined by the author's intention.

TeSelle, Eugene. *Augustine the Theologian.* London: Burns & Oates, 1970.

Troeltsch, Ernst. *Augustine, die christliche Antike und das Mittelalter.* Munich: R. Oldenbourg, 1915.

Willis, Geoffrey G. *Saint Augustine and the Donatist Controversy.* London: SPCK, 1950.

Wills, Garry. *Saint Augustine.* New York: Viking, 1999.

Zarb, S. M. "Unité ou multiplicité des sens littéraux dans la Bible?" *Revue Thomiste* 37 (1932): 251–300.

Index